DANIEL WEBSTER
AND
JACKSONIAN DEMOCRACY

THE JOHNS HOPKINS UNIVERSITY STUDIES IN
HISTORICAL AND POLITICAL SCIENCE

NINETY-FIRST SERIES (1973)

1. Daniel Webster and Jacksonian Democracy
BY SYDNEY NATHANS

SYDNEY NATHANS

DANIEL WEBSTER
AND
JACKSONIAN
DEMOCRACY

THE JOHNS HOPKINS UNIVERSITY PRESS
BALTIMORE AND LONDON

The Johns Hopkins University Press, Baltimore, Maryland 21218
The Johns Hopkins University Press Ltd., London

Library of Congress Catalog Card Number 72-10779
ISBN 0-8018-1246-1
Manufactured in the United States of America

Library of Congress Cataloging in Publication Data
will be found on the last printed page of this book.

To my father,
    Isadore Nathans,
And to the memory of my mother,
    Mina Goldstein Nathans

CONTENTS

ACKNOWLEDGMENTS

THE FLAWS OF THIS BOOK are mine; its merits belong to many. Long ago, Francis L. Loewenheim encouraged me to venture the study of a major historical figure, urging the risk of grand failure over the safety of minor success. Over the years, Louis Galambos, James Doty, and Stephen Weiswasser sustained the confidence that brought this book into being. Valuable commentaries on the manuscript by Jack P. Greene and William W. Freehling produced important revisions.

That this work exists or has any worth at all is due in large part to David Donald. Lavish with his time, incisive in his criticism, unstinting in his support, he knew how to probe and when to praise. Though this is not the book on Daniel Webster that he would have written, he encouraged me to go my own way and saw to it that I got there.

The librarians of the institutions cited in the bibliographical essay were uniformly helpful. My special thanks go to those who made labor in the Eisenhower Library of The Johns Hopkins University so easy, Miss Margaret Lough, Miss Ethel DeMuth, and Miss Adelaide Eisenhart. Elvin Strowd of the Duke University Library and Joseph Cabaniss of St. Timothy's School provided the ideal quarters in which this book was completed. My typists, Mrs. Glenn Anglin and Sylvia Boudreaux, managed their work with éclat and skill. A generous grant from the Woodrow Wilson Foundation financed the research for this study.

ACKNOWLEDGMENTS

Members of my family kept a loving vigil throughout the lumbering progress of this study. My parents, Isadore and Mina Nathans, demanded only that I please myself in my work. Daniel and Jo Ann Nathans provided a sanctuary where I could always relax and clear my thoughts. To my wife, Elizabeth Studley Nathans, fell the incompatible roles of companion and critic. Somehow she kept teaching, kept home, kept faith, and kept on, despite provocations that would have exhausted a mere mortal. Heather and Steve, my children, endured more than they knew, and made it all worthwhile.

DANIEL WEBSTER

AND

JACKSONIAN DEMOCRACY

INTRODUCTION

ALMOST EVERY GENERATION of American political leaders has produced men who have harbored doubts about the merits of political parties. The most prominent skeptic about parties in the generation that guided American government from the 1820s to the early 1850s was Daniel Webster. Congressman, senator, and twice secretary of state, Webster found it incomprehensible that "intelligent minds could differ as to . . . whether party contest and party strife, organized, systematic," and continued, were "desirable ingredients in . . . society."[1] The study that follows explores the responses of Daniel Webster, as a man and as a type of political leader, to the organized, systematic, and continued party strife that took firm root in the era of Andrew Jackson.

I

Long before Webster, leaders had been alarmed at the impact of party contention on social tranquillity. Almost to a man, those who

---

[1]Daniel Webster, "Speech at Faneuil Hall, April 3, 1825," *The Writings and Speeches of Daniel Webster*, ed. J. W. McIntyre, 18 vols. (Boston: Little, Brown & Co., 1903), 2:6. For recurrent statements of Webster's hostility to parties, see *ibid.*, pp. 6, 21-22, 25, 77-79; and 10:5-8.

1

assumed the reins of the government established by the Constitution of 1789 anguished over the place of party conflict in American life.[2] The new nation, experimenting with an untried form of government only six years after it had secured its independence, seemed to them little able to afford the divisions that party strife threatened to create or exploit. It was despite such universal anxieties that parties emerged in the 1790s. Those who came to lead the Federalist party and the Republican opposition found the issues between them too deep to reconcile by gentlemanly agreement. Both groups turned to the voters to settle their disputes; both resorted to party organization to mobilize the voters.

Even as a two-party system took shape, men in both camps retained fears about the danger of permanent party conflict.[3] The goal of many in the Democratic-Republican party, the political victors from 1800 through 1824, seemed less the mere defeat than the political extermination of their Federalist opponents.[4] Quite naturally the Federalists found in repeated defeat only confirmation of their original hostility to political parties.

Defeat led the Federalists especially to ponder the meaning of organized party conflict, and they found in it a threat to the type of leadership they represented. Elitists who believed that the best men should wisely guide a grateful citizenry, the Federalists saw mortal danger in Republican appeals for popular favor—appeals that undermined the proper relation of leader to follower. That proper relationship was one of deference, the voluntary "habit of subordination" of the multitude to the"people of the better sort." Even younger Federalists, who increasingly accepted the need for party organization and democratic electioneering, secretly kept the faith that the community was best served by an elite of wealth and talent.[5] In practice, of course, the

---

[2] William Nisbet Chambers, *Political Parties in a New Nation: The American Experience, 1776-1809* (New York: Oxford University Press, 1963), pp. 4-5, 9-10; Paul Goodman, "The First American Party System," *The American Party Systems: Stages of Political Development,* ed. William Nisbet Chambers and Walter Dean Burnham (New York: Oxford University Press, 1967), pp. 56-65.

[3] For an excellent analysis of residual doubts about parties in the early nineteenth century, see Michael Wallace, "Changing Concepts of Party in the United States: New York, 1815-1828," *American Historical Review,* 74 (December, 1968): 453-76.

[4] Shaw Livermore, Jr., *The Twilight of Federalism: The Disintegration of the Federalist Party, 1815-1830* (Princeton: Princeton University Press, 1962), pp. 21-24.

[5] David Hackett Fischer, *The Revolution of American Conservatism: The Federalist Party in the Era of Jeffersonian Democracy* (New York: Harper & Row, 1965). Fischer argues that even the younger Federalist leaders who borrowed Republican political techniques disdained party conflict in principle: "Emulation encapsulated fundamental disagreement." *Ibid.,* pp. xiii-xx, 179-97.

Federalist notion that politics were best guided by men "independent" enough to act for the whole community often meant rule by cliques of wealthy families. Nevertheless, the Federalist conviction persisted that selfless stewardship was preferable to partisan conflict.

Daniel Webster was among the Federalist leaders of the early nineteenth century who doubted that parties served the best interests of his country. For the half-century he was in public life, Webster rarely wavered from his conviction that partisan conflict did more harm than good. Though himself successively a member and leader of three parties—the Federalists, the National Republicans, and the Whigs—Webster thought a far better form of leadership was government by independent men. Gentlemen did not needlessly undermine the unity of the community or defame the character of its leaders merely to gain office. Public men properly settled issues among themselves.

As Webster anticipated the future in the early 1820s, he had great expectations. At best, the era of good feelings in politics would continue indefinitely and would revive Webster's style of leadership. At minimum, the emergence of new sectional interests would create a setting for aggressive sectional leaders and a need for brokers who could harmonize varied interests. In fact, party conflict revived, and, for all of the sectional infighting, the period from 1828 to 1844 witnessed a remarkable muting of sectional controversy in the politics of the country. Two political organizations, national in their leadership and in their electoral followings, contested for the presidency.[6] Parties catered less and less to limited sectional interests and more to broad economic concerns and universal democratic desires. The rush to prove obeisance to the popular will entrenched modern political techniques and styles. The nominating convention and the dramatic political campaign became permanent features of American life. The style of leaders and parties became as important as their stand on issues. Leaders oriented their words and deeds less to each other and more toward the voter; plain speaking, humble origins, and simple manners became required public virtues.[7] Within parties new virtues also emerged. Political inde-

---

[6]Richard P. McCormick, *The Second American Party System: Party Formation in the Jacksonian Era* (Chapel Hill: University of North Carolina Press, 1966), pp. 13–16, 353–54; *idem*, "Political Development and the Second Party System," in *American Party Systems*, ed. Chambers and Burnham, pp. 112–13; Joel H. Silbey, *The Shrine of Party: Congressional Voting Behavior, 1841–1852* (Pittsburgh: University of Pittsburgh Press, 1967), pp. 142–43; Thomas B. Alexander, *Sectional Stress and Party Strength: A Study of Roll-Call Voting Patterns in the United States House of Representatives, 1836–1860* (Nashville: Vanderbilt University Press, 1967), pp. 35, 48, 54.

[7]On the entrenchment of the nominating convention and of politics as drama, see McCormick "The Second American Party System," pp. 104–9. On the increased emphasis on

pendence gave way to loyalty to the organization; oratorical distinction yielded to managerial skill.

To the rise and entrenchment of voter-oriented partisan politics, Daniel Webster was compelled to respond. This study analyzes his efforts to survive, comprehend, and manipulate the new politics, and examines his career from the election of Andrew Jackson in 1828 to the resurgence of sectional politics in 1845.

II

Webster, of course, did have the option of abandoning politics altogether, as many alienated by partisanship and vote-mongering had done before him.[8] But withdrawal was not Webster's choice, for the revival of the two-party system coincided with the energizing of his ambition for the presidency. After the second victory of Andrew Jackson in 1832 and for almost two decades thereafter, Webster hoped that his countrymen would accept him as their leader. Webster's aspirations compelled him to fight in a contest governed by rules of political conflict not of his making or liking.

Yet, if Webster did not leave public life after Jackson's triumph in 1828, neither did he simply capitulate to the pressure for party loyalty or to the cult of humility that characterized Jacksonian politics. To be sure, Webster made his compromises. In the presidential campaigns of 1840 and 1844 he played the partisan par excellence, and from the mid-thirties on he appeased the taste of an egalitarian electorate. An elitist who once had pitied the masses as those "who meaning right" were too stupid to know what right was,[9] Webster came publicly to glorify the wisdom of the people. A statesman who as late as 1833 had described himself as "one of the great before his country,"[10] Webster soon discovered that he was truly one of the humblest. Nevertheless, his reservations about parties and electioneering "contrivances" persisted, and his was rather a struggle to survive and shape the new forms of

---

political style, see John William Ward, *Andrew Jackson: Symbol for an Age* (New York: Oxford University Press, 1955), pp. 46–78, 211; and Alexis de Tocqueville, *Democracy in America*, ed. Phillips Bradley, 2 vols. (New York: Alfred A. Knopf, 1945), 2:111–12. For the increased orientation of parties and leaders to the voter, see Lynn Marshall, "The Strange Stillbirth of the Whig Party," *American Historical Review*, 72 (January, 1967): 448–49.

[8] Fischer, pp. 4–10, 17, 25–28.

[9] Webster to [William Sullivan], January 2, 1816, Daniel Webster Papers, George F. Hoar Collection, Massachusetts Historical Society, Boston (hereafter cited as MHS).

[10] See Webster's amendments to an editorial drafted by Edward Everett for the *Boston Courier*, August, 1833, Edward Everett Papers, MHS.

politics than a surrender to the public style and party servitude he disdained. He continued to believe that statesmen had their place, that class conflict did not exist, and that the interests of all Americans were in harmony.

At first Webster's effort to fit the political style set by the Jacksonians seemed hopeless, for the simple polarities of Jacksonian appeals left little room for an Eastern gentleman, a self-confessed defender of the rights of property, a spokesman for the capitalists of Boston, New York, and Philadelphia. Given the choice between frontier generals and urban aristocrats, defenders of the people and defenders of property, honest yeomen and crafty capitalists, the electorate repeatedly opted for the wisdom of the forest, the spokesmen of the poor, and the virtues of a rural republic.

By the late 1830s, however, Webster saw a new possibility for attracting a following, even among a citizenry demoralized by Jacksonian democracy. A rift had developed between those who instigated Jackson's economic policies and those who benefited by them. Behind Jackson's program, and especially his war upon the second Bank of the United States, was his spartan hostility to "rash speculation, idleness, extravagance, and . . . deterioration of morals"[11] and his advocacy of simplicity and stability, "self-reliance and independence, economy and useful toil, honesty and plain dealing."[12] In practice, though, speculation and inflation accelerated during Jackson's presidency and lured an increasing number of Americans from economic self-sufficiency into producing their goods for market.

Webster was among the first Whigs to realize the divergence between the intent and the reality of Jacksonian economic policies and to recognize that thousands of Jacksonians wished only to join the ranks of American entrepreneurs. Webster discovered that the expansion of credit provided by Jackson's policies had raised economic expectations to new heights. Credit had made plausible Webster's rhetorical claims that the industrious could rise at will and that no permanent poor existed. The panic of 1837 gave Webster an opportunity to exploit his new awareness of what Jacksonian democracy had meant to Americans and his new sense of the reality of the national consensus he had long preached. To thousands who had dreamed of striking it rich, to thou-

---

[11] James D. Richardson, comp., *A Compilation of the Messages and Papers of the Presidents, 1789-1905*, 11 vols. (Washington, D.C.: Bureau of National Literature and Art, 1907), 3:246, 302.

[12] Marvin Meyers, *The Jacksonian Persuasion: Politics & Belief* (Stanford: Stanford University Press, 1957), p. 24.

sands who suddenly faced the threat of foreclosure of farms or stores, Webster pledged he would seek to sustain their credit and their hopes. Whigs would keep the Democratic faith.

Webster's adjustment to the issues and to the style of Jacksonian politics left him fit to cope with the voters by the end of the 1830s. He was less able to deal with the demands of his party comrades.

Nowhere were Webster's misgivings about partisan conflict more evident than in his ambivalent and troubled relationship to the National Republican and Whig parties. Webster joined the alliance opposed to Andrew Jackson belatedly and reluctantly, and his belief persisted that conflict was best resolved by consensus among leaders rather than by competition between parties. Though the initial structure of the Whig party permitted Webster and other leaders to retain considerable independence of action,[13] he chafed even under the minimal discipline imposed. To Webster and the Whigs, however, the weakness of a party with many chieftains and few faithful followers gradually became apparent. In its early years the Whig party proved unable to choose a presidential candidate, unable to agree on issues, and unable consistently to win elections.[14] Deadlock and defeat inexorably moved Webster and his comrades toward emulation of the Democrats—to demands that Whigs subordinate their personal tastes to the good of the party organization.

III

Webster's dilemma in the Jackson era went far beyond that of a single elitist politican out of his element. His was the dilemma of an entire generation of leaders reared to rule in a traditional world and forced to function in the modern one.

In the world that Webster idealized, party conflict was corrosive. Custom and deference permitted all men to assume a basic harmony of interests and enabled the mute majority to trust its leaders to seek and serve the common good. Parties challenged custom, dissolved deference, fettered leaders, and elevated conflict to a public virtue. More than the anachronism of his tastes and talents hampered Webster's adjustment to partisan strife. His difficulties were rooted in enduring doubts about modern politics. How could leaders act for the whole community when compelled to cower before constituents or party comrades? How could common good issue from the conflict of selfish interests?

[13]Marshall, "The Strange Stillbirth of the Whig Party," pp. 458–63.

[14]E. Malcolm Carroll, *Origins of the Whig Party* (Durham: Duke University Press, 1925), pp. 118–71, 216–19.

In the society it was Webster's fate to encounter, conflict was pervasive. As Webster himself reluctantly recognized, the sources of strife went deeper than party agitation. The hunger for wealth, the quest for equality, the gulf between rich and poor, and the rivalry of different sections of the country were realities. Through the medium of leaders or of parties, conflict had to be resolved. Rule by disinterested gentlemen, Webster's formula for managing conflict, was antiquated in his lifetime, but the practical defeat of his formula did not settle the questions it raised. Were there men without interests? Were there potential stewards who were impartial in their perception of the common good and untempted by ambition to betray their trusts?[15]

That parties resolved the conflicts of society more reliably than independent leaders was the judgment of Webster's contemporaries. That parties also solved the problem of generating a sense of the common good was the view of Webster's most reflective contemporary, Alexis de Tocqueville. The French aristocrat, no less committed to social harmony or more suspicious of political parties than Webster, concluded that parties made possible the mutation of self-centered individuals into citizens concerned with the common welfare. Parties involved all men in governing their affairs and compelled interest in the "destiny of the state." By organizing and operating political associations men learned the "art of adapting themselves to a common purpose." It was through political participation and a "kind of selfishness," Tocqueville thought, that a democratic citizen "interested himself in the welfare of his country."[16]

Webster was never prepared to rely on enlightened self-interest and party association to resolve all conflicts and to generate a sense of community. Convinced that stewardship and self-sacrifice were needed to serve the general good, he relied increasingly on appeals to public patriotism.[17] His dependence on patriotism as the way to secure the blessings of the traditional politics was prophetic. It was no accident that twentieth-century stewards, similarly aware of the limits and dangers of party conflict, also would summon citizens to self-sacrifice and ask men to support a New Nationalism, a Great Crusade, or a New Frontier.

---

[15] For incisive and skeptical answers to these questions, see James Sterling Young, *The Washington Community, 1800–1828* (New York: Columbia University Press, 1966).

[16] Marvin Zetterbaum, *Tocqueville and the Problem of Democracy* (Stanford: Stanford University Press, 1967), pp. 93, 96.

[17] Tocqueville himself came to the conclusion that patriotism was needed to "give public-spiritedness a foundation that would make it unshakable by mere utilitarian considerations." *Ibid.*, pp. 149–52.

PROLOGUE

"CHARACTER IS POWER"

NOTHING WAS MORE DECISIVE in the public career of Daniel Webster than his family roots. Born in 1782, the ninth child and youngest son of a New Hampshire farmer, Webster was reared in a household where New England Federalism was a family faith. His father, Ebenezer Webster, was a pioneer, soldier of the American Revolution, and devoted admirer of George Washington. Both Websters revered Washington as a statesman who acted for the "universal good" and who rightfully received "universal love." The ties of veneration between Daniel Webster and his father, between Washington and his countrymen, shaped Webster's initial ideal of optimum bonds between leader and citizen. They should be as father to son. Wise generosity should beget devotion and gratitude.[1]

I

Ebenezer Webster, though not a man of great property or wealth, transmitted to his son a faith in the mobility of American society. Webster was a leader in the small community of Salisbury, New Hampshire, and was the recipient of what the community could offer in

[1] Daniel Webster, "The Character of Washington, February 22, 1832," *The Writings and Speeches of Daniel Webster*, ed. J. W. McIntyre, 18 vols. (Boston: Little, Brown & Co., 1903), 2:79 (hereafter cited as *Writings*).

position and respect. Justice of the peace, delegate to the New Hampshire state convention that ratified the Constitution, representative in the state assembly, Ebenezer Webster was content with his modest achievements. Those accomplishments were limited, the elder Webster told his son, only because his education was poor. With good schooling a man of talent could expect to become a man of influence and enjoy the independence and perquisites of a gentleman.

Quite early Ebenezer Webster elected to give his youngest son the opportunities he never had. The frail but endearing child preferred "boyish sports" and declamation to his daily chores, and succeeded easily in delighting visitors to his father's tavern with patriotic lore and recitals from the Scripture. The huge and vigorous Ebenezer Webster decided his son was unfit for a "robust occupation" and gave "extra care" to the boy's education. Small-town schools taught Daniel Webster writing and reading, and at the age of fourteen he was sent to Exeter Academy. Tutors at Exeter and, when funds ran low, nearer home advanced him in English grammar, arithmetic, Latin, and Greek, and in 1797 his father divulged that he would send him to college. "[T]hrilled . . . overcome . . . dizzy" at the prospect, Daniel entered Dartmouth that year.[2]

Though Dartmouth was not Harvard or Yale, it was a step far beyond the village schoolhouse, and it gave the fluent and sensitive young man the credentials for choosing a profession. He chose law, despite misgivings. Law promised fame and seemed "well calculated to draw forth the powers of the mind," Webster ruminated in 1802, "but what [were] its effects on the heart?" Lawyers dealt constantly with objects of "dishonesty or misfortune" and squeezed their living from "penury (for rich folks seldom go to law)." Might not law, by "frequent repetition of wretched objects," pervert his talent to "purposes reproachful and unjust?" The young idealist chose the bar, but prayed "God to fortify [him] against its temptations."[3]

Temptations were few during Webster's two-year apprenticeship to a local Salisbury lawyer,[4] but, when he moved to Boston in 1804 to complete his legal training, enticements abounded. He secured a clerkship at the law office of Christopher Gore, a refined and prominent

[2]Daniel Webster, "Autobiography," *ibid.*, 17:7, 9-10.

[3]Webster to John Bingham, May 18, 1802, in George Ticknor Curtis, *Life of Daniel Webster*, 2 vols. (New York: D. Appleton & Co., 1872), 2:55.

[4]Thomas W. Thompson was Webster's mentor. He was a leading New Hampshire Federalist who later worked with Webster in guiding the Federalist party of the state. See David Hackett Fischer, *The Revolution of American Conservatism: The Federalist Party in the Era of Jeffersonian Democracy* (New York: Harper & Row, 1965), p. 237.

attorney, and saw Boston at its most alluring. Commerce, culture, and fashion all thrived in the hub of New England, and Webster's legal mentor was a leader at the bar and in society. Gore, who had spent many years in England, personified wealth, independence, and cultivation. As a leader of the Federalist party in Massachusetts, he also stood for authority.[5] For Gore, as for many other Bostonians of means and standing, talent, Federalism, and success seemed to go hand in hand.

Webster himself seemed to doubt that he would ever enter such glamorous circles. On the eve of his departure from Boston and of the end of his legal preparation in the spring of 1805, the young lawyer seemed reconciled to a return to New Hampshire and the comfortable obscurity of an appointment, arranged by his father, as clerk of the local Court of Common Pleas. The salary of $1,500 a year would enable him to pay off his debts and those of his brother and to support their father in his old age. Feeling that his "fortune was made," Webster was astonished when Christopher Gore advised him to reject the post and pursue the greater prospects that lay ahead. Follow "your profession, make yourself useful to your friends and a little formidable to your enemies," for greatness beckoned, the eminent lawyer told his clerk.[6]

Webster accepted his mentor's counsel. He declined the office his father had secured, worked near his home until his father's death in 1806, and then removed promptly to Portsmouth, New Hampshire, to seek his fortune. Webster left for Portsmouth committed never to repeat the hardships of his legal apprenticeship, when he had been forced to borrow money constantly to sustain himself. "I am determined," he confided to a friend, "to be under no obligations to anybody." But the young lawyer admitted to higher ambitions. "Cash ... ever did, does now, and ever will, constitute the real, unavoidable aristocracy that exists and must exist in society."[7] Webster meant to acquire wealth and all the perogatives it conferred.

II

The bustling commerce of the Napoleonic Wars made Portsmouth a prospering and promising town for a young and talented man, and Webster quickly established himself as an eloquent and effective lawyer at the bar of the state. As the young man from the country advanced,

[5] Curtis, *Life of Daniel Webster*, 1:53–59.

[6] *Ibid.*, 1:71–72; Webster, "Autobiography," *Writings*, 17:21.

[7] Lynn W. Turner, *William Plumer of New Hampshire, 1759–1850* (Chapel Hill: University of North Carolina Press, 1962), p. 30.

he developed a "commanding air,"[8] and the elite of the city gained a devoted recruit. Ambition and talent won Webster entry into the circle of leading lawyers and families of Portsmouth; once in the inner circle, his experience repeatedly indicated that the favors and fame in his world were conferred by gentlemen on other gentlemen. Within a decade he was convinced that the "masses" had little respect or use for men of worth;[9] happily, his career testified to what could be achieved despite them.

Webster's career in Portsmouth quickly came to include politics. The commanding attorney made his eloquence available to the Federalist party on numerous occasions,[10] and the occasions grew more frequent as the diplomacy of the ruling Republican party became ever more damaging to the shipping interests of Portsmouth. Embargo and the threat of war with Britain or France jeopardized the lucrative European trade of the city's shippers and merchants, and in 1812 the outbreak of war with Britain threatened to shut the port indefinitely. Webster had labored hard for the state's Federalist organization and had shown himself skillful at taking the case against Republican policies to the voters of the state.[11] When he drafted a ringing denunciation of Republican diplomacy in 1812, he seemed the natural advocate for the mercantile interests of New Hampshire in Washington.[12] The Federalist caucus chose him as one of its six nominees for Congress in 1812, the citizens of the state elected him, and in 1813 Webster began the first of two terms in the capital.[13]

The war years were bad years for the New England Federalists. Hopelessly outnumbered and consistently frustrated in their attempts to halt the war abroad or to win decisive elections at home,[14] Webster and his

---

[8]George Ticknor noted Webster's commanding air in his reminiscences of Webster; see Curtis, *Life of Daniel Webster*, 1:85.

[9]Webster to [William Sullivan], January 2, 1816, Daniel Webster Papers, George F. Hoar Collection, Massachusetts Historical Society, Boston (hereafter cited as MHS).

[10]See, for example, Webster's "Appeal to the Old Whigs of New Hampshire, February, 1805," *Writings*, 15:522-31; "Fourth of July Oration," Concord, July 4, 1806, *ibid.*, pp. 537-47; "Considerations on the Embargo Laws, 1808," *ibid.*, pp. 564-74; "Fourth of July Oration, Portsmouth, July 4, 1812," *ibid.*, pp. 583-98; and Claude Moore Fuess, *Daniel Webster*, 2 vols. (Boston: Little, Brown & Co., 1930), 1:125-26, 130-31.

[11]Fischer, *The Revolution of American Conservatism*, pp. 63, 69, 88, 238; Turner, *William Plumer*, pp. 157, 204.

[12]Daniel Webster, "The Rockingham Memorial, August, 1812," *Writings*, 15; Fischer, *The Revolution of American Conservatism*, p. 99; Fuess, *Daniel Webster*, 1:136-46.

[13]Fuess, *Daniel Webster*, 1:146-47.

[14]Shaw Livermore, Jr., *The Twilight of Federalism: The Disintegration of the Federalist Party, 1815-1830* (Princeton: Princeton University Press, 1962), pp. 10-12; James M. Banner,

Federalist comrades increasingly resorted to states'-rights arguments later associated with Southern defenders of slavery. More and more Webster came to contend that the Constitution did not permit a majority to destroy the commerce of a section of the Union; increasingly he intimated that states faced with illegal destruction of their commerce had the right to calculate the worth of the Union.[15]

Through no effort of the Federalists, the war finally ended in 1815, but for the rest of his career Webster bore the political scars of his opposition to the conflict. The young Federalist leader had indeed been partisan and often obstructionist in his fight against the war. But he had never sanctioned the secessionist threats of the more extreme New England Federalists and had not even approved the convening of the more moderate antiwar Federalists at Hartford in 1815.[16] Nevertheless, for years to come, Webster, who had not participated in the Hartford Convention, was repeatedly linked with the meeting, which was itself linked with treason.

Any gain that might have accrued to Webster and the Federalists from the fact that the Republican war had settled nothing at enormous cost was voided by the final battle of the conflict. On the dawn of January 8, 1815, General Andrew Jackson of Tennessee and his hastily assembled frontier militia routed Britain's finest troops as they attempted to capture New Orleans. Those who might have been held to account for the diplomatic and military catastrophes of the war instead basked in the afterglow of Jackson's triumph.[17]

With the war removed as a political issue for the Federalists, all hope for a party resurgence was gone, and a tired and disheartened Daniel Webster vacated his seat in Congress after 1816. Equally discouraged with the prospects of Portsmouth, whose commerce was disrupted by the upheaval of war, Webster also left New Hampshire the same year. Casting about for a new home, the thirty-four-year-old lawyer rejected Albany and New York City, and in August, 1816, returned to the hub of New England politics and enterprise, Boston.[18]

Jr., *To the Hartford Convention: The Federalists and the Origins of Party Politics in Massachusetts, 1789–1815* (New York: Alfred A. Knopf, 1970).

[15] Richard W. Current, *Daniel Webster and the Rise of National Conservatism* (Boston: Little, Brown & Co., 1955), pp. 14–18.

[16] *Ibid.*, pp. 17–19.

[17] Livermore, *The Twilight of Federalism*, pp. 11–14, 16.

[18] Curtis, *Life of Daniel Webster*, 1:156; Webster to Ezekiel Webster, March 26, 1816, *Writings*, 17:256.

III

Webster did not arrive in Boston, as he had in Portsmouth a decade before, as a young lawyer from the country in pursuit of his fortune. He came to the city as an accomplished attorney at the forefront of his profession and as the leading young spokesman of the Federalist party. Never for a moment was Webster an outsider who had to struggle for entry into the inner circles of Boston society and politics. Rather, the merchants and shipping magnates of the city welcomed him promptly as one of their own. He received their cases in court, he joined the select group permitted to buy stock in their companies and to borrow from their banks, and he broke bread with the finest families of the city. The wealthy shipping entrepreneur Thomas Handasyd Perkins, Supreme Court Justice Joseph Story, and Brahmin George Ticknor quickly numbered among Webster's devoted admirers and friends.[19]

Indeed, as he neared the age of forty, Webster was a man to admire in Boston or anywhere. At the height of his powers as a speaker and an advocate, he commanded individuals and crowds alike with his imposing physical presence and his gifted oratory. Webster's broad shoulders, deep chest, his massive and majestic forehead, his coal black hair and shaggy black brows, and, above all, his dark, luminous eyes gave him a look of awesome power which men could convey only in metaphor. In court, in Congress, or during a public address, Webster's oratory often transported his listeners. Quietly he began with the facts of a dispute; frequently he stated the case of his opponent. As he moved to establish his argument his delivery warmed, his voice deepened and rang out, his right hand hammered up and down as he drove home the plain, compelling points of his case.[20] At his best, Webster fulfilled his own definition of "true eloquence," which comes,

if it comes at all, like the outbreaking of a fountain from the earth, or the bursting forth of volcanic fires, with spontaneous, original, native force. . . . The clear conception, outrunning the deductions of logic, the high purpose, the firm resolve, the dauntless spirit, speaking on the tongue, beaming from the eye, informing every feature, and urging the

---

[19] Curtis, *Life of Daniel Webster*, 1:161–62, 192; Arthur B. Darling, *Political Changes in Massachusetts, 1824–1848: A Study of Liberal Movements in Politics*, Yale Historical Publications, no. 15 (New Haven: Yale University Press, 1925), p. 16. Other prominent Bostonians among Webster's friends included Judge Issac P. Davis, Federalist leader William Sullivan, and entrepreneurs John Lowell and F. C. Gray. See also Martin Burgess Green, *The Problem of Boston: Some Readings in Cultural History* (New York: W. W. Norton & Co., 1966).

[20] William Norwood Brigance, ed., *A History and Criticism of American Public Address*, 3 vols. (New York: McGraw-Hill, 1943), 2:688–711; Maurice G. Baxter, *Daniel Webster & the Supreme Court* (Amherst: The University of Massachusetts Press, 1966), pp. 9–11.

whole man onward, right onward to his object—this, this is eloquence; or rather it is something greater and higher than all eloquence, it is action, noble, sublime, god-like action.[21]

"It was hardly *eloquence*," wrote an observer of one of Webster's great Supreme Court summations. It "was pure reason," a "statement so luminous, a chain of reasoning so easy to be understood, and yet approaching so nearly to absolute demonstration, that he seemed to carry with him every man of his audience."[22] "Three or four times," recalled a listener at an epic Webster oration, "I thought my temples would burst with the gush of blood. . . . When I came out I was almost afraid to come near him."[23]

When Webster would again turn his talents to politics was uncertain. During his first five years in Boston he displayed some interest in public affairs, but sought no office. With other Federalist leaders, Webster hoped that the abatement of party strife after the end of the war in 1815 augured a permanent change in American politics. Believing that the issues that had divided the country since 1800 had spent themselves, and that entirely new subjects would dominate the coming years of peace and growth, Webster pressed for the complete abandonment of old disputes and traditional party lines. Successfully he counseled his Federalist colleagues to give up the contest for the presidency; with the decline of national competition he expected a new alignment of citizens and leaders. But Webster wished for far more than political flux. Exploiting the postwar euphoria of national amity, he called for the complete repudiation of conflict through political parties and for a return to politics by the best men.

The pause in party battles, Webster argued as early as 1816, gave leaders everywhere the chance to ponder the shape of American politics in the decades ahead. The essential question was whether men of talent were still required to govern the republic. The fact was, Webster believed, that the partisan strife of years past had hounded men of merit out of public life. Party leaders and party editors had venomously attacked men's reputations, had willfully distorted issues, and had made a "havoc of all virtue." The public had become accustomed to thinking

---

[21] Webster's thoughts on "true eloquence" came in his "Discourse in Commemoration of the Lives and Services of John Adams and Thomas Jefferson," a speech delivered in Boston on August 2, 1826, *Writings*, 1:131–32.

[22] Curtis, *Life of Daniel Webster*, 1:169–70.

[23] So Boston Brahmin George Ticknor responded to Webster's discourse at Plymouth Rock celebrating the two-hundredth anniversary of the landing of the Mayflower. David B. Tyack, *George Ticknor and the Boston Brahmins* (Cambridge, Mass.: Harvard University Press, 1967), p. 215.

only of party labels; citizens had all but abandoned the "rational" and "independent" appraisal of men and measures. If such tactics and customs continued, politics would come to belong entirely to professional politicians and "licentious" editors. But Webster believed that the "well-meaning and the wise" could regain a hold of public affairs. Men of talent in all parties could bring the press under control, could safeguard the reputations of distinguished citizens, and above all could quell "the violence of party spirit." The best men had only to unite. United, they would "deprecate the spirit that deprecates merit." Together, they would prove to each other and to the public that "character is power."[24]

Webster's belief that the nation might return permanently to an "Era of Good Feelings" was not unique to frustrated Federalists. The view that party conflict was an aberration, a "monster" to be endured only while the necessity was overwhelming, was widespread. The hope that the nation could return to government by "independent" voters and public-spirited leaders was commonplace after 1815. The yearning for repose had deep roots, especially among citizens who wished to affirm the fundamental harmony of American society and among those who continued to believe that party conflict spawned needless social division.[25] Eventually, of course, political parties revived and prevailed, and patrician rule went into protracted eclipse. Yet failure was not foreordained. It came only despite the opposition of Webster and others who, lacking hindsight, staked everything on their belief that parties were transient. Well into the 1830s, Webster acted on the assumption that a man's public reputation—rather than his party support—determined his political power. He went to extraordinary lengths to see to it that his own public "character" remained unsullied and untarnished.[26] He deliberately cultivated the image of a "public man" whose "disinterestedness" and "purity" gave him the credentials to negotiate states-

---

[24] Daniel Webster, "Extraordinary Red Book" and "The Battle of Bunker Hill and General Putnam," articles in the *North American Review*, December, 1816, and July, 1818, reprinted in *Writings*, 15:5-8, 44.

[25] Ronald P. Formisano, "Political Character, Antipartyism, and the Second Party System," *American Quarterly*, 21 (Winter, 1969): 683-709.

[26] Webster went to extraordinary lengths to preserve his reputation in 1828. In October of that year, shortly before the presidential election which pitted John Quincy Adams against Andrew Jackson, a Jackson newspaper in Boston had attempted to exploit old animosities between Adams and the Federalists. Adams had deserted the Federalist party in 1808, charging that certain Federalists, in their opposition to Thomas Jefferson's diplomacy, had verged on treason. In the midst of the presidential contest of 1828, Adams gratuitously reiterated his harsh judgment, and the Jackson paper of Boston gloatingly asked "why for three years," Adams had "held to his bosom, as a political councellor, Daniel Webster, a man whom he called . . . a traitor in 1808?" Shortly after the election, Webster brought a libel suit against

manlike settlements to public disputes.[27] Ultimately, no premise prepared Webster less for the party battles ahead. But no assumption—however mistaken—was more integral to his view of proper politics.

Opportunities came in the early 1820s for Webster to demonstrate to Bostonians that in their city, at least, talent and character were still potent. Citizens of Massachusetts had authorized the revision of the state constitution of 1785; Boston Federalists named Webster as one of the city's delegates to the constitutional convention of 1820. Webster was in awesome company: former President John Adams, Supreme Court Justice Joseph Story, Massachusetts Chief Justice Issac Parker, and state leaders Levi Lincoln and Josiah Quincy were among the luminaries in attendance. Questions vital to Boston were at issue, including the representation of the city in the Massachusetts legislature and the basis of suffrage in the state. From first to last, Webster guided the deliberations of the convention. His parliamentary knowledge and resourcefulness repeatedly settled all procedural disputes and, at critical junctures, his arguments decisively swayed the delegates and terminated debate.[28] Webster's dazzling performance paved the way for revisions that left Boston's power secure, and it vividly illustrated his ability to achieve a consensus among the elite of Massachusetts.

Webster emerged from the constitutional convention with an enhanced reputation[29]—and his personal stature was put to the test in the congressional election of 1822. That year began badly for Boston's Federalists, when a heterogeneous mix of Republicans and dissatisfied

---

Theodore Lyman, editor of the *Jackson Republican*. During the trial the prosecution asserted that Webster's "character . . . was the property of the public," that Lyman had imputed treason to Webster, and that the charge had created a "stain . . . on the escutcheon of his reputation." Webster called on the jury to curb the "abuses" and "slanders" of the press; if "calumny were not . . . repressed, what security for his fair reputation could a good man obtain, when he was presented as a candidate for the offices of the people?" The defense replied that it was "idle talk about [editorial] delicacy in relation to public men. Every one . . . who courts the public . . . must calculate not only to have his name but his character handled." The jury deadlocked, with ten of twelve jurors favoring conviction. For the provocative editorial, see the *Jackson Republican*, October 29, 1828; for the transcript of the libel trial, see John W. Whitman, *Report of a Trial in the Supreme Judicial Court, Holden at Boston, Dec. 16th and 17th, 1828, of Theodore Lyman, Jr., for an Alleged Libel of Daniel Webster* (Boston: Putnam & Hunt, 1828), pp. 7-8, 55-56, 64.

[27] Rufus Choate to Daniel White, April 5, 1834, Rufus Choate Papers, Dartmouth College, Hanover, N.H.

[28] *Journal of Debates and Proceedings in the Convention of Delegates, Chosen to Revise the Constitution of Massachusetts, Begun and Holden at Boston, November 15, 1820, and Continued by Adjournment to January 9, 1821* (Boston: *Boston Daily Advertiser*, 1853), pp. 29, 43-47, 304-22, 458-60, 603-4.

[29] *Boston Daily Advertiser*, October 31, 1822; and *Boston Columbian Centinel*, November 2, 1822.

Federalists challenged the authority of Boston's ruling clique. Two local disputes precipitated a challenge by the group that called itself the "Middling interest," but both controversies focused on the fundamental question of whether Boston's best men represented the common interest of the city's citizens. The structure of local elections prompted the first conflict, as Bostonians debated whether elections should continue to take place at a town meeting or instead should occur at smaller, ward polling places throughout the city. The Federalists stood by the town meeting, for, in the large public assembly, a Boston leader confided, the city's best men had every advantage. Proper leadership, thought Harrison Gray Otis, "depends on the influence and example of the most respectable persons." In a town assembly, the "force of these persons is increased by the sympathy and enthusiasm of numbers." The "class which is *acted upon* by this example and influence" was best led when "collected together," for the "old leaders have learnt the art of giving . . . salutary" guidance to a public meeting.[30] Notwithstanding Federalist objections, the city abandoned elections by town meetings. Boston Federalists invited a second rebuke in 1822 when city leaders defied the instructions of a massive town assembly. Ordered to seek laws which would permit the construction of new homes in Boston, the Federalist representatives to the Massachusetts General Court chose to ignore the town's command. Angry that the "secret influence of a FEW" had prevailed over the "known will of the majority," the "middling interest" challenged the Federalists in the city election of May, 1822. The opposition slate defeated half the Federalist candidates.[31]

When Boston's seat in the U.S. House of Representatives became vacant in the fall of 1822, the "middling interest" resumed its battle against the established Federalist leadership and ran its own candidate. To meet this challenge, the local Federalist caucus—dominated by Webster's merchant clients, legal associates, and personal friends—

---

[30]Harrison Gray Otis to William Sullivan, January 19, 1822, copy, Harrison Otis Papers, MHS; *Boston Daily Advertiser*, March 8, 1822.

[31]*An Exposition of the Principles and Views of the Middling Interest in the City of Boston* (Boston, 1822), p. 4. High prices and high interest rates had halted the erection of brick homes in 1822. State laws prohibited the erection of additional wooden dwellings, to the dismay of artisans and mechanics in the building trades and of Bostonians of modest means who wished their own homes. Early in 1822 a town assembly instructed Boston's representatives to the General Court to present and support a bill for the construction of more wooden buildings in the town. Most of the Federalist representatives were wealthy, already owned brick homes, and feared for the town and their insurance premiums if the more combustible buildings were erected. They therefore refused to comply with the instructions. *Boston Daily Advertiser*, March 7, May 9, 15, 17, and June 10, 11, 1822.

summoned him to represent the wealth, respectability, and mercantile interests of Boston in the capital. The "middling interest" portrayed their candidate, Jesse Putnam, as a man of modest means and talent who would faithfully serve his constituents. Bostonians need "no longer vote for nominations got up in private parties, or by the influence of family connections." The election would be a final rebuke to "those proud and haughty aristocrats" who had "long trampled upon" the interest of ordinary citizens.[32] To Webster's patrons, the contest was no less than a referendum on the caliber of leader Bostonians wished to have represent them in Congress. "To appreciate merit and reward it by expressions of public confidence" was "the exalted privilege conferred on the American people by the right of election." Webster was a statesman of "commanding eloquence" and "extensive learning"; his *talents . . . are known to all.*" The duty of voters was to defer to "men who know your *best interests*," who selflessly "represent every interest of their community." Webster was such a man. He had an *"unspotted reputation."* "His disinterestedness is proverbial." If these claims were considered insufficient, Federalist editors reminded the citizens of Boston that the congressional contest of 1822 was no ordinary election. In the current uncertainty of national politics, it was likely that the House of Representatives would select the next president. What "a momentous interest will then hang over the cabals of the capital! and what less than the destinies of a nation may depend on the influence of a single man!" Now was no time to send to Washington a representative who was "merely respectable." The city should dispatch a leader whose "extensive influence" and great experience would give Boston a voice in the great choice ahead.[33]

Webster's reputation brought the Federalist candidate a smashing victory—and illuminated the harsh specifics of rule by men of merit.[34] His rivals were on the mark when they charged that the "aristocrats" had beaten them by bringing out "their *Goliath.*"[35] Nonetheless, in the years to come, Webster continued to cultivate the congenial role of the

[32] *Independent Chronicle and Boston Patriot*, November 2, 1822; *Boston Patriot & Daily Mercantile Advertiser*, November 1, 1822.

[33] *Boston Columbian Centinel*, March 20 and October 26, 30, 1822; *Boston Daily Advertiser*, October 23, 31, 1822.

[34] Webster's candidacy in the November congressional contest decisively reversed the setback suffered by the Federalists in the May city elections. In the first May ballot, Federalist candidates received 51 percent of the total vote. In the May runoff vote, Federalists dropped to 46 percent of the total. In the November congressional election, Webster won 62 percent of the votes cast. *Boston Daily Advertiser*, May 5, 17, and November 5, 1822.

[35] *Independent Chronicle and Boston Patriot*, November 2, 1822.

disinterested statesman. The contest of 1822 illustrated the continuing vitality of "character" in politics and fixed for a dozen years Webster's public image and preferred political strategy.

The potency of Webster's reputation led the Federalists of Boston to ask him again to serve in Congress, but other qualifications soon were needed to sustain the Federalist party of Massachusetts. Federalists were jolted when their candidate for governor lost in the fall of 1823, and that loss and subsequent defeats made it clear that Federalism in Massachusetts, like Federalism in New England, was dying.[36] By the time Webster took his seat in Congress in December, 1823, it was apparent that elite survival required men who could bring to Massachusetts a spirit of reconciliation and "Good Feelings"—men who could unite hitherto hostile factions of Federalists and Jeffersonian Republicans.

Webster readily accepted the role of harmonizer among the gentlemen of Massachusetts and labored to bring former Federalists and Jeffersonians together. He sought to mute old antagonisms by denigrating political parties and sought to create unity by eulogizing New England and the future.[37] For Federalists he continued to prescribe cautious self-effacement; from Republicans he solicited tolerance and fairness in dealing with their former rivals.[38]

Webster's strategy of Federalist and Republican fusion achieved considerable success in Massachusetts. Webster was twice re-elected to the House of Representatives after 1822; Levi Lincoln, son of Jefferson's attorney general, accepted Federalist support for the governorship and overwhelmed the opposition between 1825 and 1832. When one of Massachusetts' senators vacated his senate seat in 1827, and the popular Lincoln chose to remain governor, fusion triumphed with the selection of Webster by a state assembly dominated by Republicans.[39]

Webster's work as congressman and senator from Massachusetts was not, however, one of unimpeded harmony and triumph. He occasionally had to battle against recalcitrant Republicans who favored a

[36]Livermore, *The Twilight of Federalism*, pp. 117-19; Darling, *Political Changes in Massachusetts*, pp. 40-53.

[37]Webster to Joseph Story, May 12, 1823, *Writings*, 17:325; Daniel Webster, "The Election of 1825, Boston, April 3, 1825," *ibid.*, 2:1-10; Livermore, *The Twilight of Federalism*, pp. 113-20, 134-35.

[38]Webster, "The Election of 1825," *Writings*, 2:1-10; Webster to Ezekiel Webster, July 20, 1827, Daniel Webster Papers, Dartmouth College, Hanover, N.H.

[39]Curtis, *Life of Daniel Webster*, 2:293-304; Darling, *Political Changes in Massachusetts*, pp. 46, 52-54.

"narrow & bigoted policy" against ex-Federalists and to reiterate that former Federalists would cooperate only on *"equal terms,* with a proper self-respect—& with our proper influence."[40]

Economic as well as political changes brought dangers. In the 1820s, the economy of Massachusetts was changing from one dominated by trade and mercantile interests to one increasingly influenced by cotton and woolen textile manufacturers. Merchants and manufacturers stood opposed on the issue of a national tariff. Commercial men favored a low tariff and untrammeled imports and exports; industrialists tended to back a high tariff which would protect "infant" American factories and well-paid American wage-earners from British competition. As manufacturing achieved parity with trade in Massachusetts, Webster correctly read the future and changed from staunch support of "free trade" in 1824 to endorsement of a high protective tariff in 1828.[41] Fortunately for Webster, however, the forces for and against protection in Massachusetts were not in mortal conflict. Many leading manufacturers had begun as merchants and kept social and family ties to men of commerce. Merchants, also reading the signs of changing times, diversified and soon bought stock in new factories.[42] Despite his difficulties, Webster was able to continue to play the role of harmonizer.[43]

Exactly because Webster was able to keep together the gentlemen and leading social and economic groups of Massachusetts, he and the other leaders of politics rarely had to confront serious discontent from the citizens of the state. Yet the roots of discontent were there. Long-standing tension existed between Boston and the interior of Massachusetts. Economic changes, just beginning, threatened the rural way of life.[44] Some old and distinguished families, such as the Adamses, refused to make their peace with the parvenu wealth and parvenu politicians. But most of the latent disputes would wait until the 1830s to surface. For the moment, as long as the major leaders agreed among themselves, dissent found little voice.

[40]Webster to Ezekiel Webster, July 20, 1827; Ezekiel Webster to [Daniel Webster], March 17, 1828; Webster Papers, Dartmouth.

[41]See Webster's speeches on the tariff, April 1 and 2, 1824, *Writings,* 5:94–149; and May 9, 1828, *ibid.,* pp. 228–47.

[42]Darling, *Political Changes in Massachusetts,* pp. 1–39; Oscar Handlin, *Commonwealth: A Study of the Role of Government in the American Economy: Massachusetts, 1774–1861* (New York: New York University Press, 1947), pp. 131–36, 173–74, 196–99.

[43]Webster was able to smooth over his shift on the tariff in a speech to a dinner meeting of Boston manufacturers and merchants on June 5, 1828; see *Writings,* 2:11–24.

[44]Handlin, *Commonwealth,* p. 199; Daniel Webster, "Speech on the Tariff, Boston, October 2, 1820," *Writings,* 13:8, 10, 17–19, 21.

IV

By the mid-1820s, Webster had every reason to hope that the tactics and talents that had brought his rapid rise in Massachusetts would prove equally effective in national politics. As he sought to join gentlemen of different parties but common interests in his own state, he hoped for a similar fusion of like-minded leaders in the capital.

Webster recognized that old party labels and "angry [recollections] of past differences" stood in the way of a realignment of political men, but he also knew that clear party distinctions were proving more and more difficult to maintain in the 1820s. With the Federalist decision to abandon the presidential field after 1816, Webster calculated that the Republicans would not survive total success. Suppressed ambitions and differences among Republican factions would eventually require the aid of former Federalists. When the Republicans deadlocked, all men of "talent, standing," and "public service" could turn to the "new questions" facing the country.[45]

Circumstances proved ripe for an attempt at political fusion in 1825, and Webster seized his chance. The presidential election of 1824, uncontested by the Federalists, had resulted in a stalemate among four Republicans. William H. Crawford of Georgia and Henry Clay of Kentucky had trailed in the election; John Quincy Adams of Massachusetts was second; and first in the running, though without a clear majority of popular or electoral votes, was the hero of the Battle of New Orleans, General Andrew Jackson of Tennessee. The decision went to the House of Representatives in March, 1825. Though Clay had already given his support to Adams, it proved insufficient to give the New Englander the presidency. Webster, hitherto silent on a choice, solicited and won Adams' pledge that Federalists would be treated fairly by his administration, especially on the matter of presidential appointments. Decisively, Webster threw his influence and the election to Adams.[46] The

---

[45] Webster, "The Election of 1825," *Writings*, 2:6, 8. Neither the structure of the government established under the Constitution nor the residential pattern of the Washington community had favored strong party allegiances. Both the Constitution and living arrangements encouraged fragmentation of power, and, in fact, since the departure of Jefferson, leaders had listened more to their constituents, consciences, and messmates than to party dictates. Within the Republican party, eloquence, etiquette, and courtesy won influence. There was every reason for Webster to think that, with party labels voided, Federalists and Republicans would find no difficulty in governing together. For a seminal discussion of parties, leadership, and the Washington community, see James Sterling Young, *The Washington Community, 1800–1828* (New York: Columbia University Press, 1966), pp. 9–10, 53–55, 63–64, 79–82, 97–109, 112–42.

[46] Henry Warfield to Webster, February 3, 1825, *Writings*, 17:377–80; Livermore, *The Twilight of Federalism*, pp. 172–83.

new president and his followers became known as the National Republican party.

Webster hailed the ensuing union of men of high character and nationalist sentiments as marking a "new era" in American politics, and sketched his vision of the future to a Boston assembly in April, 1825. Political men would forget outmoded labels and regroup around "present interests" and "new questions." In "the wonderful spirit of improvement and enterprise which animates the country," West, North, and South would "naturally exert . . . power in favor of objects in which" each was interested. Necessarily, the North would want "united counsels and united efforts" to support its concerns. If new parties did in fact arise, they would be very different from those of the past. They would not be "organized and systematic party combinations . . . continued and preserved for their own sake." Nor would their "bond of union" be adherence to "particular *men.*" Rather, statesmen, at last freed from the "mutual crimination and recrimination" of disputes long dead, would form "associations . . . to support principles."[47]

But Webster did not perceive in 1825 that the entry of Andrew Jackson into the contest for the presidency had challenged the old Federalist premises and given a new direction to American politics. From the beginning, Jackson was an outsider among the ruling groups in Washington. A military hero, his political credentials included neither administrative experience nor parliamentary dexterity nor oratorical talent. Stories of the barroom brawls and frontier duels of the Tennessee General led some even to imagine that Jackson was a "barbarian" and a "perfect savage." Of course, the Tennessee planter and aristocrat was no savage at all; his civility and dignity startled and delighted Webster's wife when she finally met him in 1824.[48] Yet the instincts of most established political leaders were quite correct. By nature Jackson was bold, direct, and pragmatic. Despite his outward decorum, he had little of the inner punctilio and deference to precedent that characterized his gentlemen rivals.

Jackson nevertheless compelled respect among established state and national leaders because of his potency as a presidential candidate. The general's appeal was transcendent; a battlefield hero, a man associated with no one section, and a symbol of the national pride, frontier energy, and will to success that characterized the age, he was the perfect candidate.[49]

---

[47] Webster, "The Election of 1825," *Writings*, 2:6, 10.

[48] Grace Fletcher Webster to James W. Paige, January 6, 1824, James W. Paige Papers, MHS.

[49] John William Ward, *Andrew Jackson: Symbol for an Age* (New York: Oxford University Press, 1955), pp. 18, 29, 44–45, 56–57, 69, 157–78, 166–67, 213.

Webster played a decisive role in bringing Adams success and Jackson defeat in the presidential contest of 1824,[50] but, for Webster and the style of politics he represented, the victory was Pyrrhic. Jackson emerged from his defeat in the House of Representatives in 1825 persuaded that both he and "the people" had been wronged by cliques in the capital. Convinced by Adams' choice of Clay as his secretary of state that a "corrupt bargain" had denied him the presidency, Jackson resolved at once to seek victory and vindication in the presidential contest of 1828. Though Jackson welcomed and received help from important leaders in Congress, his experience convinced him that he must rely predominantly on the people for aid. At best, congressmen had shown that they represented interested minorities. At worst, they had shown they would defy the will of their constituents to advance their personal ambitions. Disdain for Congress and the elites they served,[51] as well as the logistics of winning the presidency, impelled Jackson to take his cause to the country and to endorse extraordinary steps to mobilize the electorate on behalf of his candidacy.

To be sure, Jackson both needed and received support from congressional leaders. Many were propelled into alliance with Jackson by the ineptitude of President Adams. Cheerless, aloof, and independent to a fault, Adams had little tact and abysmal political instincts.[52] From the moment he used his first message to Congress to endorse a sweeping system of federal programs, ranging from national canals to national observatories, and to proclaim that in the consideration of such measures congressmen should not "be palsied by the will of our constituents," his administration was in difficulty. Whatever the appeal of Adams' individual proposals, many of which Congress accepted, the hostile response to the president's over-all program suggested the difficulties of forming a coalition around common interests.[53]

Ambition as well as alienation brought leaders into the Jacksonian ranks. Little apprehending the man or the future, leaders like Martin Van Buren of New York and Vice-President John C. Calhoun of South Carolina gambled on manipulating the Old Hero once he was elected president. They brought their powerful local followings in the East and the South to Jackson's support and simultaneously sought to rally a

---

[50] Livermore, *The Twilight of Federalism*, pp. 172-83.

[51] Robert V. Remini, *The Election of Andrew Jackson* (Philadelphia: J. B. Lippincott, 1963), pp. 29, 67-68.

[52] Samuel Flag Bemis, *John Quincy Adams and the Union* (New York: Alfred A. Knopf, 1956), pp. 63-73, 136-40.

[53] Remini, *The Election of Jackson*, pp. 36-39; Webster to John Sergeant, March 3, 1826, John Sergeant Papers, Historical Society of Pennsylvania, Philadelphia (hereafter cited as HSP).

majority of congressmen, and through the congressmen their local constituencies, to the candidate's cause.

But Jackson and his supporters looked beyond the capital in the pursuit of the presidency, and in so doing altered the political environment in which Webster and his fellow leaders were forced to work. Jacksonians succeeded in creating a loosely structured but effective national organization outside Congress to link together state political organizations and to mobilize the electorate. A partisan press, uninhibited in its attacks on Adams and other members of the National Republican coalition,[54] helped weld together local political machines. To energize the electorate, Jacksonians distributed propaganda all over the country and financed political entertainment on an unprecedented scale and with exceptional coordination.[55]

Not that Jacksonian propaganda instructed the voters on where Jackson stood on the central issues of the 1820s—quite the opposite. Webster and the National Republicans gradually came to accept Henry Clay's "American System," a bold and explicit program for national development. Federally sponsored internal improvements, funded by revenue from the sale of public lands and from a protective tariff, became hallmarks of the National Republican program and constituted lures to those in the West who wanted rapid economic development and to those in the East who favored a high tariff to protect domestic industry. A clear position on sectional issues, the National Republicans believed, must be the backbone of any alliance. But, to Webster's surprise and chagrin, the Jacksonians proved able to build a political federation of Western, Southern, and Middle Atlantic voters without taking a stand on sectional issues.[56]

Jackson knew that sectional disputes could splinter his precarious political alliance and that clarity could ruin his candidacy. Hence he equivocated, endorsing a "judicious tariff" and remaining mute on other issues. Jackson's silence and ambiguity left his energetic local organizations free to interpret his meaning as they wished. Even when Jacksonian congressional leaders were forced to confront the tariff in

---

[54] *Milledgeville Georgia Southron*, n.d., cited in *Washington National Intelligencer*, August 1, 1828; letter to *Richmond Enquirer*, n.d., cited in *ibid.*, October 6, 1828. Few National Republicans could have uttered that "the defeat of the foe will not be sufficient; we should only be satisfied with his *utter destruction. A solitary stab through the heart* will never do: his body should be covered with a *thousand wounds*. . . . Let every man then *plunge his dagger deep into the bosom of the foe*, and *brandish aloft its dripping point.*"

[55] Remini, *The Election of Jackson*, pp. 76-98, 119-20; Clay to Francis P. Brooke, September 24, 1827, *The Works of Henry Clay, Comprising His Life, Correspondence, and Speeches,* ed. Calvin Colton, 10 vols. (New York: G. P. Putnam's Sons, 1904), 4:179 (hereafter cited as *The Works of Henry Clay*).

[56] Daniel Webster, "Speech at Faneuil Hall, June 5, 1828," *Writings*, 2:21-23.

1828—an issue so delicate to Webster's New England constituents that he had hesitated to confront it himself—they did not commit their candidate. Jacksonian leaders knew the General needed support from both the antitariff South and the protariff states of Pennsylvania and New York in 1828.[57] Northern Jacksonians in Congress therefore concocted a bill to reward manufacturers in Pennsylvania and New York as well as producers of raw materials in the West. Hurt most by the bill were Southerners opposed to a higher tariff and New England manufacturers and shippers penalized by the expected higher costs of raw materials. Feeling betrayed by their Northern comrades, Southern Jacksonians sought to block any amendments which might make the bill more palatable to New England and gambled that the merchants and manufacturers of the region would force their representatives to oppose and thus defeat the tariff.[58] But the Southern strategy backfired. After much agony,[59] Webster and many other New England congressmen joined Northern Jacksonians to pass the high-tariff schedule. The resulting "Tariff of Abominations" was "monstrous" to Henry Clay and abominable to the South,[60] but Jackson escaped unscathed. Southerners supported him, notwithstanding the Tariff of 1828, on the assumption that he would remedy the inequity once in office.

Responding to the Jacksonian challenge, the National Republicans were not lax in seeking to mobilize local editors and organizations on Adams' behalf.[61] Nevertheless, in essential and prophetic respects, the National Republicans failed. Unable to generate much personal loyalty

[57]The best analysis of the tangled manuevers behind the Tariff of 1828 is Robert V. Remini, "Martin Van Buren and the Tariff of Abominations," *American Historical Review*, 63 (July, 1958): 903–17. See also *idem, The Election of Jackson*, pp. 171–80.

[58]For Southern strategy and tactics, see Charles M. Wiltse, *John C. Calhoun*, 3 vols. (Indianapolis and New York: The Bobbs-Merrill Co., 1944–51), 1:369–72. See also Robert Y. Hayne to Thomas W. Ward, January 21, 1828; and Jonathan Goodhue to Ward, January 11, 1828, and February 4, 1828; Thomas W. Ward Papers, MHS. For evidence of hostility to the tariff among New England shippers, see Israel Thorndike to Webster, April 28, 1828; Israel Thorndike to Nathaniel Silsbee, April 28, 1828; and Levi Lincoln to Webster, April 19, 1828; Daniel Webster Papers, New Hampshire Historical Society, Concord (hereafter cited as NHHS). See also Nathaniel Silsbee to Ward, December 22, 1827, Ward Papers.

[59]Abbott Lawrence to Edward Everett, December 28, 1827, Edward Everett Papers, MHS; Webster to J. E. Sprague, April 13, 1828, copy, Webster Papers, NHHS; Nathaniel Silsbee to T. W. Ward, December 22, 1827, Ward Papers; Webster, "Speech at Faneuil Hall, 1828," *Writings*, 2:11–24.

[60]Clay to Peter Porter, April 2, 1828, Peter B. Porter Papers, Buffalo Historical Society, Buffalo, N.Y.; Robert Y. Hayne to Levi Woodbury, July 10, 1828, Levi Woodbury Papers, Library of Congress, Washington, D.C. (hereafter cited as LC); James Hamilton to Martin Van Buren, July 31, 1828, Martin Van Buren Papers, LC; *Washington National Intelligencer*, July 31, 1828.

[61]Webster and Clay, who led the work of financing and organizing the Adams campaign, were hampered by the president's refusal to aid their efforts. Adams rebuffed requests that he use executive patronage to install officers who would work for his re-election, declined speaking

to the president,[62] unable to weld together party newspapers and local followings as effectively as the opposition, the Adams campaign organization was no match for that of the innovative Jacksonians.[63] More traditional tactics failed the incumbent party. The National Republicans never generated the support in Congress and the country that they expected from the administration's stand on economic issues.[64] They proved incapable of meeting "*malignant & unprincipled*" Jacksonian propaganda[65] with "*information, light,*" and "knowledge of the . . . measures of the administration."[66] Above all, they proved unable to rally enough men of strong "*personal* character" and local influence[67] to offset the supremacy of Jackson's organization.

By 1828 Webster sensed all too well that Andrew Jackson had assembled an "association of persons holding the most opposite opinions . . . on the leading measures of public concern," and that Jackson's coalition had united "in little, or in nothing, except the will to dislodge power from the hands in which the country" had placed it. The senator also knew that Jackson's success represented an "exceedingly dangerous and alarming" threat to the politics for which Webster was tailored.[68] Whether Jackson had found a lasting new way to generate political power, Webster and the defeated National Republicans waited to see.

---

engagements designed to rally the faithful, and disdained all other activity that might be construed as electioneering. See Webster to Clay, November 5 [1827], Henry Clay Papers, LC; Edward Everett to Abbott Lawrence, October 29, 1827, Edward Everett Letterbooks, MHS; Everett to John McLean, August 1, 1828, John McLean Papers, LC; E. Malcolm Carroll, *Origins of the Whig Party* (Durham: Duke University Press, 1924), pp. 13–16.

[62] Francis Baylies to Harrison Gray Otis, March 3, 1827, Otis Papers, MHS.

[63] Clay complained of the "divisions" in Massachusetts; Webster repeatedly urged Adams' friends to "*bestir*" themselves" and "rally friends"; he complained that the Adams party in New York was "badly managed" and timid, unlikely to survive either "the disease" or "the doctor." Clay to Everett, April 5, 1827, Edward Everett Papers, LC; Webster to Richard Peters, April 10, 1827, Thomas Cadwalader-Richard Peters Papers, HSP; Webster to Clay, November 5 [1827], Henry Clay Papers, LC.

[64] Clay hoped New Yorkers in 1828 were "beginning to open their eyes" to the threat Jacksonians represented to the tariff. "All that surprizes me is that they have not before perceived it." Clay to Peter Porter, January 14, 1828, Porter Papers.

[65] William Plumer to John Quincy Adams, April 16, 1827, William Plumer Papers, LC.

[66] Webster to Ezekiel Webster, March 11, 1828, Webster Papers, Dartmouth. The National Republicans were not above using scandal, and national leaders did little to obstruct the vilification of Jackson and his wife over their alleged adultery. For reports of other dubious charges, see the *Washington National Intelligencer*, May 17, 1827; and Henry Lee to Jackson, September 17, 1828, Andrew Jackson Donelson Papers, LC. It was more typical of leaders like Webster and Clay, however, to hope that Jackson could be destroyed with argument rather than slander. Hence Webster wrote to Clay that a recent speech exposing Jackson had prostrated the old warrior: "I can not think General Jackson will ever recover from the blow which he has received." Webster to Clay, August 22, 1827, *The Works of Henry Clay*, 4:170.

[67] Webster to Ezekiel Webster, March 31, 1828, Webster Papers, Dartmouth. See also Webster to Richard Peters, April 10, 1827, Cadwalader-Peters Papers; Webster to Clay, October 13, 1828, Henry Clay Papers LC; *Washington National Intelligencer*, September 5, 1828.

[68] Webster, "Speech at Faneuil Hall, 1828," *Writings*, 2:20–21.

I

A GENTLEMEN'S OPPOSITION

W HETHER RENEWED PARTY STRIFE and Jacksonian party organization would become permanent features in American politics was uncertain in 1828. As they sought to understand
the causes of their defeat in 1828 and to formulate a strategy for
ensuring that Jackson would serve but a single term in the White House,
National Republican leaders chose to see the Jackson menace as evanes-
cent. Disappointed in defeat, Webster and Clay nonetheless felt that
their loss was not shattering. They had borne the onus of a dour,
unpopular president against a military hero. They thought the referendum was entirely personal;[1] issues had had little bearing on the outcome.[2] How Jackson would deal with any leading controversies—the
protective tariff and internal improvements—was unknown. Few
guessed what he would do with the patronage system; none thought
even to question his views on the Bank of the United States. Though
they feared the worst of Jackson, Webster and Clay shared the uncer-

---

[1] Clay to Francis P. Brooke, January 10, 1829, copy, Henry Clay Papers, Library of Congress, Washington, D.C. (hereafter cited as LC).

[2] Webster to Ezekiel Webster, February 5, 1829, *The Writings and Speeches of Daniel
Webster*, ed. J. W. McIntyre, 18 vols. (Boston: Little, Brown & Co., 1903), 16:186–87 (here-
after cited as *Writings*); Clay to Webster, November, 1828, in George Ticknor Curtis, *Life of
Daniel Webster*, 2 vols. (New York: D. Appleton & Co., 1872), 1:335.

tainty of his backers as to how the president would stand on contro-versies.[3] But of one thing they were sure. The vagueness that had allowed Jackson to bring together his unlikely alliance of mutually hostile leaders could not last forever. When equivocation gave way be-fore clarity, so too would the tenuous Jackson coalition.

National Republican strategy thus continued to be based on the traditional political code, developed in the quarter-century when coali-tions of congressmen sought to dominate the government.[4] It looked to congressional leaders rather than directly to voters for political support; leaders presumably had local followings which they could guide as they desired. To achieve political victory, one clustered together leaders of sufficient weight to overawe a coalition of lesser weight. It was per-fectly sensible to assume that Jackson's victory had come substantially through such a combination and to assume further that, once disillu-sioned, leaders would defect and bring themselves and their followings to the Nationals. Fissured at the top, the Jacksonian coalition would cleave to the bottom.[5]

The National Republicans waited for the foe to divide. The Jackson party would disintegrate of its own jealousies and contradictions;[6] there was no need for overt National Republican opposition. On the contrary, opposition would only, in Webster's words, "check discontent and schisms among our opponents."[7] Determined not to prolong the life of the enemy beyond its natural span, Webster, Clay, and other National Republicans concurred on a course of passive resistance.[8] Clay

[3] Webster to Ezekiel Webster, January 17, 1829, *Writings*, 17:467; Clay to Francis P. Brooke, December 25, 1828, *The Works of Henry Clay, Comprising His Life, Correspondence, and Speeches*, ed. Calvin Colton, 10 vols. (New York: G. P. Putnam's Sons, 1904), 4:215 (hereafter cited as *The Works of Henry Clay*).

[4] Lynn Marshall, "The Strange Stillbirth of the Whig Party," *American Historical Review*, 72 (January, 1967): 445–68.

[5] Josiah S. Johnston to Clay, December 12, 1829, Thomas Jefferson Clay Papers, LC; Clay to Brooke, April 24, 1830, *The Works of Henry Clay*, 4:261–62. For a brilliant analysis of the limitations of government by congressional coalition, see James Sterling Young, *The Washington Community, 1800–1828* (New York: Columbia University Press, 1967), pp. 110–53.

[6] Clay to Josiah S. Johnston, July 18, 1829, Thomas Jefferson Clay Papers. For similar forecasts of factionalism by Democrats, see James C. Curtis, *The Fox at Bay: Martin Van Buren and the Presidency, 1837–1841* (Lexington: The University of Kentucy Press, 1970), p. 27.

[7] Webster to Clay, May 29, 1830, *The Works of Henry Clay*, 4:275. See also Josiah S. Johnston to Frank Johnston, December 1, 1828, Josiah S. Johnston Papers, Historical Society of Pennsylvania, Philadelphia (hereafter cited as HSP). Jacksonians had in fact counted on the opposition to oppose. "It is most fortunate for our party," regency Democrat Churchill C. Cambreleng wrote Vice-President-elect Martin Van Buren, "that we start with an opposition—it unites the main body of the old republican army and relieves us at once of a parcel of mere hangers on. . . . We . . . know our enemies and our motto should be those who are not for us are against us. We shall now have . . . a party administration . . . governed by party principles." Cambreleng to Van Buren, March 1, 1829, Martin Van Buren Papers, LC.

[8] Clay to Webster, November 30, 1828, in G. Curtis, *Life of Daniel Webster*, 1:335–36.

left the capital in temporary "retirement," removing a frequent target for the Democrats. The opposition abandoned formal meetings. Publicly and privately the leaders passed the word: "the nation wants repose." They relied on the repentance of the "better part" of the Jackson party; the Nationals would "recall them to their duty by kindness."[9] Webster remained in Washington to guard against Jacksonian attacks on any "great interests."

I

Exactly as National Republicans hoped, Jackson disappointed many between 1829 and 1832. The opposition exploited Democratic "divisions and jealousies" with "insidious skill," complained Jackson's capital newspaper, by "appealing to the pride of independence among their individual opponents" and asking deceitfully, " 'Art thou in health my brother?' "[10] Yet, to the dismay of Webster, Clay, and other National Republican leaders, Jackson's coalition failed to dissolve.

Sooner than Webster expected, he was called on to obstruct a major effort to unify the president's followers in Congress. Curiously enough, Jacksonian congressmen sought to use the tariff—which seemed the dispute most likely to shatter Jackson's party[11]—as the issue to unite the coalition. For every Northerner who supported Jackson because of the tariff, there stood a Southerner who backed the General in 1828 only in the expectation that he would disavow the "Tariff of Abominations" and seek its reduction.[12]

To make Southern concern over the tariff clear, moreover, South Carolina revived the doctrine of "nullification"—the claim that a state had the right to void a federal law it judged unconstitutional—first used by Jefferson and Madison in 1799 against Federalist laws curbing free speech and press. After passage of the Tariff of 1828, John C. Calhoun secretly drafted a pamphlet which attacked the new law as unconstitutional and which invoked anew the remedy of state nullification of a law of Congress. Though the South Carolina legislature had Calhoun's *Exposition* on nullification circulated anonymously, the state took no

---

[9] Glyndon G. Van Deusen, *Henry Clay* (Boston: Little, Brown & Co., 1937), pp. 230-32; Clay to H. H. Niles, November 25, 1828, Henry Clay Papers, LC; Clay to Brooke, May 12, 1829, *The Works of Henry Clay*, 4:233.

[10] *United States Telegraph*, November 18, 1829.

[11] Clay to Josiah S. Johnston, July 18, 1829, Thomas Jefferson Clay Papers.

[12] Robert V. Remini, *The Election of Andrew Jackson* (Philadelphia: J. B. Lippincott, 1963), pp. 172-80; William W. Freehling, *Prelude to Civil War: The Nullification Controversy in South Carolina, 1816-1836* (New York: Harper & Row, 1966), pp. 136-38.

further action in 1829.[13] Nevertheless, its threat was widely discussed and gave a menacing edge to the tariff dispute.

Webster, of course, fundamentally disagreed with the doctrine of nullification. It endangered the tariff and the interests of his section, but, equally important, it threatened the authority of the national government as he had increasingly come to defend that authority in the 1820s. Throughout that decade, before the Supreme Court and in Congress, Webster had become the leading exponent of a broad construction of the powers granted to the federal government by the Constitution and the foremost advocate of the absolute supremacy of federal law.

The leaders of South Carolina in fact looked on nullification as a last resort; they preferred to bring down the tariff through new federal legislation. When Jackson remained noncommittal on tariff reduction,[14] Southern and Western Jacksonians took the matter into their own hands and sounded out one another on the possibility of a sectional bargain. Westerners would cast their votes for a lower tariff; Southerners would give their support to efforts to reduce the price of public lands and ease the restrictions on Western settlement.[15]

The formal bid for alliance came late in 1829. In December, Senator Samuel Foot of Connecticut introduced a resolution to limit the sale of public lands. Whatever Foot's purpose, Thomas Hart Benton, the gargantuan and loquacious senator from Missouri, found in the resolution the seeds of an Eastern conspiracy. New England and other manufacturing states meant to choke off emigration to the West in order to keep labor abundant and cheap for Northern factories. The high tariff—for which Benton had voted in 1828—was part of the same plot to aid manufacturers at the expense of Northern workers, Southern taxpayers, and Western settlers. The West and South held common grievance against the Northeast; they should make common cause against the tariff. In reply, Senator Robert Y. Hayne of South Carolina indicated that, in exchange for votes against the high tariff, the South would certainly support the right of Western states to survey, sell, and settle Western lands as they saw fit.[16]

At this point Webster intervened decisively to waylay the prospect of a Southern-Western alliance, which not only would have isolated New

---

[13]Those who wished the state actually to void the tariff were temporarily rebuffed. Freehling, *Prelude to Civil War*, pp. 173-76.

[14]*Washington National Intelligencer*, December 4, 1829.

[15]Charles M. Wiltse, *John C. Calhoun*, 3 vols. (Indianapolis and New York: The Bobbs-Merrill Co., 1944-51), 3:53-66.

[16]*Ibid.*; *United States Telegraph*, January 23, 1830.

England politically and damaged its manufacturing interests but would have cemented a strong coalition of Jacksonian congressmen. Though it had been Benton and not Hayne who had leveled the assault on the East, Webster chose deliberately to "reply" to the South Carolinian. In the winter of 1829/30 the senator from Massachusetts defended the services of the East to the West and compared them favorably to the labors of the South. More important, Webster successfully shifted the debate from the issue of land policy and the tariff to the question of the South's loyalty to the Union. Provoking Hayne into a defense of nullification, Webster lured the South Carolinian away from his effort to win tariff redress through a Southern-Western majority in Congress and into a defense of his state's right to veto a federal law.[17]

Once Hayne accepted the challenge to vindicate nullification, Webster was able to drive a wedge between the nationalist West and the states'-rights South. Recapitulating the arguments Calhoun had formulated the previous year, Hayne asserted that sovereign states had created the Constitution and that, therefore, they had a sovereign right to interpret, and if need be nullify, a federal law. Webster countered that the people—not the states—had ratified the Constitution and that, therefore, only the tribunal of the people, the Supreme Court, could pass on the constitutionality of the laws. State nullification was tantamount to treason, and Webster appealed to the nation to rebuke the nullifiers and affirm the Union. To the "Union we owe our safety at home, and our . . . dignity abroad. It is to that Union that we are chiefly indebted for whatever makes us most proud of our country." In a stirring peroration, Webster called out to all patriots:

When my eyes shall be turned to behold, for the last time, the sun in heaven, may I not see him shining on the broken and dishonored fragments of a once glorious Union; on States dissevered, discordant, belligerent; on a land rent with civil feuds, or drenched . . . in fraternal blood! Let their last feeble and lingering glance, rather behold the gorgeous ensign of the republic . . . blazing on all its ample folds, as they float over the sea and over the land. . . . Liberty *and* Union, now and forever, one and inseparable![18]

Though the debate over Foot's resolution dragged on for four months and ended inconclusively, the South failed in 1830 to win a

---

[17] Freehling, *Prelude to Civil War*, pp. 183–86; Wiltse, *John C. Calhoun*, 3:53–66; Edward Everett to Alexander H. Everett, March 11, 1830, Edward Everett Papers, Massachusetts Historical Society, Boston (hereafter cited as MHS). Hayne was led to abandon his original strategy, Everett believed, "by the ardor of debate, habitual scorn of the North, hatred of Webster, and a confused notion, that it is always a safe policy to abuse Eastern federalists."

[18] Daniel Webster, "Second Speech on Foot's Resolution," *Writings*, 6:74–75.

reduction of the tariff and, as it was soon to discover, had by its espousal of nullification incurred the wrath of Andrew Jackson himself.[19]

The debate with Hayne enormously enhanced Webster's prestige and he emerged from the Great Debate as the "Defender of the Constitution" and a hero of Unionists everywhere.[20] But, as was to happen repeatedly, success in dividing the Jacksonian congressional coalition did little to strengthen the National Republicans. Calhoun and others in the South deeply resented the president's refusal to help bring down the tariff, and within a year the vice-president openly broke with Jackson. But, though a bitter Calhoun thought that Jackson had "debased, distracted, and corrupted" the country,[21] he could not and did not transfer his loyalty to an opposition which overtly favored a high tariff and a strong national government. Through 1831 Clay and Webster also had little use for a "monstrous union" of nationalists and nullifiers, and Clay advised the opposition to "march onward, straight forward, with our principles uncompromised and untarnished."[22] Instead of defecting to the National Republicans, states'-rights men increasingly turned away from both parties and toward ever-growing reliance on the threat of nullification to change the tariff.[23]

The president not only frustrated important Southern members of his coalition, but disappointed many Western Jacksonians as well. Nonetheless, Jackson's firm hold on the party persisted. Many Westerners favored federally sponsored internal improvements for their section, but Jackson used his veto power to block several internal improvement bills passed by Congress. The first of the vetoes came in May, 1830,

---

[19] For Western dissent from nullification, see James Brown to Johnston, April 8, 1830, Josiah S. Johnston Papers, HSP; and Clay to Johnston, May 9, 1830, *The Works of Henry Clay*, 5:267. For Jackson's hostility to the nullifiers, see Robert Hayne to Levi Woodbury, July 30, 1831, Levi Woodbury Papers, LC; and Wiltse, *John C. Calhoun*, 2:67–73. Webster even convinced some Southerners that nullification was revolution. See [John Campbell] to James [Campbell], April 23, [1830], David Campbell Papers, Duke University Library, Durham, N.C.; Benjamin Watkins Leigh to William H. Crawford, January 16, 1831, William Crawford Papers, Duke; *Southern Patriot*, n.d., quoted in the *Washington National Intelligencer*, July 1, 1830.

[20] Warren Dutton to Webster, March 4, 1830, in George Jacob Abbott Papers, Yale University, New Haven, Conn.; Stephen White to Joseph Story, February 28, 1830, Story Family Papers, *Essex Institute Historical Collection*, 69 (January, 1933); Amos Lawrence to Webster, March 3, 1830, Daniel Webster Papers, New Hampshire Historical Society, Concord (hereafter cited as NHHS); *Boston Columbian Centinel*, March 6, 1830. New England friends saw to it that copies of Webster's speech spread freely throughout the country. Thomas Handasyd Perkins to Nathan Hale, February 27, 1830, Hale Family Papers, LC.

[21] Wiltse, *John C. Calhoun*, 2:86–99; Calhoun to Samuel D. Ingham, February 11, 1832, John C. Calhoun Papers, South Caroliniana Collection, University of South Carolina Library, Columbia.

[22] Clay to Thomas Speed, May 1, 1831, Henry Clay Papers, Dartmouth College, Hanover, N.H.

[23] Freehling, *Prelude to Civil War*, 219–59.

when Jackson rejected a bill for federal aid to help build the Maysville Road, which ran from Lexington to Maysville in the heart of Clay's Kentucky. The veto, grounded on the constitutional argument that the proposed road would lie solely within the borders of a single state and therefore was not entitled to national aid, deeply angered Clay—and Clay and Webster believed it would anger and alienate the entire West as well.[24] But Jackson's subsequent approval of other internal improvement bills, together with the limited constituency affected by the Maysville bill, mitigated the impact of the veto in the West, and even Kentuckians proved indifferent to the affront.[25] Western congressional support of the president remained strong.

It was Jackson's use of patronage, however, which Webster and other National Republicans relied on most confidently to drive penitent statesmen back to their proper place in the gentleman's opposition. Jackson's "leading measure," Webster asserted in 1829, had been the creation of a party built on patronage. The president's appropriation of "all offices . . . for *his* use, and to reward *his* friends," made "all good men sick of the government." The appointment of "third-rate men," distinguished only by their slavish loyalty to Jackson, insulted and threatened every man of "independence and . . . character."[26] Many Democrats agreed, and privately complained that Jackson's appointments had "disgraced" the country. The "plebian" character[27] of the president's choices struck numerous gentlemen as an offense to "the moral sensibilities of the nation" and as an affront to "every man of honor and intelligence."[28] Jackson's insistence that in a democracy anyone was fit to hold office suggested to his contemporaries that the president meant to displace gentlemen officeholders with partisan functionaries of little status—and that office would be made a reward for party loyalty rather than for talent and virtue.[29] National Republican leaders fully expected senators to reject Jackson's "most objectionable" appointments.[30] Rejection would "break the charm" of Jackson's

---

[24]Webster to Clay, May 29, 1830, *The Works of Henry Clay*, 4:274-76; Webster to Jeremiah Mason, June 4, 1830, *Writings*, 16:204-5. The Maysville veto "seals the fate of Jackson in all the West," wrote Clay in June. Clay to Peter Porter, June 13, 1830, Peter B. Porter Papers, Buffalo Historical Society, Buffalo, N.Y.; Clay to Edward Everett, June 18, 1830, Edward Everett Papers, MHS.

[25]Clay to Everett, August 14, 1830, Edward Everett Papers, MHS.

[26]Webster's draft of an article on "Mr. Clay," subsequently published in 1829, in the Webster Papers, Dartmouth.

[27]Cambreleng to Van Buren, March 1, 1829, Van Buren Papers, LC.

[28]John Campbell to David Campbell, February 20, March 26, 1829, Campbell Papers.

[29]Marshall, "The Strange Stillbirth of the Whig Party," pp. 455-58.

[30]Clay to Johnston, April 6, 1830, *The Works of Henry Clay*, 4:257; Webster to Ezekiel Webster, February 23, 1829, Webster Papers, Dartmouth.

apparent invincibility, put the "mark" of senatorial rejection on the president and his choices, and "thereby dissolve the party."[31] Webster acknowledged that the "out-door popularity of General Jackson" deterred many congressmen from defeating his nominations, yet he remained confident that the "burning fire of discontent" must "some day break out. When men go so far as to speak warmly against things which they yet feel bound to vote for, we may hope that they will soon go a little further." But, though Jacksonian congressmen grumbled, they did not rebel, and they showed lamentably little "indignation" or "repentance."[32]

By the fall of 1831, the fact was that, despite intraparty rivalries, disquieting economic policies, and appointments unpopular with many congressmen, Jackson's coalition had remained largely intact and National Republican tactics had failed.[33] In part, Jackson had proved far more skillful as a sectional broker than leaders of the opposition cared to acknowledge or admit. In part, Jackson had held the allegiance of dissatisfied leaders because he had declared his intention to seek, and was likely once more to win, the presidency. As long as the president's party was likely to win, it was hard for a politician to desert. The discontented could only hope that Jackson's strength was his personal popularity, and that, once he vacated the presidency, men with talent and strong sectional support would again rule the nation.

II

National Republicans had assumed not only that Jackson's party would dissolve when its leaders divided, but that its disaffected leaders could in turn be united and could draw with them their local followings. But, as the fidelity of Jacksonians in the capital had challenged the hope that the disappointed would desert the president, so the experiences of Webster and Clay in their own localities challenged the assumption that strong sectional leaders could automatically command their local followings.

In Massachusetts, Webster's hegemony rested on the continued alliance of former Federalist and Republican leaders. Strong and influen-

---

[31] Everett to Levi Lincoln, February 17, 1830, Levi Lincoln Papers, American Antiquarian Society, Worcester, Mass.; Clay to Everett, August 20, 1831, Edward Everett Papers, MHS.

[32] Webster to Warren Dutton, May 9, 1830, *Writings*, 16:500–501; Clay to J. B. Harrison, June 2, 1829, copy, Henry Clay Papers, LC.

[33] In the words of one Clay correspondent, "the quiescent policy, which it was deemed expedient for us to act upon during the last year, . . . is not fitted to make converts." Alexander H. Everett to Clay, October 29, 1830, Henry Clay Papers, LC.

tial personalities—former Republican Levi Lincoln in the governor's chair, Webster in the Senate, and Massachusetts' John Quincy Adams in the White House—attached their personal followers to the coalition, and the disparate group reinforced its authority with appeals to sectional pride. Jacksonians had flung "sneers, contumely, reproach . . . against New England," Webster told a Boston audience in the campaign of 1828. They must not be rewarded. "If there be one among ourselves who can be induced, by any motives, to join in this cry against New England, he disgraces the New England mother who bore him, the New England father who bred and nurtured him." As he would do repeatedly in the future, Webster admonished the voters of Massachusetts: " 'This above all,—to thine own self be true.' "[34] True to themselves, Bay Staters in 1828 gave the National Republicans a patriotic and resounding majority.[35]

The dispute over a protective tariff tested Webster's coalition in Massachusetts and saw the senator again exploit local patriotism to defeat a challenge. Webster, who had reversed his former opposition to protection and voted for the extremely high tariff of 1828,[36] had made his peace with most of Boston's merchants over his vote,[37] but important groups in the state and in the city remained dissatisfied. Dissenters included many shipowners, shipbuilders, and carpenters, and in 1830 they challenged the National Republican nomination of a manufacturer, Nathan Appleton, for congressman from Boston and Suffolk County.[38]

Antitariff men argued that the tariff benefited only the privileged and hurt the workingman. With equal vigor Webster and his colleagues

---

[34] For the origins of the fusion of Federalist and Republican leaders, see Arthur B. Darling, *Political Changes in Massachusetts, 1824-1848: A Study of Liberal Movements in Politics*, Yale Historical Publications, no. 15 (New Haven: Yale University Press, 1925), pp. 41-47, 52-53. For Webster's appeal to New England patriotism, see his "Speech at Faneuil Hall, June 5, 1828," *Writings*, 2:22, 24.

[35] Richard McCormick discusses the general use and importance of sectional allegiances in the presidential contests of 1824-40 in *The Second American Party System: Party Formation in the Jacksonian Era* (Chapel Hill: University of North Carolina Press, 1966), pp. 46, 91, 329-32. In 1828, Jacksonians had revived old animosities between Adams, who had deserted the Federalist party twenty years before, and the Federalist wing of the Massachusetts National Republicans. It had been all Webster could do to keep the ancient feud from dividing the party. With Adams' defeat, Webster and his state organization relied more than ever on local patriotism and the firm alliance of leaders to keep the state party united. Lynn W. Turner, *William Plumer of New Hampshire, 1759-1850* (Chapel Hill: University of North Carolina Press, 1962), p. 332.

[36] For statements of Webster's public positions on the tariff, see *Writings*, 13:5-21, 5:94-149, 228-48, and 2:11-24.

[37] *Ibid.*, 2:11-24.

[38] Darling, *Political Changes in Massachusetts*, pp. 143-46.

contended that all in Massachusetts were workers—"there is scarcely an idler among us"—and that all gained from the protection of the state's industry.[39] But Webster sought as well to shift the issue from the merits of the tariff to the implications of defeat of the tariff candidate. Defeat would be a triumph of *"Nullification."* It would "show a want of attachment to the Constitution," he told a Boston audience on the eve of the election. Would Massachusetts "depart from N. England, & stand alone? . . . For myself, I shall hold on."[40] Pride and profit convinced the voters of Boston to give a close victory to Webster's hand-picked candidate.[41]

With his state coalition seemingly dependent on appeals to sectional pride, Webster was compelled to be exceedingly cautious in his public support of Henry Clay. Jacksonian partisans had pictured the Southwestern slaveholder as a duelist and profligate; in an anonymous article Webster sought to counter that portrait by depicting Clay as a gentleman and statesman.[42]

Watching carefully for signs of Clay's strength in the West in 1830 and 1831, Webster was repeatedly disappointed. He and Clay fully expected that Jackson's veto of the Maysville Road and other internal improvements projects would bring a resounding rebuke to the president in the Western state elections of 1830—and especially in the legislative contests in Kentucky. Instead, Clay's partisans barely escaped defeat by the Jacksonians. Though backed strenuously by Clay, men "of talent, & much local influence & connexion" won only "very small" majorities. Clay explained that "local causes [and] divisions" had rendered it impossible to make the veto and "the Presidential question every where bear on the election." But the slim victory and further setbacks in Kentucky left Webster "uneasy." "I am sorry to say it," Webster wrote his Massachusetts colleague Levi Lincoln, but "there seems to be . . . something hollow, in Mr. Clay's western support. It gives way, in the moment of trial."[43]

---

[39] *Boston Columbian Centinel,* October 30, 1830.

[40] Webster's address at Faneuil Hall in October, 1830, is not published in any collection of his speeches. Reports of the speech can be found in the *Boston Daily Evening Transcript,* November 2, 24, 1830. My quotations are taken from Webster's manuscript notes of the address, found in the Webster Papers, Dartmouth.

[41] Alexander Everett to Clay, October 29, 1830, Henry Clay Papers, LC.

[42] The draft manuscript of this article is in the Webster Papers, Dartmouth. Edward Everett reported publication of the article; see Everett to Clay, September 16, 1829, Edward Everett Letterbooks, MHS.

[43] Clay to Everett, August 14, 1830, Edward Everett Papers, MHS; Clay to Brooke, August 17, 1830, *The Works of Henry Clay,* 4:283; Webster to Levi Lincoln, December 25, 1830, Webster Folder, American Antiquarian Society.

The extent of Webster's public support for Clay in fact depended heavily on Clay's ability to rally the voters of his own section. If Clay demonstrated he could win votes in the West, then a greater commitment to him by the New Englander was worth the risk. If Clay's Western following was unreliable, lavish endorsement of him in parochial New England would burden Webster and Massachusetts National Republicans with the liabilities of a Westerner and a loser. Webster's doubts about Clay's credentials as a presidential candidate persisted, and for the better part of 1830 and 1831 the Massachusetts senator counseled caution when pressed to advance the Kentuckian's candidacy.

Clay, growing steadily more impatient, urged Webster and other opposition leaders to abandon passive resistance to Jackson and to enter his name as the National Republican candidate. Inaction blinded the country to the "incompetency of the President," and submission to Jackson's "most objectionable acts" made a mockery of congressional "dignity [and] independence." In mid-1830 Clay argued that "the time is now past" to "leave the other party to its own divisions." The opposition could no longer "conceal" itself; its friends were growing "uncertain"; "our flag should be unfurled."[44]

Webster responded to Clay's pressure with pleas for continued patience. In early 1830 it was Webster's "firm belief" that, "if we . . . let the Administration . . . have their way, and follow out their own principles, they would be so unpopular that the General could not possibly be re-elected." A formal nomination by Clay's friends in the capital "would not be popular enough in its character and origin, to do good" and "would excite jealousies . . . which are now fast dying away."[45] Webster advised his Massachusetts colleagues to turn away from "larger subjects" and to concentrate on uniting the party in New England.[46] When Clay's friends in Washington asked Webster to draft a formal "nominating document" in early 1831, he at first did "nothing." Only after lengthy prodding did he finally consent to draft a paper attacking Jackson and naming Clay the opposition's standard-bearer. Even then, so tepid and ambiguous was Webster's language—he made no

---

[44]Clay to Johnston, April 6, 30, 1830; Clay to Adam Beatty, July 19, 1830, *The Works of Henry Clay*, 4:257, 265, 281; Clay to Edward Everett, August 14, 1830, Edward Everett Papers, MHS.

[45]Webster to Clay, April 18, May 29, 1830, *The Works of Henry Clay*, 4:259-60, 275; see also Webster to John Woods, April 24, 1830, Webster Papers, NHHS.

[46]Webster to Levi Lincoln, December 25, 1830, Lincoln Papers. Webster also blocked an attempted nomination of Clay by members of the Massachusetts National Republican party. Edward Everett to Alexander Everett, December 28, 1830, Edward Everett Papers, MHS.

direct mention of Clay—that party stalwarts were in doubt about whom the manifesto had nominated.[47]

If Webster did indeed have doubts about Clay as the party nominee—as distinct from doubts about the timing of Clay's nomination—they seemed fully warranted by the outcome of the state elections of 1831. Again the opposition was beaten badly in the Western states; again the party suffered a close call in Clay's Kentucky. Clay himself was "mortified" by the result and concluded that his failure in the West made his "election . . . hopeless." He offered to withdraw, but was dissuaded by friends who argued that his abdication would shatter the party in critical states.[48]

In the fall of 1831, however, Webster abruptly asked Clay to reassume the parliamentary leadership of the opposition—and the Massachusetts senator seemed to recognize that Clay's return to Washington would clench his candidacy. Through intermediaries Webster quashed all talk that he himself wished to displace Clay as the candidate. The news of party setbacks in the West only rendered his zeal for Clay "*more decided* and open than . . . ever . . . before."[49] Whatever "regret was felt in this quarter, that [the Kentucky] results were not more strongly in our favor," Webster wrote Clay in October, 1831, was offset by the "debt of gratitude to the good men of Kentucky, for the firmness with which they have breasted" the Jacksonian "storm." Webster called on Clay to end his retirement and return to the capital. "I speak in unaffected sincerity and truth, when I say that I should rejoice, personally, to meet you in the Senate." It would be an "infinite gratification," Webster concluded, "to have . . . your lead."[50]

What prompted an end to Webster's hesitation and called forth his effusive plea for the Kentuckian's leadership was a new and ominous threat to New England interests. South Carolina had initiated steps to make good on its threat of nullification; Jacksonians had indicated they were ready to modify the "Tariff of Abominations," untouched since 1828. A "formidable" coalition, Webster reported to Clay, was preparing to assault not "only the Tariff, but the Constitution itself." "Every thing is to be debated, as if nothing had ever been settled."

[47] The document was published anonymously in the *Washington National Intelligencer*, March 5, 1831. See also Edward Everett to Alexander Everett, March 10, 1831, Edward Everett Papers, MHS.

[48] Clay to Johnston, August 20, 1831, Henry Clay Papers, LC; Edward Everett to Alexander Everett, December 8, 1831, Edward Everett Papers, MHS.

[49] Edward Everett to Josiah S. Johnston, August 26, 1831, Johnston Papers; G. Eustis to Clay, September 12, 1831, Henry Clay Papers, LC; Alexander Everett to Henry Shaw, September 25, 1831, *ibid.*

[50] Webster to Clay, October 5, 1831, *The Works of Henry Clay*, 4:318.

Whatever the limits of Clay's authority in the West, Webster, New England, and the opposition needed his support and parliamentary mastery in the capital. Wrote Webster to Clay, "we need your arm in the fight."[51]

Clay returned to Washington in December, 1831, as the new senator from Kentucky, and, with his coming, passive resistance to Andrew Jackson formally ended. That tactic, in fact, had long since proved bankrupt. Whether Jackson's congressional coalition could survive the more active assault that Clay had long advocated, and that he now prepared to make, remained to be seen. At issue, too, were the consequences Clay's success might have. The experiences of both Webster and Clay had cast doubt on the premise that leaders could automatically command their local followings. As Clay worked skillfully to revive congressional independence and to detach congressional leaders from the Democratic coalition, he tested whether citizens would follow their leaders in defecting from Andrew Jackson.

III

In 1832 the National Republican coalition dissolved, and in all but name the Whig party emerged. The convictions of the National Republicans—a belief that talent should rule, a corollary that unfit men would rule poorly, and a conviction that national politics was the business of gentlemen leaders—transferred to the Whigs. The success of Andrew Jackson and his political party had challenged the validity of these beliefs and had undermined the power of those who shared them. Stressing new issues, which clarified the emergence of party rule and the growth of presidential power, the gentlemen of the opposition swelled their ranks and put to the country the question of the place and the power of traditional political leadership.

Leading members of the new coalition included Webster, Clay, and John C. Calhoun. The alliance of the two patrons of high tariff and internal improvements with the antitariff nullifier of South Carolina was not wholly anticipated and was never comfortable. Mutual hostility to executive encroachment on congressional authority made cooperation desirable, and the temporary resolution of the tariff dispute made the tenuous alliance possible.

Cooperation between the nationalists and the nullifier first came in early 1832. Since the moment of Jackson's inauguration, his vice-president, John C. Calhoun, and his secretary of state, Martin Van

---

[51] *Ibid.*

Buren of New York, had been rivals for his favor and for the right to succeed him. Calhoun had lost the contest, but lingering bitterness had plagued the party and the cabinet, and, to end the anomosity, Van Buren had persuaded Jackson in the spring of 1831 to accept his resignation and to reorganize the cabinet. Jackson had named a new cabinet thoroughly hostile to Calhoun and had appointed Van Buren minister to England.[52] Van Buren's nomination came before the Senate for its approval in January, 1832, and Webster, Clay, and Calhoun joined to oppose the appointment. The reasons for rejection were dubious, but they brightly illuminated the opposition's strategy for the year ahead. Webster and others asserted that, while secretary of state, Van Buren had instructed the previous minister to England to disregard the position of the preceeding administration on a commercial dispute with Britain. The minister was to inform the British that the American public had repudiated the "late administration" and had brought to power a new government free to act differently in the controversy. Webster declared that Van Buren's instructions had sacrificed "true patriotism and sound American feeling . . . to mere party"; the appointment was therefore not a "fit and proper nomination." What was at issue, however, was more than a single appointment. Van Buren was the symbol of the new breed of politician who promoted "the interests of his party at the expense of those of his country." He was the representative of all the manipulators who had driven "statesmanship" and "dignity" and "elevated regard for country" from the citadel of power. The man and all he stood for required public "rebuke."[53] The Senate vote was a tie, and, as vice-president, Calhoun cast the deciding nay vote; he exulted that Van Buren's defeat "will kill him, sir, kill him dead." In fact, however, Van Buren's rejection made him a party martyr and insured his nomination as the Democratic candidate for vice-president. The opposition was delighted nonetheless. To place the status of statesmen before "every independent freeman in the United States" was "exactly the point."[54]

For cooperation among opposition senators to continue in 1832, however, the tariff dispute had to be settled somehow. South Carolina's threat to nullify the highly protective Tariff of 1828 and the unavoidable specter of rebellion implicit in that threat brought the issue to a head. Almost all agreed that the earlier "Tariff of Abominations" was a

---

[52] J. Curtis, *Martin Van Buren*, pp. 34-37.

[53] Daniel Webster, "Remarks . . . on the Nomination of Mr. Van Buren as Minister to Great Britain, January 24, 1832," *Writings*, 6:89-96.

[54] *Ibid.*, p. 96; Clay to Francis Brooke, February 21, 1832, *The Works of Henry Clay*, 4:326.

"monster" and that duties must be reduced.[55] Even Webster and the New England manufacturers favored "conciliation," provided that the "principle of protection" was preserved.[56]

Exactly who would lead the movement for tariff cuts and how deep the reductions would be was uncertain in 1832. Calhoun, who had resigned from the vice-presidency and had returned to the Senate in 1832 to speak for South Carolina, had hoped that Jackson would take the lead in arranging a compromise. Jackson's secretary of the treasury did in fact recommend a general reduction of duties that would very nearly have vitiated protection, but the absence of direct presidential leadership led Calhoun to condemn Jackson for an "ignominious and criminal silence."[57] Clay meanwhile sought to save protection by proposing cuts in duties on goods marginal to manufacturers; he tried to persuade the South that such a tariff would reduce its burdens while aiding the factories of the North and bringing in revenue for internal improvements of the West.[58]

Ultimately, a more genuine compromise emerged which, though it fully satisfied neither protectionists nor nullifiers, effectively quieted the tariff question for most of 1832. The compromise measures, arranged largely through the efforts of Jacksonian leaders, won the backing of protectionist congressmen, whose negative votes might otherwise have killed the bill, as well as the support of many Southerners who feared that the lack of any tariff law at all would throw all the Southern states into the arms of the nullifiers. The result of this improbable coalition was a "most unexpected & astonishing" two-to-one majority for the tariff compromise in both the House and the Senate.[59]

With the tariff controversy temporarily settled, Webster and Clay were able to focus on a new issue, the issue they thought would most likely accomplish the long-sought goal of disrupting Jackson's coalition. No institution was more sacred or central in the established circles of politics and finance than the Bank of the United States. Its operations were coextensive with the Union, it lent liberally to men of character

---

[55]Calhoun to Samuel D. Ingham, July 31, 1831, deCoppett Collection, Princeton, University, Princeton, N.J.; Louis McLane to Gulian V. Verplanck, November 6, 1831, Gulian V. Verplanck Papers, New York Historical Society, N.Y., N.Y.; Clay to Brooke, October 4, 1831, *The Works of Henry Clay*, 4:314; Jackson to Van Buren, December 6, 1831, Van Buren Papers, LC.

[56]Nathan Appleton to Harrison Gray Otis, January 11, 1832; and Webster to Otis, [July 7, 1832]; Harrison Gray Otis Papers, MHS.

[57]Calhoun to Ingham, January 13, 1832, Calhoun Papers, South Caroliniana Collection.

[58]Van Deusen, *Henry Clay*, pp. 251–53.

[59]Edward Everett to Alexander Everett, July 1, 1832, Edward Everett Papers, MHS; Webster to Otis, [July 7, 1832], Otis Papers.

and promise, and it had found uncommon favor among both parties in both halls of Congress.[60] In the West and the South especially, where the cause of the tariff and of internal improvements had brought disappointing results, the Bank had made extensive investments[61] and presumably could count on extensive support among those interested in its credit. Jackson, in successive annual messages to Congress, had indicated his hostility to the Bank and had called for reform of the Bank's "abuses" before its charter came up for renewal in 1836. There was every reason to think that, if the Bank applied for early recharter, Democratic friends of the Bank would combine with the opposition to pass the bill. There was equal reason to calculate that the president, given his earlier attacks on the Bank, would veto a recharter and thus allow the opposition to make both the Bank and his expected veto the major issues in the coming presidential campaign.

Having anticipated a Jackson veto, most National Republican leaders now welcomed it. A veto would allow them to draw into the vortex of politics thousands who had a vested interest in the loans and the stability made possible by a national bank. It would allow the National Republicans to tap the energies of hundreds of men of business and talent who hitherto had been indifferent to politics and untroubled by Jackson. It would, thought Webster, surely anger voters in the crucial state of Pennsylvania, where the Bank was located.[62] It would likewise alienate "Jackson members from the West . . . sensible to the benefits" the Bank brought "their Constituents."[63] The Bank, Webster judged, had an "inherent popularity that will and must carry it through."[64]

Yet, though he sensed the advantages the Bank issues would bring the opposition, Webster seemed far less sanguine than his colleagues over the "bright" prospect[65] of a presidential veto. He was fully aware that a veto would permit the opposition publicly to expose the changes that Andrew Jackson had wrought in American politics. But he remained privately uncertain whether the opposition should make Jackson's revolution the central issue of the 1832 campaign.

Personally, Webster believed that Jackson had brought "excessive party spirit"—the "greatest danger . . . of our time"—into government.

[60] See Jean Alexander Wilburn, *Biddle's Bank: The Crucial Years* (New York: Columbia University Press, 1967).

[61] For a report on the sectional distribution of Bank funds, see U.S., Congress, *Senate Documents*, 22nd Cong., 1st sess., 1832, S. Doc. 27 ("Report of the Secretary of the Treasury").

[62] Webster to Harrison Gray Otis, June 8, 1832, Otis Papers.

[63] Joseph Kent to Richard Smith, January 14, 1832, Etting Papers, HSP.

[64] Webster to Stephen White, June 28, 1832, *Writings*, 17:520.

[65] Clay to Hezekiah C. Niles, July 8, 1832, Henry Clay Papers, LC.

The president and his "sinister and selfish" partisans had taken the country far from the ideal form of leadership, where independent men, unafraid of being "outnumbered, or outvoted, or outmanaged, or outclamored," acted "honestly for universal good."[66] Webster knew all too well that Jackson and his party had undermined the bases of authority of leaders like himself. The president had used the veto power to deny legislative rewards to the constituents of congressional leaders; Jackson's followers had used the press to assassinate the character and standing of gentlemen opposed to him.[67] Appointments of *"third-rate men"* loyal only to the president had helped sustain the party organization and the network of newspapers that had brought Jackson to power.[68] It was fully possible, Webster knew, that Jackson had found a way to maintain a political alliance that dispensed with the support of men of talent and of powerful sectional leaders. Webster might hope that Jackson's party would collapse when the popular Old Hero retired in 1836, but there was the ultimate danger that the president's machine would survive him.[69] Some less popular man, bereft of talent but deft at political management, might use the Jacksonian organization to prevent the rightful resurgence of gentlemen leaders.

Exactly how to combat the Jacksonian challenge seemed still to trouble Webster. Everything in his experience as a Federalist suggested that opposition only fed partisanship. He had urged for a decade that balm, not strife, would soften party lines. Perhaps such doubts accounted for the fact that, while Webster's comrades felt a Bank veto would "finish" the president[70] and welcomed it exultingly, Webster confined himself to conjecture over whether Jackson would challenge Congress and so powerful an institution as the Bank of the United States.[71]

With the aid of Democratic congressmen the bill for the Bank's recharter passed on July 4 and within a week, as expected, Jackson vetoed the bill. His veto message exceeded all the expectations of the opposition. It boldly asserted the president's right to override the judgment of Congress and even that of the Supreme Court in determining

---

[66]Daniel Webster, "The Character of Washington, February 22, 1832," *Writings*, 2:75, 79.

[67]For Webster's views of the Jacksonian press as the villifier and traducer of "character," see articles he wrote for the *Washington National Intelligencer*, August 2, 7, 11, 1832; and his "Speech at Worcester, October 12, 1832," *Writings*, 2:114.

[68]*United States Telegraph*, December 4, 1829.

[69]See the series of editorials written for the *Boston Daily Advertiser*, cited in the *Washington National Intelligencer*, October 20, 1832.

[70]Clay to Niles, July 8, 1832, Henry Clay Papers, LC.

[71]Webster to Biddle, May 14, 1832, Nicholas Biddle Papers, LC; Webster to James W. Paige, June 5, 1832, James W. Paige Papers, MHS.

the constitutionality and utility of laws. It suggested that the congressmen who had voted for the bill meant to perpetuate a monopoly and to give unfair advantages to the privileged over the poor. It appealed over the heads of congressmen to the people to sustain the president.[72] Jackson's message, gloated the president of the Bank, had the ring of a "manifesto" to a "mob." It would end "the domination of these miserable people."[73]

Indignantly, Webster replied to Jackson's veto in the Senate. The president had demonstrated his contempt for Congress and had sought to inflame the people against their representatives. Jackson's logic and constitutional arguments were unworthy of notice by "respectable" men.[74] The president's message, Webster warned, "calls us to the contemplation of a future which little resembles the past." It "extends the grasp of executive pretension over every power of the government." The message denied "the authority of the Supreme Court to decide on the constitutional questions"; it "denied to Congress the authority of judging what powers may be constitutionally conferred on a bank." But this was "not all." The veto

manifestly seeks to inflame the poor against the rich; it wantonly attacks whole classes of people, for the purpose of turning against them the prejudices and the resentments of other classes.

Though a "state paper," the veto found "no topic too exciting for its use, no passion too inflamable for its address and solicitation."[75] The question before Congress and the country was now whether "the people of the United States are mere . . . man-worshippers."[76]

Though seemingly content that the issue was now joined, Webster privately was alarmed at the extent to which Jackson had coddled the "prejudice" and "passion" of the voters. He could handle Jackson's constitutional argument, though it was "such miserable stuff" that he hated to "condescend to give it respectful notice." Yet, as Webster drafted and redrafted his reply to the veto for distribution to the country, he was "not satisifed." He wondered if as propaganda his

---

[72] James D. Richardson, comp., *A Compilation of the Messages and Papers of the Presidents, 1789–1905*, 11 vols. (Washington, D.C.: Bureau of National Literature and Art, 1907), 2:577–78, 582, 590–91; Marshall, "The Strange Stillbirth of the Whig Party," pp. 448–49.

[73] Biddle to Clay, August 1, 1832, *The Works of Henry Clay*, 4:341.

[74] Daniel Webster, "The Presidential Veto of the United States Bank Bill, July 11, 1832," *Writings*, 6:180.

[75] *Ibid.*, pp. 179–80. For Webster's reiteration of these objections during the campaign of 1832, see his "Speech at Worcester," *ibid.*, 2:98, 106–7, 112.

[76] Webster, "The Presidential Veto," *ibid.*, 6:155.

address was "too *forensic*, too much in the manner of legal argument, for general reading, or extensive usefulness."[77]

Well might Webster and his colleagues have wondered further to what extent their provocation of the president had helped fulfill their worst premonitions. How far had they forced Jackson toward a strategy of "exciting the multitude"? How much had they compelled the president to seek the aid of the people in order "that he might be in a situation to despise the leaders"?[78] Before the issue of recharter was forced in 1832, the president had regarded the Bank and the leaders of Congress with ambivalent suspicion. It was challenge that crystallized his hostility and hastened his orientation to the voters alone. It "seems to me," Jackson wrote a trusted friend ten days after the veto, "that providence has had a hand in bringing forward the subject at this time to preserve the republic from [the Bank's] thraldom and corrupting influence."[79]

Victory in 1832 went to the General, and in retrospect the results of Jackson's second triumph seem clear. The contest fixed the Bank and executive encroachment of the power of Congress as paramount issues for a decade. In turn, those issues crystallized party premises about who should govern. The National Republican crusade for the Bank and the prerogatives of Congress exposed the bond between the opposition and the established leaders of politics and finance. That strategy deepened Jackson's suspicion of the wealthy and the wise, spurred him to call on the people to save him and themselves from the privileged, and sped the change of Democratic orientation from leaders to voters. Jackson succeeded, and left the opposition disabled by its own strengths. Its appeal attracted the very men who were least fit for the new politics—those who were unwilling to blemish honor by making demeaning pleas to the voter, those who were reluctant to yield command for the good of organization. The election allied and antiquated a whole breed of politicians.

---

[77]Webster to Biddle, August 25, September 24, 1832, Biddle Papers, LC.

[78]Martin Van Buren, "Notes on Conversations with Jackson," n.d., Van Buren Papers, LC.

[79]Jackson to Amos Kendall, July 23, 1832, Andrew Jackson Papers, LC; Marshall, "The Strange Stillbirth of the Whig Party," pp. 458-59.

II

THE POLITICS OF PATRIOTISM

THE PRESIDENTIAL CONTEST of 1832 had rendered the gentleman-leader an anachronism, and Daniel Webster was among the out-moded. Yet, along with others, he hoped the changes of 1832 were not final. Webster sensed that, if the methods, issues, and parties became permanent, he would be affected profoundly. Not only would the election then bind him to his uneasy alliance with Clay and Calhoun, rivals in ambition and outlook, but the place for Webster's kind of leadership would vanish. The "public man," as Webster repeatedly referred to him, settled disputes—and offices—not by pleas to the uninformed but by reasoned negotiation with other public men. He and others of the better class ruled public affairs selflessly; Tocqueville's doubts and Marx's later denials notwithstanding, Webster's leader could transcend self-interest to serve the whole community. But a public man could be successful only when trusted by the community to do what was best for all, and only when independent enough to act as reason required. Partisan conflict destroyed trust, as party discipline fettered reason, and the recent campaign had made a virtue of both evils.

At the end of 1832 nothing seemed less likely than a cessation of party wars, but that is just what happened. In December, faced with the threat of state nullification of a federal law, the victorious president stunned the country with a stinging attack on state's rights and a de-

48

fense of national supremacy. Swiftly Webster responded by moving to forge an alliance with the president and to translate the peril of disunion into a new sense of national community. For a year, through public patriotism and private negotiations, Webster simultaneously pursued two goals. He positioned himself to lead his own coalition by exploiting his stature as a nationalist. But, more energetically, he fought to obliterate old parties—and to form an enduring union of Unionists.

I

The tumult of the election had overshadowed an ominous fact: in the waning days of the campaign, South Carolina had made good on its threat to void the federal tariff by state law.[1] The state's immediate goal was to force a further reduction of the tariff, but its nullification ordinance also forced the issue of whether the government should capitulate with a pistol at its head. Without an explicit rebuke of nullification, tariff cuts might set a precedent for extortion. Concessions to preserve the Union might then only hasten its end. Yet, if some form of rebuke seemed indispensable, it could not be so harsh as to provoke war or to rally other Southern states—all of whom had formally rejected nullification—to South Carolina's defense. How to concede without appeasing, how to chasten short of war, was the delicate problem that confronted the country, the Congress, and the president.

For his part, as the crisis came to a head, the senator from Massachusetts was gloomy. The president's early silence on the tariff and the nullifiers, he felt in mid-October, had encouraged South Carolina to act in the first place.[2] To make matters worse, John C. Calhoun, who had resigned from the vice-presidency to return to the Senate as the nullifiers' spokesman,[3] had recently published the "ablest and most plausible, and therefore the most dangerous vindication of that form of revolution, yet done."[4] Rumored presidential remedies—hangings, an inva-

---

[1] The nullification ordinance and laws of November 24-27, 1832, authorized South Carolina citizens to refuse to pay duties and empowered the government to resist enforcement of the tariff by force.

[2] Daniel Webster, "Speech at Worcester, October 12, 1832," *The Writings and Speeches of Daniel Webster*, ed. J. W. McIntyre, 18 vols. (Boston: Little, Brown & Co., 1903), 2:121-23 (hereafter cited as *Writings*).

[3] For a discussion of Calhoun's hope to ward off more radical steps by his fellow South Carolinians through the doctrine and policy of nullification, see William W. Freehling, *Prelude to Civil War: The Nullification Controversy in South Carolina, 1816-1836* (New York: Harper & Row, 1966), pp. 155-59, 175-76.

[4] Daniel Webster to James Kent, October 29, 1832, James Kent Papers, Library of Congress, Washington, D.C. (hereafter cited as LC).

sion of South Carolina—seemed as portentous as the danger itself. As Webster set out in early December for the capital and the climactic confrontation, there seemed little prospect that Jackson would adopt Webster's formula for handling the crisis: a summons to the "good and the wise" for counsel, an admonition to the country that "the Union is in danger"; and a call for the aid of all patriots.[5] On the contrary, there seemed every chance that the president would do too little or too much—that he would totally sacrifice protection or lead the country headlong into civil war.

But, as Webster rode toward the capital, Jackson moved against the nullifiers. His proclamation of December 10, which reached Webster in New Jersey, declared that the "laws of the United States must be executed" and that disunion "by armed force is *treason.*" Jackson appealed to South Carolina for prudence and to the nation for support. The president might have ended on this note of firmness and patriotism, but the proclamation went on to denounce nullification in terms Webster had shaped over the years in the battle against states' rights. Jackson rejected the argument that nullification was a constitutional form of redress and a nonviolent alternative to secession. The government, he declared, was formed by the people—not by the states—and, hence, no state could challenge it. Nullification was but a prelude to secession; South Carolina's ordinance—"incompatible with the existence of the Union, contradicted expressly by the letter of the Constitution, unauthorized by its spirit, inconsistent with every principle on which it was founded"—was rebellion.[6]

Instantly Webster saw profound changes in the making. Here, at last, was proof that the president was sound on the Constitution. Here, at last, was an intimation that the president would not sacrifice the tariff to the nullifiers. Here, at last, was a summons for the good and the wise to rally around the Union. Of his firm personal support for Jackson, Webster was now certain, but, perhaps fearing—and rightly so—that Massachusetts antipathy for Jackson would lead some at home to hold back support for the proclamation and wishing to have a public chance quickly to announce his own stand, he ordered his coach back to Boston. As he sped home, he settled on his course. He would see to it that

---

[5] Webster, "Speech at Worcester," *Writings*, 2:121-23.

[6] James D. Richardson, comp., *A Compilation of the Messages and Papers of the Presidents, 1789-1905*, 11 vols. (Washington, D.C.: Bureau of National Literature and Art, 1907), 2:643, 648. For a sophisticated comparison of the views of Webster, Jackson, and John Quincy Adams on the meaning of "liberty" and of the Union, see Major L. Wilson, " 'Liberty and Union': An Analysis of Three Concepts Involved in the Nullification Controversy," *Journal of Southern History*, 33 (August, 1967):331-55.

Massachusetts responded to Jackson's call swiftly and unequivocally, and he would announce the state's support for the president himself. Webster returned to a Boston stirred by the president's stand. "The proclamation takes prodigiously," Edward Everett's wife reported. "We are all quite in love with the President," exclaimed another correspondent.[7] Yet, as Webster probably expected, some had their doubts. The proclamation contained "the true principles of the Constitution," affirmed Supreme Court Justice Joseph Story, but would the president enforce them? Webster's close friend Rufus Choate thought the document mere verbal flourish, a ringing prelude to tariff surrender. Most National Republican leaders, including John Quincy Adams, wished to wait and see if Jackson's deeds would match his words and wanted to delay an endorsement at least until the state legislature met later that month. But Webster drove for prompt approval of the president's stand. Two days after his return, a petition began to circulate which called for a public rally to support Jackson, and shortly thereafter a meeting was set for December 17.

When Webster addressed the Faneuil Hall assembly on the gray, rainy morning of the seventeenth, his speech reflected his private premonition that bloodshed was now likely.[8] No one knew whether the audience would meet again as citizens of the United States, for "this doctrine of nullification means resistance to the laws by force. It is but another name for civil war." If the government now failed to keep the states in their places, "from that moment the whole Union is virtually dissolved." Between anarchy and union, Webster proclaimed, "my choice is made. I am for the Union as it is"—and hence for the proclamation.[9]

---

[7] Charlotte Everett to Edward Everett, December 16, 1832, Edward Everett Papers, Massachusetts Historical Society, Boston (hereafter cited as MHS). MHS; Theodore Sedgwick to Nathan Appleton, December 18, 1832, Nathan Appleton Papers, MHS.

[8] Joseph Story to Richard Peters, December 22, 1832, Thomas Cadwalader–Richard Peters Papers, Historical Society of Pennsylvania, Philadelphia (hereafter cited as HSP); Rufus Choate to [Jonathon Shove], December 25, [1832], in *Essex Institute Historical Collections*, 69 (January, 1933):84; John Quincy Adams to Charles Francis Adams, December 25, 1832, letterbook copy, John Quincy Adams Papers, MHS; Webster to Levi Lincoln, December 10 [1832], Levi Lincoln Papers, MHS.

[9] Whether nullification was in fact "but another name for civil war" is open to question. Among the nullifiers themselves, secession and the possibility of civil war had actually been considered among the recourses to the tariff—and rejected. Nullification was thought a "conservative" measure, a peaceful alternative to secession. Peace would prevail and union would continue if federal officials declined to enforce the laws. But, if nullification was not necessarily "resistance to the laws by force," it clearly was resistance to the laws. Webster properly questioned how long a government could sanction civil disobedience by states before that government either dissolved in anarchy or suppressed the disobedient.

Convinced that Jackson, for one, would not be timid, Webster insisted that support of the proclamation required support of the president. When "the standard of the Union is raised and waves over my head—the standard which Washington planted on the ramparts of the Constitution—God forbid it that I should inquire whom the people have commissioned to unfurl it and bear it up." Both the cause and the president would have Webster's "zealous cooperation."[10] On December 21, days after Webster had again left for Washington, a close friend and member of the Massachusetts General Court surprised the legislature by moving that Jackson be invited to visit Massachusetts. Reluctantly the legislature acquiesced, agreeing privately that, should Jackson actually come, "those who did not like it" would "simply do nothing."[11]

The words of Webster and the act of his friend suggest that already he anticipated that nullification might produce a new alignment of men and parties. Crisis would unite the country; patriotism would supplant partisanship; former foes would see their common interest in the Union. If Jackson wanted a new era of good feelings, Webster had signaled that New England was ready to make its peace.

II

In fact, Jackson had no special wish to make his peace with Webster or New England. He was above all interested in quelling nullification, and to that end would work with any allies. Jackson initially had hoped to pacify South Carolina and other Southerner states with moderation. In his message to Congress on December 4—a week before the proclamation—he not only had ruled out a request for additional military authority to deal with the nullifiers, but had reversed his previous stand on the tariff. Through 1832 Jackson had always spoken, albeit vaguely, of his approval of a "judicious" tariff to protect American labor. Now he linked the tariff to the same monopolistic interests which conspired for the Bank of the United States and called for tariff reduction.[12] His moderate approach, however, was short-lived. After his message of December 4 had gone to press, the president received word that the South Carolina state convention had passed an ordinance voiding the Tariffs of 1828 and 1832. Outraged, Jackson dedicated himself from that moment on to the supreme goal of crushing *"treason"* at "all hazards and

---

[10]Daniel Webster, "Speech at Faneuil Hall, December 17, 1832," *Writings*, 13:40-42.

[11]Peter Paul Francis Degrand to Nicholas Biddle, July 4, 1833, Nicholas Biddle Papers, LC.

[12]Freehling, *Prelude to Civil War*, pp. 265-67, 288.

at any price."[13] Tariff reform became entirely secondary in the president's priorities, and the stage was set for cooperation with Webster and the other Unionists.

The nationalist zeal of Jackson's proclamation accurately reflected Jackson's determination to preserve the Union without temporizing;[14] the proclamation's purpose and doctrine necessarily linked the president with Webster. Many Democrats recoiled from Jackson's apparent endorsement of an omnipotent central government. Churchill C. Cambreleng, a congressman from New York and a confidant of Van Buren, thought that a patriotic plea for the Union without a word of doctrine would have carried "every man in the nation but a nullifier." The gratuitous theorizing of the proclamation had confused Northern Democrats, thoroughly frightened Southerners, and elicited the "unbounded approbation of every ultra federalist from Maine to Louisiana."[15] Despite suggestions that he mute doctrinal pronouncements that affronted the sensibilities of states'-rights Democrats, Jackson steadfastly refused to modify a word of the proclamation and stood by its sentiments privately and publicly throughout the crisis.

Democrats and Southerners were not the only ones frightened by the turn of events. Henry Clay also was fearful. The inconsistency between the proclamation and the message did not escape him, but the menacing tone of the proclamation seemed more like the real Jackson—the military chieftain eager for decisive battle. The alacrity with which Webster and Boston had endorsed the proclamation— and Jackson personally— also seemed precipitate and ominous to Clay. Events pointed to civil and political danger. Hence, when Webster met with Clay in late December, as the Massachusetts senator was again en route to Washington, the Kentuckian not only spoke of possible new reductions of the tariff but showed Webster a draft of a preamble which explicitly surrendered the right of Congress to lay duties for protection.[16] Clay's purpose was

---

[13] Joel R. Poinsett to Jackson, November 29, 1832; Jackson to Poinsett, December 2, 1832; and [Jackson] to Edward Livingston, December 4, 1832; *The Correspondence of Andrew Jackson*, ed. John Spencer Bassett, 7 vols. (Washington, D.C.: Carnegie Institute of Washington, 1926-35), 4:491-95 (hereafter cited as *The Correspondence of Andrew Jackson*). For a persuasive account of Jackson's change of priorities during the nullification crisis, see James C. Curtis, *Fox at Bay: Martin Van Buren and the Presidency, 1837-1841* (Lexington: The University of Kentucky Press, 1970), pp. 40-44.

[14] Jackson to Van Buren, December 15, 1832, *The Correspondence of Andrew Jackson*, 4:500-501.

[15] Churchill C. Cambreleng to Van Buren, December 18, 1832, Martin Van Buren Papers, LC; Edward T. Tayloe to Benjamin O. Tayloe, February 6, 1833, Tayloe Family Papers, Alderman Library, University of Virginia, Charlottesville.

[16] Webster to Hiram Ketchum, January 20, 1838, in George Ticknor Curtis, *Life of Daniel Webster*, 2 vols. (New York: D. Appleton & Co., 1872), 1:454-55.

to sound Webster out on a tentative plan to avert civil war, but Webster was aghast. If any doubts lingered about working with the president, they now vanished. Jackson seemed the only salvation of the tariff and the Union.

But, when Webster arrived in Washington, he discovered that the priorities of the president were not at all the same as the goals of Democratic congressmen. Congressional Democrats talked not of the proclamation but of compromise.[17] The House Ways and Means Committee, led by Democrat Gulian C. Verplanck of New York, had prepared a bill in late December to cut duties in half by 1834.[18] "I never saw our friends so desponding," the bewildered senator confessed on January 1. "Great and extraordinary efforts are put forth" to push the Verplanck bill through Congress, he reported, and by January 4 he feared that it was inevitable that *"party discipline*, operating on members of the Government, " would scuttle the tariff. Yet, with uncanny accuracy, Webster still believed that Jackson opposed immediate compromise. *"E contra*, I fancy he would prefer the undivided honor of suppressing nullification now, and to take his own time hereafter to remodel the tariff."[19]

Amidst this confusion, Jackson's request on January 16 for additional powers to quell possible resistance to the law by South Carolina cleared the air for Webster. He correctly saw the message as Jackson's signal that the nullification question would be "seen thro', & that no modification of the Tariff would do any good." At last, he wrote, "people begin to see . . . what nullification is, & what must be done to put it down."[20] The call for new power was so distasteful to Southern Democrats and so embarrassing for their Northern colleagues[21] that it fell to Webster to lead the bill through the Senate. Almost at once after receiving the message, Webster's Senate Judiciary Committee unanimously reported a measure giving the president new powers to deal with the nullifiers. Southerners were angry. Virginia's states'-rights sen-

---

[17] Andrew Jackson Donelson to John Coffee, December 18, 1832, Andrew Jackson Donelson Papers, LC; Cambreleng to Van Buren, December 29, 1832, Van Buren Papers, LC; Webster to Henry Kinsman, January 1, 1833, Daniel Webster Papers, Dartmouth College, Hanover, N.H.

[18] Freehling, *Prelude to Civil War*, p. 288.

[19] Webster to Kinsman, January 1, 1833; and Webster to Warren Dutton, January 4, 1833, Webster Papers, Dartmouth. Webster to William Sullivan, January 3, 1833, in G. Curtis, *Life of Daniel Webster*, 1:437. For corroboration of Webster's judgment, see Jackson to Van Buren, January 13, 1833; and Jackson to Poinsett, January 16, 1833; *The Correspondence of Andrew Jackson*, 5:2–6.

[20] Webster to [unidentified correspondent], January 18, 1833, Webster Papers, Dartmouth.

[21] Cambreleng to Van Buren, February 5, 1833; and Thomas Hart Benton to Van Buren, February 16, 1833; Van Buren Papers, LC.

ator, John Tyler, predicted the "closest and most fraternal embrace" between the administration and Webster. Dining at the White House a week after Jackson's request, he resentfully noted "Mr. W. there in all his glory."[22]

In thinking that Jackson now preferred force in his dealings with South Carolina, and Webster as his agent in Congress, Webster and the Southerners had partially misjudged Jackson's intentions. The president had relied on South Carolina Unionists to counter any armed resistance to the collection of duties. Only when he received reports that the state's antinullification forces were inadequate had he reluctantly called for more federal authority. Though enemies of the legislation dubbed it the "Force Bill," the measure was in fact designed to avoid armed force and to warn headstrong South Carolinians, before they went too far, that unless the laws were executed Jackson would send troops.[23] Determined to see the measure passed and aware that it embarrassed his friends, Jackson encouraged Webster's leadership and showed him the courtesies of a comrade-in-arms.

But more than presidential courtesies led Webster to think that Jackson had committed himself to disciplining South Carolina. In February, Democratic plans for a tariff cut went awry; Jackson nonetheless stuck by the "Force Bill." Webster took the failure of compromise and the president's firmness as further proof of a hard-line executive policy. In fact, Jackson's purposes were more complex. Though he was willing for Democratic congressmen to attempt a peaceful settlement based on tariff concessions, the president remained reluctant to yield anything under threat of nullification, and he did not exert himself to force through a compromise. Compromise failed when party discipline broke down and New York Democratic congressmen refused to back the Verplanck bill. Repeatedly they voted with other protariff representatives to delay a final ballot, and by late January it became clear that they would help defeat the bill.[24]

At this point Webster might have been pleased. His careful acts and Jackson's exigencies had brought about cordial relations with the president; Jackson had not retreated before the nullifiers; and Democratic

---

[22] John Tyler to John Floyd, January 22, 1833, John Floyd Papers, LC.

[23] Freehling, *Prelude to Civil War*, pp. 282–86.

[24] Jackson to Van Buren, January 13, 1833; and Jackson to Poinsett, January 24, 1833; *The Correspondence of Andrew Jackson*, 5:3, 12. See also Silas Wright to Azariah C. Flagg, February 25, 1833, Azariah C. Flagg Papers, New York Public Library, New York, N.Y. Wright reported that the tenacity of the New York delegation in holding onto the tariff of 1832 "threw this subject out of the hands of the administration and into the hands of the new coalition." See J. Curtis, *Martin Van Buren*, pp. 41–43.

concessions were dead. If Webster could keep the issue of nationhood paramount and isolated, there seemed every chance that the new question would obliterate old divisions.

Yet Webster knew that Clay was determined to try his hand at compromise, and, with the demise of the Verplanck bill, rumors spread of a new tariff measure—drafted by Clay and approved by Calhoun. By February 8, alarmed that mounting pressures for conciliation would tempt Jackson to accept even a Clay bill, and reasoning that the president would still prefer first to quell nullification and then to adjust the tariff himself, Webster hastily drafted his own ideas on the timing and substance of a settlement.

In a memorandum almost certainly intended for Jackson's eyes, Webster pledged full support of the "administration in executing the laws" without "mingling other topics" with that support. While Webster would not give up the *"principle"* of protection, he would cooperate in reducing the federal revenue to the "just wants of the government" and, to that end, in revising the tariff. But tariff cuts, he added—in words calculated to remind Jackson of his own previous statements about protection—must have a "just regard, to the necessities of the Country in time of war, to the faith plighted by existing & previous laws to the reasonable protection of capital, & especially to the security of the interests of *labor & wages."* Then Webster offered concessions. If, in the coming year, Congress did not vote to distribute among the states the mounting income from the sale of public lands, that revenue should go directly to the Treasury. The surplus would then justify a lower tariff. If, on the other hand, distribution did pass, Webster would approve "some measure . . . to limit, practically," congressional grants for internal improvements to such projects "as in their nature transcend the powers & duties of separate States." Meanwhile he advanced a solution to the present crisis. First, a "feigned or real" test case on the constitutionality of duties for protection only should be brought before the Supreme Court. Second, Jackson should back a moratorium on tariff revision. During the delay, a special Senate committee would travel to major Northern cities seeking information on tariff sentiment and would report back in the fall with a bill to adjust the revenue to the needs of government.[25]

---

[25] Daniel Webster, "Principles," an undated document published in *Writings*, 15:104-5. My conclusion that Webster meant this paper for Jackson's eyes is admittedly speculative. At least on two other occasions, however, Webster drafted similar briefs which stated his position and sought presidential endorsement of it. See Daniel Webster, "Suggestions to Joel R. Poinsett on the Northeastern Boundary, March 9, 1839," *ibid.*, pp. 119-22; and Shaw Livermore, Jr., *The Twilight of Federalism: The Disintegration of the Federalist Party, 1815-1830* (Princeton: Princeton University Press, 1962), pp. 174-79.

Had this plan ever reached Jackson, he would surely have been skeptical about it. The proposal that Jackson be firm now and benevolent later might have attracted the old warrior, but the essence of the scheme seemed to call for a continuance of the public debt and hence the customary excuse for high duties. The opinions about the tariff that Webster proposed to collect—from leaders of Boston, Providence, New York, Philadelphia, and Pittsburgh—could provide only a view of the country's needs which was least likely to endanger protection. The court test of the tariff's constitutionality, though typical of Webster's reliance on a usually sympathetic judiciary in matters of national powers, ignored the truth that Jackson had repeatedly declared public opinion and his own judgment to be superior to judicial precedent. Indeed, Webster's entire proposal assumed that Jackson was perfectly ready to reverse previous commitments, and that he was now eager to consult the good and the wise, the bench, bar, and counting house, in making his public decisions.

If any part of Webster's plan reached or tempted Jackson, he never indicated it. Jackson had little choice but to swallow a Clay-Calhoun compromise on the tariff. By itself, the "Force Bill" had the ring of a first shot, and the last thing Jackson wanted was to give South Carolina an excuse for war or to drive other Southern states to its aid. Though Jackson continued to show friendship for Webster, he did nothing to obstruct Clay.

Clay moved swiftly. Convinced that Jackson aimed to destroy protection as well as nullification, he reached agreement with Calhoun on the same day Webster worked out his plan, February 8. On the eleventh he presented his bill to the Senate and proposed a gradual reduction of all duties over a nine-year span. Reductions would be small at first, larger later; the most severe cut would not come until 1842, when all duties would fall to the nonprotective rate of 20 percent or below.

The Jackson "Force Bill" and the Clay tariff compromise moved through Congress together. Webster did battle with Calhoun on the first and with Clay on the second. To Calhoun, who warned that the "Force Bill" would be "resisted at every hazard, even that of death," and who argued that the true issue of nullification was whether an oppressed minority had legal recourse against majority tyranny, Webster made his standard reply. Nullification and its logical offspring, secession, were not rights under the Constitution. Either claim was an "absurdity; for it supposes resistance to Government under the authority of Government itself; it supposes dismemberment, without violating the principles of union; it supposes opposition to law, without crime"; it "supposes the total overthrow of Government, without revolution." Webster ridiculed the idea of giving to each section, or to each state, the power to veto the decision of the whole country; that was minority tyranny. The majority must rule, generally ruled well, and, in the case of the doctrine of nullification, had ruled.

But, if Webster was persuasive on the probable effects of nullification on the government's authority, he appeared more vulnerable, and Calhoun seemed stronger, on a crucial point of fact. Calhoun contended that the historical origin of the Constitution gave states a right to judge, and if necessary to nullify, acts of the federal government. Of course, no such right was specified in the document, but Calhoun argued that the Constitution had been a "compact" among sovereign states. Like parties to any compact, states retained the right to suspend their obligations if the other parties violated the letter or spirit of the agreement. This was not the right of violent revolution. It was the peaceful and legitimate right of nullification. Clashing with the "compact" theory, Webster argued that the Constitution derived its authority from the "people," who had merely acted through the medium of the states. Only the people, through their national institutions of court, Congress, and executive, could legally change or suspend the Constitution. A recent study of the origins of the federal Constitution suggests that Webster was actually closer to the truth about the process of ratification than Calhoun. In any case, Webster was certainly closer to the romantic interpretation of the past and to the public sentiment about the Union which prevailed by the 1830s.[26] Sensing that the real strength of his argument lay more in current conviction than in the record of the past, Webster quickly skipped over whether the states or the people had conceived the Union and focused instead on the present. Calhoun's doctrines had "no succor from public sympathy; no cheering from a patriotic community." No logic, no historical quibbling, could reverse the verdict of public opinion.[27] As to Calhoun's prophecy of conflict, Webster did not want war. But, if blood did flow, Webster would stand "where the blows might fall thickest and fastest" and to his last breath exhort his countrymen, *"To the Rescue. To the Rescue!"*[28]

The oratory of neither senator seemed to have much impact on the outcome of the "Force Bill," and even most Southerners judged the law

---

[26] Gordon Wood, *The Creation of the American Republic, 1776-1787* (Chapel Hill: University of North Carolina Press, 1969), chap. 8, and esp. pp. 354-63 and 532-36.

[27] U.S., Congress, *Register of Debates in the Congress of the United States* (Washington, D.C.: Gales & Seaton, 1833), 22nd Cong. 2nd sess., December, 1832-March, 1833, 9:554-87; see pp. 553-56, 570, 586-87 (hereafter cited as *Register of Debates*).

[28] *Register of Debates*, 9:587; report of Webster's speech in *Boston Daily Evening Transcript*, February 26, 1833.

an unfortunate necessity. After efforts to postpone the bill failed, only a remnant of eight Southern senators stood to oppose the measure by February 19. The dissenting eight decided not to sanction the bill with their presence—even to oppose it—and, on the final vote, only John Tyler said nay to the measure, which passed, 32 to 1.[29]

Webster failed to ward off Clay's compromise, however. With no success, he called on Congress to settle one issue at a time, to send a committee from both houses and all sections to canvass the country on the tariff, and to postpone action until they received a report conceived in tranquillity rather than in fear. Vainly he argued that the Clay measure granted concessions under threat of force and thus encouraged future threats. Futilely he charged that Clay's "compromise" in fact surrendered the principle of protection, even if surrender was to be postponed until 1842.[30] Clay simply replied to all these claims that his bill was not a sellout and that delay would only bring a still lower tariff measure at the next session of Congress. New York Democrats seemed to agree that Clay's was a milder bill than the one they had just blocked, and, with their votes and Southern cooperation, Clay's tariff passed.[31] Jackson signed the bill into law on March 2.

Confused and angry, Webster missed the essential truth of Clay's claim that his was a better measure for protectionists than any that was likely to pass the next, more Jacksonian Congress, which would take office on March 4. Calhoun and others had gone along with Clay's plan, which postponed meaningful tariff cuts until 1842, only because they feared further delay might bring war. Had congressional Democrats had the votes in the spring of 1833, they would have permitted far greater and more immediate reductions in the tariff.

Webster rather comprehended the cooperation of Clay and Calhoun as a plot for the presidency: Clay had traded the tariff for Southern support. Awkward facts which did not jibe with this appraisal were ignored by the senator. He did not stop to wonder at Calhoun's conspicuous refusal to sanction a permanent Southern alliance with Clay, or to ask how Calhoun, at the nadir of his national influence, could have made anyone president. Nor did Webster linger to ask why Clay should sit limply by in the face of Webster's own overtures to Jackson and Webster's seeming readiness to risk civil war for textile mills. Gener-

[29] *Register of Debates*, 9:246, 404, 601, 689.

[30] *Ibid.*, pp. 478-79; 727-29; Webster to Benjamin F. Perry, April 10, 1833, in G. Curtis, *Life of Daniel Webster*, 1:457-58; Webster to Joel Poinsett, May 7, 1833, Pierpont Morgan Library, New York, N.Y. (photostatic copy, Webster Papers, Dartmouth).

[31] *Register of Debates*, 9:481, 729-42.

ous in judging his own motives and Jackson's, Webster did not allow his thinking to go beyond Clay's treason. Sensing the public was unaware of the scope of that betrayal, Webster prepared to publish a copy of the sacrificial tariff plan Clay had shown him in December. Only at the last minute did a friend dissuade him.[32]

Webster soon found himself all the more irked when Clay coolly calmed Northern anxieties over the compromise. A Clay emissary easily soothed Massachusetts industrialists with the revelation of the secret benefits of the bill. It not only averted a worse measure and gave them time to become independent of protection; it also gave established mills a greater hold on their markets, by removing the high-tariff shield which had encouraged the proliferation of smaller competitors. By March 19, Clay's intermediary reported from Boston that the bill was "*now* considered a good one—and will be *extremely* popular when fully understood."[33] Businessmen could not publicly praise Clay, lest praise stir new Southern demands or demean the struggle of their Massachusetts senator. But privately they cooed. Abbott Lawrence, a leading Boston manufacturer who had initially opposed the lower tariff, now smothered Clay with thanks. The bill was an unbounded "dictate of wisdom"; it "greatly promoted" New England's interests; Clay was "never more popular." Critical Boston editors suddenly fell silent on the tariff—"and will remain so," Lawrence assured Clay.[34]

Even before Clay had turned protectionist anger into applause, Webster had decided to sustain his good relations with the president. Plausibly anticipating that South Carolina hotheads would portray the Clay compromise as but a first victory and would make prompt new demands for the total emasculation of the tariff, Webster expected the nullification crisis to continue.[35] The expected challenge would again require that the two leaders work together, and none could say for how long or with what results.

Jackson, equally unsure that the worst was over, possibly uncertain of his Southern support should the nullification threat not subside, and

---

[32] Webster to Ketchum, January 18, 20, 1838, in G. Curtis, *Life of Daniel Webster*, 1:454-55.

[33] Peleg Sprague to Clay, March 19, 1833, Henry Clay Papers, LC; Harrison Gray Otis to George Harrison, March 11, 1833, Harrison Gray Otis Papers, MHS.

[34] Abbott Lawrence to Clay, March 26, 1833, *The Works of Henry Clay Comprising His Life, Correspondence, and Speeches*, ed. Calvin Colton, 10 vols. (New York: G. P. Putnam's Sons, 1904), 5:357-58 (hereafter cited as *The Works of Henry Clay*).

[35] Webster to Benjamin F. Perry, April 10, 1833, in G. Curtis, *Life of Daniel Webster*, 1:457-58; Webster to Poinsett, May 7, 1833, photostatic copy, Webster Papers, Dartmouth.

no doubt pleased in any case to divide Henry Clay's National Republican alliance, encouraged the Northern senator's attentions. He complimented Webster personally on his reply to Calhoun, and soon afterward a Jackson senator offered to show Webster a list of tentative government appointees for the Eastern states (which Webster declined to examine). Secretary of State Edward Livingston, thought by most to be the author of the nullification proclamation, had repeated talks with Jackson in February and early March about Webster's political future, and Webster found relayed reports of the conversations cheering.[36]

By mid-March, spurred by an exaggerated sense of betrayal and the irritation of being outflanked in his home state, Webster was ready to go beyond courtesies. He moved to make permanent the bond forged with Jackson in their joint defense of the Union and the Constitution. In a summer of mutual manipulation, of testing and tempting, Webster sought to break ground for his own presidential candidacy and for a new political party—a party of patriots.[37]

III

To that alliance there were substantial obstacles. The most obvious was the still unsettled dispute over the Bank of the United States. Jackson had tacitly agreed to Webster's proposal that the war on nullification be unmingled with other topics, but the truce was threatened in April by intimations of new presidential moves against the Bank. Word spread that Jackson was preparing to rechannel government deposits from the national bank to selected state banks. Removal of the deposits would not only curb the Bank's lending power and depress its stock. It would signal that Jackson meant to see the bank war through and would dash all lingering hopes for a bank compromise.

But the danger was as much an inducement to cooperation as a deterrent. If Webster could forestall removal and then negotiate a settlement on the Bank with Jackson, he would in a stroke eliminate the great issue between parties and pave the way for a lasting alliance with the president. The style of negotiations exactly suited Webster's notion of proper politics. He would reason with the president through Livingston and other personal contacts; Jackson's concessions would gain Webster's support and the attachment of New England; Jackson would

---

[36] Memorandum dictated by Webster in 1838, in G. Curtis, *Life of Daniel Webster*, 1:464.

[37] Webster to Perry, April 10, 1833, *ibid.*, p. 458; Webster to Poinsett, May 7, 1833, photostatic copy, Webster Papers, Dartmouth.

abandon conflict and would bid his coalition to follow suit. With dispute gone, a new coalition would result. This was the correct form of politics: conflict was negotiated; leaders led; followers followed.

In his venture to deal directly with Jackson on the Bank issue, Webster had the backing of the president of the Bank. Though Nicholas Biddle had given unstinting support to the National Republicans in the recent election, his first loyalty was to the Bank, and he encouraged and closely followed Webster's efforts.[38] Meanwhile, however, Biddle labored to keep relations among Webster, Clay, and others from breaking down totally. Biddle knew that, if Webster failed and Jackson did remove the deposits, he would need the aid and cooperation of all friendly senators.

Intractable obstacles to Webster's alliance with Jackson were the vested political interests of men in the Jackson and Clay coalitions who stood to lose from such an arrangement. New York Democrats, such as Martin Van Buren, Benjamin F. Butler, and Churchill C. Cambreleng, had long opposed any form of "amalgamation." Party distinctions were indispensable to party survival, thought Benjamin Butler. The *"moral qualification"* of independent men did not prevent quite selfish conduct by them. The "safety of the republic & the good of the People" required Democrats "to keep up & adhere to old party distinctions, & to make *political consistency"* an "indispensable requisite to public office."[39] Van Buren, in particular, depended on party discipline and Jackson's blessing for his promotion to the presidency. A threat to either might thwart his plans; Webster's threat to both was an immediate danger.

Clay had equal reason to fight a new political alliance, especially along the lines Webster envisaged. A Constitution and Union party would isolate Clay and Calhoun. The prospect discomfited, not only because Clay and Calhoun plainly distrusted one another, but also because all in opposition to a party of patriots would be branded anti-Unionists. Even if the movement for a new party failed, Webster's possible defection to the Democrats threatened havoc for the Whig league of sectional leaders.

Against these substantial odds Webster moved to lay the foundation for his candidacy and, if possible, a new party. Moving first to buttress

[38] Thomas Payne Govan, *Nicholas Biddle: Nationalist and Public Banker, 1786–1844* (Chicago: University of Chicago Press, 1959), p. 261; Webster to Biddle, April 7, 8, 10, 1833, Biddle Papers, LC.

[39] Benjamin F. Butler to Van Buren, May 6, 1829, Benjamin F. Butler Papers, New York State Library, Albany, N.Y.

the alliance with Jackson, he pressed in mid-March for an understanding on the Bank and sought a meeting with Secretary of State Livingston. Since by this time Livingston was in the capital, and Webster in Boston, Webster suggested a meeting in New York City in April, before Livingston embarked for his new post as U.S. minister to France. Webster urged haste, because he feared that at any moment Jackson might take the irrevocable step of removing the deposits from the Bank. The senator slipped into New York, where he awaited Livingston's reply or arrival, and meanwhile relayed to Biddle all hints about Jackson's plans.[40] Campbell P. White, a New York Democrat who had just returned to the city from the capital, told Webster on April 7 that Jackson had decided on removal, then assured Webster on April 8 that the deposits question was *as far from being settled as ever.*" Before White—who was in fact sounding out New Yorkers on removal for Jackson—left again for Washington the next day, Webster warned him of the "impropriety & impolicy of this war on the Bank." "He seemed earnestly to concur," Webster reported to Biddle. They discussed the state of parties and the prospects for the future. White promised a "full conversation with the President."[41]

In fact, Jackson never for a moment thought of abandoning the war with the Bank or his resolve to remove the federal deposits from the Bank's vaults. The president avoided a commitment to Webster on the Bank issue only because he had no wish to divulge his plan prematurely. Livingston, who may well have been in the dark anyhow, continued to postpone a reply to Webster's request for a meeting, and the two did not meet until July 18. By then, Livingston was leaving the cabinet to become minister to France, and it is unlikely that he had authority to speak on issues or possible offices. He did want Webster connected with the administration, however, and apparently reiterated Jackson's personal sentiments of attachment and gratitude to the Massachusetts senator.[42] Meanwhile, Jackson indicated an eagerness at least to continue the show of good feeling. He accepted the Massachusetts legislature's

[40]Draft of letter, Webster to [Edward Livingston, March 21, 1833], Daniel Webster Papers, New Hampshire Historical Society, Concord (hereafter cited as NHHS); Webster to Biddle, April 7, 8, 10, 1833, Biddle Papers, LC.

[41]Webster to Biddle, April 7, 8, 10, 1833, Biddle Papers, LC.

[42]Throughout the spring and summer of 1833, Jackson made clear to his confidants and cabinet members his irrevocable intention to remove the deposits. See, for example, Jackson to the Members of the Cabinet, March 19, 1833; Jackson to Rev. Hardy M. Cryer, April 7, 1833; Jackson to Van Buren, June 6 and July 24, 1833; Jackson to Tilgham A. Howard, August 20, 1833; *The Correspondence of Andrew Jackson,* 5:32–33, 52–54, 106–7, 142–43, 165–66. For Webster's protracted attempts to gain an audience with Livingston, see Webster to John Davis, April 15, 1833, John Davis Papers, American Antiquarian Society, Worcester, Mass.;

invitation to visit the state, and had Webster informed in April of his plan to journey to New England in June.[43] Webster was delighted—as well he might have been, since he had arranged the invitation—but he was himself preparing for a tour of the West the same month. But both men seemed wary of too much camaraderie. Webster asked the president to alter his plans so that he could welcome Jackson personally to Boston, and Jackson lamented that his schedule was fixed.[44] So the two leaders went on with their separate arrangements, content for the time with a tacit moratorium on the Bank and a continued exchange of the symbols of friendship.[45]

Webster left for the West in late May, visiting Albany, Buffalo, Cincinnati, Pittsburgh, and cities between. He canvassed the possibilities for a Union party. Time and again he warned his audiences that the nullification threat remained and spoke of a "deep determination among the politicians of the South to produce a separation."[46] In numerous private meetings, Webster took care to add sentiments congenial to local interests, variously endorsing the Bank, the tariff, internal improvements, and Anti-Masonry. But mainly he encouraged the view that the "great approaching political division of the whole country is to be between Unionists and anti-Unionists." Privately he urged the establishment of newspapers "devoted to this question exclusively" and assured editors and local leaders of "regular contributions from the Massachusetts delegation in Congress."[47] The envisioned chain of newspapers would be headed by a new paper in Washington, the *Examiner*, which began publication while Webster was en route. Webster did not yet come out openly for a new party, lest he lose all standing with his old coalition before a firm agreement with Jackson was reached, but the *Examiner* explicitly advocated the destruction of present parties. Only *"names"* now perpetuated old divisions, the paper declared; those "once known as federalist" now were Jackson's "most prominent supporters," and so-called *"Democrats"* were "among his most inveterate

---

Norman D. Brown, "Webster-Jackson Movement for a Constitution and Union Party in 1833," *Mid-America*, 66 (July, 1964):162; and *idem, Daniel Webster and the Politics of Availability* (Athens: University of Georgia Press, 1969), chaps. 2 and 3.

[43] Lewis Cass to Webster, April 17, 1833, in G. Curtis, *Life of Daniel Webster*, 1:460–61.

[44] Webster to Cass, n.d., *ibid.*

[45] Webster to Cass, n.d., *ibid.*; William T. Barry to Van Buren, July 7, 1833, Van Buren Papers, LC; Daniel Webster, "Speech at Cincinnati, June 20, 1833," reported in *Boston Daily Evening Transcript*, July 29, 1833; *idem*, "Speech at Pittsburgh, July 8, 1833," *Writings*, 2:143.

[46] *Boston Daily Evening Transcript*, July 29, 1833.

[47] Brown, "Webster-Jackson Movement," p. 159.

opposers and revilers." Surely all could see that present party lines must dissolve.[48]

Meanwhile, Webster arranged for New England to be on her best behavior for Jackson's visit. It was "well understood," reported a Bostonian, "that Jackson shd. be very kindly recd & that those who did not like it shd. simply do nothing."[49] Webster's friend Stephen White, who had made the motion for the General Court to invite Jackson to Massachusetts, accompanied Webster as far as Buffalo and then returned to Boston to supervise the city's welcome personally.

The *Boston Daily Evening Transcript* set the tone for the reception of the president on June 20. Jackson, it announced, "comes in an era of good feelings—when party spirit is at rest, and finds no immediate cause for action."[50] Bostonians hailed the Old Hero. Thousands of children lined his route to the city and cheered as he passed by; artillery roared; and, when the vast crowd spilling over the Boston Commons sighted him, they erupted with a thunderous ovation. Jackson was delighted. It "cannot be denied," noted Biddle's bank agent in Boston, "that a sympathy is excited, in his breast," for the Webster men. Stephen White organized a more formal assembly for the next day and led the testimonials with a toast to the new "Era of Good Feelings." Even Joseph Story joined the fellowship with public praise of the proclamation. "Observe," wrote Biddle's agent after the visit, that "Jackson is kindly recd at the *East* 'without distinction of party';—&, at the same time, Webster is kindly recd, *at the West, without* distinction of *Parties.*"[51]

Elated by his reception in the West, and apparently undaunted by his earlier and inconclusive talk with Livingston, Webster by August was optimistic over the prospects for a new party. "There is no telling what drill & discipline may effect," he wrote a friend. "But at present the great majority are all Constitutional, all liberal, all right. Old political heats seem in a great measure to have subsided."[52] The *Boston Courier* seemed to reflect Webster's optimism, as it often reflected his views, when it declared the time ripe for a reorganization of parties. "Let the principles of the President's Proclamation," the *Courier* urged on

---

[48] *Washington Examiner*, August 22, 1833.

[49] Degrand to Biddle, July 4, 1833, Biddle Papers, LC.

[50] *Boston Daily Evening Transcript*, June 20, 1833. Party spirit would be revived soon enough. Jackson drafted his final plan for removal of the deposits while basking in the "good feelings" of his Boston reception. Jackson to William J. Duane, June 26, 1833, *The Correspondence of Andrew Jackson*, 5:111–28. The only remaining question, Jackson wrote, was the "time when this change should commence."

[51] Degrand to Biddle, July 4, 6, 1833, Biddle Papers, LC.

[52] Webster to Samual P. Lyman, August 10, 1833, copy, Webster Papers, Dartmouth.

August 8, "be the principles on which to raise up this new organization." Let us have "no Jacksonians nor National Republicans, as party men—let us have no Free-masons nor anti-masons, no Southrons or Northmen—but let all be for the principles of the Proclamation." Let "the watchword be UNION AND THE CONSTITUTION."[53]

Others, however, made harsher appraisals of Webster's tour and of the chances for a fusion of parties. John McLean, a Supreme Court justice and a presidential quadrennial, thought Webster a fool if he believed the attentions of the Jackson men were sincere. Webster was their poorest presidential possibility; to strengthen him was to weaken the anti-Jackson party. Duff Green, a friend of Calhoun and editor of the *Washington Daily Telegraph*, played on the same theme, imploring Webster's friends not to endanger the Southern wing of the Clay-Calhoun opposition to Jackson—and Webster's presidential chances—by running him on the proclamation. Rufus Choate, one of Webster's closest advisers, counseled against being "carried away" by the "recent flow of good feeling." The fact was that, in Massachusetts, "Jackson men . . . are Van Buren Men," and National Republicans must "keep our own ranks."[54]

That Jackson ever seriously considered a new party is doubtful. Since all evidence suggests that Jackson looked on Van Buren as his successor, the president certainly did not intend to boost the New Yorker's rival. Whether Jackson was Machiavellian in his dealings with Webster is another matter. Jackson did seem to think Webster a useful ally, at least while nullification remained a danger to the country, and perhaps thereafter. The president did not see as clearly as Van Buren and later historians that his strength lay "in the multitude," and not in the leaders allied to him,[55] and he doubtless viewed Webster's attachment to him, or at least detachment from the opposition, as a tactical advantage. Whatever Jackson's plans, the reopening of the Bank issue soon decided the Webster question for him.

IV

By September, 1833, events had overtaken political calculations, for it had become clear by the fall that the tariff compromise would hold.

[53]*Boston Courier*, August 8, 1833.

[54]John McLean to John W. Taylor, September 7, 1833, John W. Taylor Papers, New York Historical Society, New York, N.Y.; Duff Green to Biddle, September 22, 1833, Biddle Papers, LC; Rufus Choate to Webster, August 12, 1833, cited in Brown, "Webster-Jackson Movement," p. 162.

[55]Notebook, n.d., Van Buren Papers, LC; Arthur M. Schlesinger, Jr., *The Age of Jackson* (Boston: Little, Brown & Co., 1945), p. 51.

South Carolina, though it voided the "Force Bill," had revoked its ordinance of nullification. With that act, the prospects for a Union party in the South had gradually vanished, and throughout the country the sense of crisis abated. More important, after an ardous summer of secret negotiations, Jackson's aide, Amos Kendall, had constructed a network of state banks—soon dubbed "pet banks"—that were to receive the government deposits. On September 25, the administration announced that it would no longer deposit funds with Biddle's Bank of the United States.

For Biddle and most others, removal[56] clearly ended all hope of reaching an understanding with the president. Quickly Biddle turned to friends in Congress for help and again invested complete leadership in Clay. Since the Bank was temporarily unpopular, Biddle's congressional supporters agreed to mute all direct defense of the institution and to stand instead on the issue of law: executive removal had illegally usurped congressional powers. While Biddle used the loss of deposits as an excuse to curtail loans, and financial distress resulted, Clay sought a Senate vote condemning removal.[57] The old coalition accepted the title of the Whig party, and hoped that congressmen alienated by King Andrew's new usurpation, their followers, and those converted by financial pressure would eventually add enough to the Whig ranks to make possible a permanent remedy, recharter.[58]

Biddle confidently expected that Webster would now rejoin Clay and Calhoun to lead the pro-Bank coalition. Despite reports of continued coolness toward the Kentuckian, Webster seemed ready. All was amicable when he and Biddle met in Philadelphia on November 30. Biddle entrusted Webster with a protest against removal from the directors of the Bank, left it to Webster's discretion when he would present the petition to Congress and initiate debate on removal, and apparently elicited a pledge of cooperation with Clay.[59]

But, from the moment he reached Washington in early December, Webster resisted commitment to the opposition and sought to avert a clash with Jackson. He delayed the Bank directors' protest, and, when pressed about it, asked huffily if the Bank did not trust his judgment on the matter. He sniped at Clay, and, when the Kentuckian urged the Senate to reject Jackson's hostile nominees to the Bank's Board of

---

[56]The government deposits were not actually removed; they were discontinued. Contemporaries, however, referred to the action as the "removal" of the deposits.

[57]Govan, *Nicholas Biddle*, pp. 255–57, 261–62.

[58]*Ibid.*, pp. 261–62.

[59]Webster to Biddle, November 27, 1833; and Horace Binney to Biddle, December 11, 1833; Biddle Papers, LC.

Directors, denounced the move as a needless provocation of the president.[60]

Clearly reluctant to rejoin Clay and Calhoun, Webster believed that compromise with the president was still possible. Continued "discussion," Webster wrote Biddle, "must have very great effect" on the subject of recharter. The "present distraction & distress," if "aired efficiently," would carry home "the necessity of the Bank." But tactics must be decorous and largely confined to correcting "every misstatement." If the opposition embattled Jackson prematurely, Webster implied, the president would almost certainly not retreat. Until the pressure did its work, restraint should rule the Whigs.[61]

Webster's hope that panic and calm reasoning might change administration policy was simply wrong. The Bank issue was more to Jackson than a matter of finance or pique; it was power. Repeatedly the Jacksonian press charged that Biddle's "monster," defying public control, had used its control of the currency to influence editors, legislatures, and congressmen.[62] Removal was an indispensable step to reduce the Bank's corrupting power. The logical antidote to that power was dispersal; hence, Jackson ruled out any central bank and opted instead for an experimental network of government-connected state banks to supervise the currency.[63] The "pet banks" of course made some quick friends for the Democrats,[64] but the decentralized system also fit with Jackson's faith that local institutions lent themselves more easily to public control. Citizens who were able to seek redress for wrongs in the state legislature could better influence bank policy, and, when necessary, national government could cope better with dispersed power than with concentrated authority. With the "pet banks" being chosen and governed by the executive rather than by Congress, effective public rule was assured. Whereas sectional minorities or personal bargains often blocked the majority will or consistent policy in Congress, the president—the only officer elected by a national majority—could supervise the banks with dispatch and consistency. Jackson's policy on internal improvements had followed the same logic. Locally sponsored improve-

[60]Binney to Biddle, December 11, 1833; Webster to Biddle, December 19, 1833; and J. G. Watmough to Biddle, December 22, 1833; Biddle Papers, LC.

[61]Webster to Biddle, January 2, 1834, *ibid.*

[62]Govan, *Nicholas Biddle*, pp. 237, 241–42.

[63]Jackson knew that the creation of a new central bank would only support the claim that his goal all along had been to substitute a pro-Jackson monster for an anti-Jackson one.

[64]See Frank Otto Gatell, "Spoils of the Bank War: Political Bias in the Selection of Pet Banks," *American Historical Review*, 70 (October, 1964):35–58.

ments were acceptable because they were better subject to public control.

Webster kept the faith that Jackson would come round, but he did not rely solely on neutrality and time to convert Jackson. On December 12, the senator reminded the president that his influence was valuable and still available if Jackson wanted it—and Jackson was tempted. As the president knew, the Whigs controlled, or at least seemed to control, the Senate. But a routine partisan vote on the formation of Senate committees found Webster aligned with the Democrats; he and six other New England senators voted to delay the selections until absent senators arrived. Clay, who until that moment thought he had enough votes to control the appointments, was incredulous. If Webster and his colleagues continued to vote with the Democrats, there was a chance the administration might end up controlling the committees and the Senate. Since the Jacksonians already ruled the House, the Whig forces then would have no legislative forum at all. Tennessee Democrat Felix Grundy reported to Jackson that this was Webster's proposition exactly. He was ready to help weight the committees and hence all their reports in favor of the Democratic minority; reciprocal kindness presumably would bring further senatorial and sectional help. As the capital buzzed, Jackson, doubtless eager to discomfit the gentlemen of the opposition in any way possible, pondered the bait, but he delayed a decision until the arrival in Washington of his vice-president-elect.[65]

Martin Van Buren had long anticipated such an interview, crucial to him and the Democratic party, and in a free discussion with Jackson on December 15 he bared the Webster issue with clarity. A party was known by the enemies it kept, and Webster was an enemy. Cooperation between the pro-Bank ex-Federalist and the president would only confuse loyal Democrats, Van Buren told Jackson. Webster would not long remain an ally without making demands, and one of those would doubtless be compromise on the issue of a national bank. But on this issue, Van Buren observed, Jackson did not intend to compromise. Without speaking of the merits of the bank war or of removal, about which his previous reticence indicated reservations,[66] Van Buren stressed that the commitment was made. The public name and internal discipline of the party now required consistency. Even if Webster made

---

[65] Brown, "Webster-Jackson Movement," pp. 165-67.

[66] See Frank Otto Gatell, "Sober Second Thoughts on Van Buren, the Albany Regency, and the Wall Street Conspiracy," *Journal of American History*, 52 (June, 1966):3-39; and Van Buren to Jackson, October 2, 1833, Van Buren Papers, LC. For Van Buren's stand on the removal of the deposits, see J. Curtis, *Martin Van Buren*, pp. 45-46.

no demands or totally abandoned his former views, Van Buren concluded, the reward of alliance would merely encourage political infidelity. Jackson would revive the very system which had victimized him in 1825, the system of "intrigue" whereby gentlemen sought the presidency through bargains with one another instead of through majorities. Jackson listened, assented, told Grundy to drop the scheme, and never spoke of the matter again.[67]

The rejection of Webster and fusion, if perhaps inevitable, was nonetheless symbolic. Jackson had chosen the Bank issue as the test of Democratic loyalty and had turned down the no less appealing but far more sectional issue of nullification. But Jackson had done more—he had passed final judgment on traditional politics. He had chosen, over a return to personal negotiation and good feeling, to stay with his organization and to pursue his goals through conflict. Jackson's choice cast the mold of future Democratic leadership; all succeeding Democratic presidents until the Civil War—Van Buren, Polk, Pierce, and Buchanan—were dedicated organization men. None was the favorite of colleagues, a charismatic figure, a sectional titan; none had exceptional polish, eloquence, or could lay claim to the affections of his section—all hallmarks of a traditional leader like Webster. Rather, each rose by virtue of his skill at management and by his fidelity to the Democratic party. In turn, success for the party came to depend on its ability to make good without personalities, and in particular on its ability to survive the loss of its central personality in 1837. Party creed replaced the Old Hero, and, here again, the rejection of Webster was crucial. An entente with Webster would have blurred the clarity and consistency required for a creed and organizational integrity. Bank war became the party's creed and was synonymous with Jackson himself. When the presidency passed to Van Buren, creed replaced charisma as the cement of the party.

The party of patriots was finished; the rest was anticlimax. Though Webster sensed a setback when Democrats allowed the Whigs to control the Senate committees, he still fought to keep the door open for compromise. He did so against mounting pressure and suspicion. Normally the Whigs would have made him chairman of the Senate Finance Committee and used it as a pro-Bank forum, but by December 19, Clay and

---

[67]John C. Fitzpatrick, ed., "The Autobiography of Martin Van Buren," in American Historical Association, *Annual Report, 1919* (Washington, D.C.: Government Printing Office, 1920), 2:676-79, 707, 710-11. Van Buren loathed Webster and cannot be trusted for impartial reports about him. Webster's procrastination on the Bank petition and his votes in the Senate seem to verify Van Buren's testimony in this instance.

others had lost patience with him and had maneuvered to create a special committee led by Calhoun to investigate removal. Clay relented when Webster demanded the assignment himself, yet even then Webster won the post only with Democratic help. Clay's doubts proved correct when Webster continued to do nothing. The Whigs finally gave up waiting for Webster to come around on the question of executive appointments and rejected Jackson's Bank nominees on December 30. Furious, Webster said the "premature" action deeply compromised him, and he threatened to withdraw his help from the Bank's battle. Only after three separate visits from a pro-Bank congressman did Webster allow his "wounded . . . feelings" to be soothed.[68]

Despite such bluster, Webster was increasingly despondent over his frustrations as an honest broker. As early as December 21 he unburdened his woes to a Boston correspondent, who could only sympathize that the "mad pranks of Old Andrew" had indeed jolted hopes for fusion. The *Boston Courier* of December 27 conceded that "at this moment" the party of patriots was faltering. Though the *Courier* reiterated that Webster belonged "to no party, except the friends of the Union," straddling became less and less manageable.[69] By January 2, even as he urged Biddle to step up the Bank's economic squeeze and proposed a Senate inquiry into the cause of the crisis, Webster privately questioned whether more debate and delay would serve any purpose.

Yet, assuming that the government did not restore the deposits, *"what then? Can Congress adjourn, leaving things where they are now?"*[70] Webster felt that Jackson "must be brought to *some* reasonable terms," and he devised one more plan for settling the crisis. He arranged for a conspicuously nonpartisan Boston assembly to adopt resolves which he himself had drafted and then used their plea for relief to present his solution to the Senate on January 20.[71] The first step in his solution was restoration of the deposits. While insisting that removal had caused the present distress, Webster absolved the government from malice. Restoration would simply be an admission that removal had

[68] Edward Everett to [Henry D. Gilpin], December 19, [1833], Henry D. Gilpin Papers, HSP. See also Webster to Biddle, December 19, 1833; Binney to Biddle, January 6, 1834; and Watmough to Biddle, December 30, 1833; Biddle Papers, LC.

[69] Stephen White to Webster, December 27, 1833, Webster Papers, NHHS; *Boston Courier*, December 27, 1833.

[70] Webster to Biddle, January 2, 1834, Biddle Papers, LC; Webster to Levi Lincoln, January 8, [1834], Lincoln Papers.

[71] Webster to Nathan Appleton, January 17, 1834, Appleton Papers; Charles Francis Adams, ed., *Memoirs of John Quincy Adams*, 12 vols. (Philadelphia: J. P. Lippincott & Co., 1876), 9:76–76 (January 13, 1834).

"operated more deeply and more widely than was expected" and would not be a commitment to recharter.[72] Webster admitted, however, that some new national bank was necessary and proceeded to propose one. He designed it to "overcome all scruples & reconcile all conflicting interests: whether between the East & the West, the N. & South or between Phila. & N. York." Indeed, Webster's plan went to remarkable lengths to overcome states'-rights objections to a national bank. No branch of the bank would be created in any state without the permission of its legislature; states would be permitted to tax the branches to the extent they taxed their own state-chartered banks; and, though the capital of the bank would increase, all new stock would be purchased and presumably held by the states and would give them a measure of influence they formerly lacked.[73]

Ten more days of administration silence, however, convinced even Webster that the president would "not go back, & cannot go forward." Yet desperately he waited for some formal sign, estranging even the few Whigs who still judged his motives charitably.[74]

On January 30, the administration's answer to Webster's overture finally came. Though he praised the "open and manly ground" taken by Webster, New York Democratic Senator Silas Wright rejected compromise categorically. A national bank in any form was unconstitutional. Wright's position, Van Buren wrote his son, was the "creed by which we mean to stand or fall."[75]

Just before a disappointed Webster rose to reply the next day, a colleague told him that Wright had privately gloated that " 'we shall carry this question with *the people for the poor always hate the rich.*' " It was the final goad. In a "style of the most vehement impassioned & thrilling eloquence & argument," full of rebuke and fire, Webster denounced the administration and its decision to resume the politics of conflict.[76] The deplorable appeal to class jealousy sought to play off the passions of the laboring man against his interests, Webster thundered, to "prevail on him, in the name of liberty, to destroy all fruits of

---

[72] Samuel Jaudon to Biddle, January 15, 1834, Biddle Papers, LC; *Register of Debates*, 23rd Cong., 1st sess., 1834, 10:294–95.

[73] Watmough to Biddle, January 20, 1834, Biddle Papers, LC. Webster coupled these public concessions with a private plea to the Bank to "be *most unyielding*" in the charade of winding up its concerns; he stated flatly that success depended on panic.

[74] Webster to C. H. Thomas, January 28, 1834, Webster Papers, MHS.

[75] *Register of Debates*, 10:402; Martin Van Buren to John Van Buren, Van Buren Papers, LC.

[76] Rufus Choate to [Warwick Palfrey, Jr.], January 31, 1834, *Essex Institute Historical Collections*, 69 (January, 1933):86–87.

liberty." The Bank served "all interests" by stabilizing the currency; indeed, it served the laborer most, for he suffered most from fluctuations. To Webster, the man who sought to obscure "the public good, to overwhelm all patriotism, and all enlightened self-interest, by loud cries against false danger," showed "himself the wreckless enemy of all."[77]

With these words Webster belatedly joined the Whig fold. He did not abandon his faith that the community was best served when public men negotiated conflict through the medium of genuine nationalist emotions. But his brief experience did make it questionable whether nationalism could continue to shape political alignments without the constant threat of war. For those who looked to political parties as better instruments of national unity than emotion, and to party conflict as a better vehicle for the dispute and settlement of issues than public men, Webster's loss was at least a temporary triumph.

A Webster-Jackson party of patriots was Webster's last easy route to check the politics of conflict. Success might have resurrected the public man, atrophied the opposition of 1832, and elevated Webster to a commanding position for the presidency. Failure clarified the meaning of 1832 and forced Webster to go the harder route. He had to take his candidacy to his party, embittered by his near defection, and his altruism to the people.

---

[77] *Register of Debates*, 10:440–42.

III

WHY NOT WEBSTER?

W EBSTER TARDILY ENLISTED in the Whig coalition in February, 1834, and at once faced perplexing problems. Still a determined presidential candidate, he had to seek support from a party antagonized by his attempt at alliance with Jackson.[1] Reluctantly a Whig, he had to work with Senate colleagues whom he had battled for most of the previous year.

Webster found it difficult to re-establish a congenial relationship with Whig leaders in the Senate or to take up the Whig standard of "executive usurpation." John C. Calhoun had devised South Carolina's policy of nullification, and in response Henry Clay had, in Webster's judgment, all but eviscerated the protective tariff. To meet the nullification and tariff challenges of 1833, Webster had supported Andrew Jackson, fully endorsed Jackson's claims of presidential power to define and suppress insurrection, and finally sought a permanent alliance of the two Unionists. Webster's vigorous support of broad presidential prerogatives in 1833, as well as his recent, if futile, courtship of Jackson, made it both

---

[1] William Ward, Jr., to Thomas Wren Ward, January 5, 1834, Thomas W. Ward Papers, Massachusetts Historical Society, Boston (hereafter cited as MHS); Samuel Bell to William Plumer, Jr., January 18, 1834, William Plumer Family Papers, New Hampshire State Library, Concord; *New York Daily Advertiser*, January 25, 1834.

difficult and distasteful, under the best of circumstances, for him to regress to the Whig attack on the "tyranny" of "King Andrew."

I

The appeal of "executive usurpation" had been dormant since 1832, but Jackson's offensive against the Bank of the United States late in 1833 had led Clay and Calhoun to revive the issue. Jackson's removal of the deposits conveniently allowed the Whigs, divided internally on the merits of the Bank but united against the excesses of the president, to focus again on the question of who legally controlled the national revenue and on the larger issue of congressional-versus-executive rights. Whigs insisted that control of the revenue belonged exclusively to Congress, and that the president had once again usurped the rights of the legislative representatives of the people. The issue of Jackson's "tyranny" allowed the Whigs to evade their own disagreements and simultaneously to lure support from Democratic congressmen who were angered by Jackson's further erosion of their power.[2]

Against this Whig strategy, Webster now balked. Fresh from his battle against nullification, he could hardly wish the Whigs to be party to still another tacit sacrifice of national authority. The coalition had already yielded on internal improvements and the tariff, and now it seemed ready to mute the principle of a national bank to appease further those who were seeking to curb national authority.[3]

The issue of principle aside, however, Webster still thought that Jackson sooner or later would have to return the deposits to the Bank of the United States, largely because of the financial panic and political outcry that removal had prompted. Webster believed the Whigs would hence do just as well to keep the need for a bank in the forefront of politics as to stress exclusively the alleged tyranny of the president. Petitions for relief and the restoration of the deposits, now beginning to flood the Congress, suggested that the president had seriously underestimated the

[2] Clay to R. H. Wilde, April 27, 1833, Henry Clay Papers, Cole Collection, Alderman Library, University of Virginia, Charlottesville; Glyndon G. Van Deusen, *Henry Clay* (Boston: Little, Brown & Co., 1937), pp. 279, 282; Thomas Payne Govan, *Nicholas Biddle: Nationalist and Public Banker, 1786-1844* (Chicago: University of Chicago Press, 1959), pp. 261-62.

[3] For Webster's preoccupation with the erosion of national power by both Democrats and nullifiers, see his speeches at Worcester and Pittsburgh, October 12, 1832, and July 8, 1833, respectively, in *The Writings and Speeches of Daniel Webster*, ed. J. W. McIntyre, 18 vols. (Boston: Little, Brown & Co., 1903), 2:106-7, 144-46, 153-54 (hereafter cited as *Writings*). Calhoun had a similar understanding of the larger issue. See Calhoun to James Edward Calhoun, May 21, 1834, in J. Franklin Jameson, ed., "Correspondence of John C. Calhoun," American Historical Association, *Annual Report, 1899* (Washington, D.C.: Government Printing Office, 1900), 2:338.

extent of support for the Bank. Though there was truth to the charge that the petitions were "managed" by merchants and Whig politicians eager for the restoration of the deposits, support for the Bank transcended party lines, and none could deny that hundreds of mechanics and artisans had endorsed restoration. Webster noted that Democratic congressmen were wavering under the pressure, and he insisted, with some justice, that Jackson's congressional party could be split as easily over the Bank issue as over the president's "usurpations."[4]

Webster proposed, therefore, that the Whigs not only fight for congressional rights but endorse and seek a temporary recharter of the Bank. Because temporary, a recharter of from four to six years could win support from Democrats who were eager to satisfy the cry for relief but were unwilling to commit themselves to a permanent recharter.[5] Almost certainly, however, Webster anticipated the move as a prelude to the eventual charter of another permanent national bank. Sure that a temporary recharter would restore business confidence, terminate the depression, and prove that prosperity turned on a bank, Webster could plausibly expect that both the Whig party and the principle of a national bank would be vindicated. Moreover, if Webster succeeded in wresting even a temporary recharter from Congress, whether or not Jackson vetoed the measure, Webster would further his party's goal of riving Jackson's coalition and be entitled to an authority in Whig councils which was far superior to the one he had.

Such was the structure of the Whig party in 1834, however, that opposition to Webster's scheme among the Whigs was sufficient to thwart the recharter proposal. The Whig triumvirate allowed no one man to set policy—or to further his ambitions—without the consent of the others, and in this instance both Calhoun and Clay exercised their power to veto Webster. Calhoun opposed Webster's recharter plan with one of his own, and Clay obstructed them both.[6] The outcome was six weeks of deadlock between February and mid-March.

---

[4] Robert V. Remini describes the difficulty Democrats had in mobilizing their nominal House majority in his *Andrew Jackson and the Bank War: A Study in the Growth of Presidential Power* (New York: W. W. Norton & Co., 1967), pp. 135–37. For corroboration see George McDuffie to Biddle, February 22, 1834, Nicholas Biddle Papers, Library of Congress, Washington, D.C. (hereafter cited as LC). For Webster's hope that he could "turn a majority in the H. of R." on the recharter issue, see Webster to John B. Wallace, February 12, 1834, John B. Wallace Papers, Historical Society of Pennsylvania, Philadelphia (hereafter cited as HSP); *Washington Examiner*, February 5, 1834; and Webster's post-mortem on his strategy, *Writings*, 7:31–33, 37, 41, 46.

[5] *Writings*, 6:272–80.

[6] Calhoun to Littleton Tazewell, May 27, 1834, copy, John C. Calhoun Papers, South Caroliniana Collection, University of South Carolina Library, Columbia; U.S., Congress, *Register of Debates in the Congress of the United States* (Washington, D.C.: Gales & Seaton, 1834),

In the interim, Jackson, whose hold on the congressional Democrats had been shaken by the bank panic and by a deluge of petitions for relief from men of all parties and occupations, marshalled his forces. With the rallying cry that the issue was not relief or the legality of removal but the power of the Bank, Jackson countered by encouraging meetings and by bringing pressure to bear on individual congressmen. By mid-March, the endangered Democratic majority in the House was secure once more. Webster's scheme and Whig paralysis had only strengthened the president's hold over his congressmen and hardened the party's anti-Bank creed.[7]

Thus, when Webster offered a formal motion to the Senate on March 18 to take up his Bank recharter plan, he knew the bill had no chance of succeeding.[8] United, the Democrats immediately pounced on the motion as proof that the real issue was not executive tyranny, not "law or no law," but "bank or no bank," and they quickly maneuvered debate from Clay's still-pending resolves about usurpation to the Bank issue.[9] Clay insisted at once that all Whigs drop recharter and return to his resolutions. Webster, hoping now only to establish a claim as a disinterested patriot who had given his all in search of financial relief, held out for another week. But, when Clay threatened to table the recharter motion, Webster, to avoid obvious embarrassment, capitulated and tabled his own bill on March 25.[10] Denouncing the removal of the deposits as a rash, deluded, and insane experiment, he blamed the nation's economic distress on executive tyranny and declared that the issue before the country was the "SUPREMACY OF THE LAWS."[11]

Webster had lost his battle to lead the Senate's Whigs. Events proved Clay correct in his judgment that avowal of recharter was suicidal, and in little more than a year Webster himself would publicly concede that the Bank cause was hopelessly unpopular.[12] Meanwhile, the issue of

---

23rd Cong., 1st sess., December, 1833–June, 1834, pp. 217–19 (hereafter cited as *Register of Debates*); Calhoun to J. E. Calhoun, February 3, 1834, in Jameson, "Correspondence of John C. Calhoun," p. 332.

[7]Remini, *Jackson and the Bank War*, pp. 154–66; Daniel Webster, "Speech of May 20, 1834," *Writings*, 7:31–32.

[8]Webster, "Speech of May 20, 1834," *Writings*, 7:31–32; Webster to Biddle, February 28, 1834, Biddle Papers, LC.

[9]*Register of Debates*, 23rd Cong., 1st sess., 1834, pp. 1020, 1032–34, 1044–45 (March 20, 25, 1834).

[10]James Watson Webb to [unidentified correspondent], March 23, 1834, Biddle Papers, LC: Choate to Daniel White, April 5, 1834, Rufus Choate Papers, Dartmouth College, Hanover, N.H.; *Register of Debates*, 23rd Cong., 1st sess., pp. 1044–45 (March 25, 1834).

[11]Daniel Webster, "Speech of March 28, 1834," *Writings*, 7:26.

[12]Biddle complained to Webster for saying this in the Senate. Biddle to Webster, April 6, 1835, Biddle Papers, LC.

executive usurpation had preserved the Whig majority in the Senate and had reaffirmed Clay's leadership there.

II

The need for other tactics to enhance his influence in Whig councils was all the more evident as it became clear that Clay, as a Whig, and Calhoun, as the aspiring leader of states'-rights Southerners, would remain among Webster's rivals for the presidency in 1836. Though Clay had told his friends through much of 1833 that another uphill fight for the White House had "no charms" for him and that "the country had better try other Sentinels,"[13] by late that year his hopes waxed again. Certain that Calhoun had no chance, and doubtful that Webster could unite the party, Clay saw himself as the only man able to bring North and South together.[14] Still less prepared to step aside for Webster was Calhoun. He regarded the Whigs and Jacksonians as equal evils, and he quietly labored to form a states'-rights ticket which he would head in 1836.[15]

In the spring of 1834, Webster firmly believed that his only hope lay with the North. Calhoun's presidential aspirations had been eclipsed by his role in the nullification crisis, and Clay still bore the stigma of having led the party to defeat in 1832. Webster felt that, if he could unite all anti-Democratic factions in the North, as Clay had been unable to do in 1832, his rivals would have to accede to his candidacy as the only one fit to challenge the Democrats in 1836.

Webster turned to the work of strengthening his claim as the leading Whig of the North. Once more he and his partisans carefully stressed that he sought only to serve his country as a disinterested statesman. He had initially cultivated the role of harmonizer of all interests in the

---

[13] Clay to Francis Brooke, May 30, 1833, August 2, 1833, *The Works of Henry Clay, Comprising His Life, Correspondence, and Speeches*, ed. Calvin Colton, 10 vols. (New York: G. P. Putnam's Sons, 1904), 5:362, 369 (hereafter cited as *The Works of Henry Clay*).

[14] Henry Gilpin to Joshua Gilpin, October 15, 1833, Henry D. Gilpin Papers, HSP; Clay to Peter B. Porter, April 11, 1834, Peter B. Porter Papers, Buffalo Historical Society, Buffalo, N.Y.; Clay to Benjamin W. Leigh, August 24, 1834, Benjamin W. Leigh Papers, Alderman Library, University of Virginia, Charlottesville.

[15] Calhoun To Francis W. Pickens, January 4, 1834; Calhoun to Christopher Van Deventer, January 25, 1834; Calhoun to J. E. Calhoun, May 21, 1834; Calhoun to Lewis W. Coryell, August 10, 1834; and Calhoun to Duff Green, September 20 and November 16, 1834; in Jameson, "Correspondence of John C. Calhoun," pp. 327, 330, 338, 340–43. Though Professor Wiltse states that Calhoun avoided the presidential issue in 1834, Calhoun's correspondence suggests the South Carolinian retained hopes of being a states'-rights party choice in 1836. Charles M. Wiltse, *John C. Calhoun*, 3 vols. (Indianapolis and New York: The Bobbs-Merrill Co., 1944–51), 2:233.

"Era of Good Feelings," and he again assumed the congenial mantle of honest broker in 1834. Webster played the role of public man with conviction; throughout the Jackson era he sought to shape the new politics in such a way as to leave a place for the traditional leader. Yet he also exploited his own reputation as exemplar of the older tradition. He understood perfectly that many citizens still believed, despite the revival of parties, that public conflicts could be best resolved by wise and independent public men.[16] Hence, throughout Webster's doomed campaign to win a limited recharter for the Bank, a deliberate goal had been the reinforcement of a public image that conveyed to all—Democrats and Whigs, merchants and mechanics—an "impression . . . of his honesty & purity & disinterestedness."[17] When Webster spoke for relief, he spoke on behalf of all classes. He characterized himself as a man summoning "all of intellect, all of diligence, all of devotion to the public good," to meet the common crisis. And he condemned those Jacksonians who exploited recession in order to array "one class against another."[18] Webster conceded that partisans who sought to pit the poor against the rich sometimes succeeded; by such means "little men occasionally become great."[19] But for Webster the aspirations of all were in fundamental harmony, and it was the task of the statesman to blend interests together.[20] Throughout 1834 and 1835, as Webster and his supporters pursued the presidency, they campaigned not just for the candidate but for his model of leadership.

Webster recognized, however, that a favorable image alone would not bring him the office he sought. To become the candidate of the North, he believed he had to win the assistance of the Northern financial community. At the most tangible level, Webster sought a $100,000 fund from business friends with which to finance his campaign. Webster assumed that removal and the stringency which followed would certainly galvanize the laggard among the business community to political action. But he may have worried, as did his Washington newspaper, that the "merchants are money-makers and the last men who busy themselves in politics."[21] Hence, he left nothing to chance. At the height of

---

[16] Ronald P. Formisano, "Political Character, Antipartyism, and the Second Party System," *American Quarterly*, 21 (Winter, 1969):683–709.

[17] Rufus Choate to Daniel White, April 5, 1834, Choate Papers, Dartmouth; Watmough to Biddle, February 7, 1834, Biddle Papers, LC'

[18] Daniel Webster, "Speech of January 31, 1834," *Writings*, 6:269.

[19] Daniel Webster, "Speech of March 18, 1834," *ibid.*, 7:95.

[20] *Ibid.*; see also Webster's address of March 15, 1839, *ibid.*, 2:196.

[21] *Washington Examiner*, February 1, 1834. For a persuasive analysis of the movement of New York's men of wealth into the Whig party, see Frank Otto Gatell, "Money and Party in

the debate over recharter, even as he denounced those Jacksonians who sought to inflame the "poor against the rich," Webster manipulated class tensions to his own advantage. Seven times in a single speech, he warned that the coming "war-cry" of the Democratic party was to be the *"natural hatred of the poor to the rich."* Webster had heard of the strategy by rumor, but there was no mistaking "the omen. . . . I see the magazine whence the weapons of this warfare are to be drawn. I hear already the din of the hammering of arms preparatory to the combat." He sounded the alarm against the "clamor and violence," the "false and fraudulent appeals," that lay ominously ahead.[22] Webster conceded in subsequent debate that he himself had heard no Democrat discuss class war. But he did not retract his warning, and he arranged for his campaign lieutenant, Congressman Edward Everett of Massachusetts, to reiterate the message of danger to Northern businessmen. In a confidential letter drafted to solicit $1,000 donations from each of 100 businessmen, Everett predicted a war of "numbers against property." To prevent anarchy, men of wealth must rally to Webster's cause. The amount of money procured by these alarms is unclear, but by August, Webster was satisfied with the pledges of financial help he had obtained.[23]

In return for aid from Whig businessmen of New York City, Webster lent his support to a major Whig effort in 1834 to dislodge Tammany Hall Democrats from control of the city's politics. Whig merchants sought to make the city election of April and the congressional contest of November referenda on the fiscal policies of the president. They put to the test Webster's contention that all classes were united in opposition to Jackson's removal of the deposits. Whig warnings were blunt. If Jackson persisted in his "unlawful" policy of removal, all citizens could expect to suffer "inevitable ruin."[24] Merchants would feel the distress first, but, as they were forced to retrench, recession would soon reach the cartmen and porters, mechanics and day laborers, and all others "mutually interested" in prosperity. Relief was "IN THE HANDS OF THE PEOPLE"; citizens must repudiate Jackson's actions "THROUGH THE MEDIUM OF ELECTIONS." In "order to devote their undivided

Jacksonian America: A Quantitative Look at New York City's Men of Quality," *Political Science Quarterly*, 82 (June, 1967): 235–52.

[22] Webster, "Speech of January 31, 1834," *Writings*, 6:258–69.

[23] Everett to [Thomas W. Ward], February 18, 1834, Edward Everett Letterbooks, MHS; Webster to Everett, April 25, 26, June 2, August 1, 1834, Edward Everett Papers, MHS; Everett Diaries, August 5, 1834, vol. 147, MHS.

[24] *New York Daily Advertiser*, February 4 and March 25, 1834.

attention to the great business of reform at the polls," New York merchants agreed to close their stores for the three days of balloting in mid-April.[25] To make certain that reform went well, merchants dispatched their clerks and employees to polling places to remind the city's laborers of the stakes of the election and to observe them as they voted.

Webster gave his full approval to the attempt of the New York Whigs to demonstrate the interdependence of all classes in the April election. Repeatedly he predicted in the Senate that "overwhelming defeat at the ballot-boxes" would prove that "mechanics, laborers, traders, manufacturers, and merchants" had united as one in opposition to removal.[26] Dining with a group of New York merchants on the evening of April 2, he told them "in the most emphatic manner" that their "great struggle" was the key to the future of the country.[27] Though Democrats denounced Whig tactics as blatant intimidation, the Whigs fared well in the election, winning a majority of seats on the city council and losing the mayor's contest by less than 200 votes. Webster was in the city on the evening of the victory, and he used the occasion to quash any lingering doubts about his allegiance to the Whig party. He reminded the triumphant New Yorkers that he "had been educated, from my cradle, in the principles of the WHIGS of 1776."[28] New Yorkers seemed happy to have Webster in their midst, and were delighted when city cartmen, seamen, laborers, and mechanics sought out the senator at his New York lodgings to pay him tribute. Hundreds of common citizens "pressed forward and seized the hand of the man who is so firmly seated in the hearts of the American people," a Whig journal reported on April 16, and Webster responded with a pledge to "preserve our glorious Constitution."[29] The next day, Webster formally received thousands of "mechanics and workingmen" with the "utmost cordiality." For those who missed the significance of these encounters, a Whig

---

[25] *Ibid.*, March 21, 22, and April 8, 1834. For a full discussion of New York City elections in 1834, see Walter Hugins, *Jacksonian Democracy and the Working Class: A Study of the New York Workingmen's Movement, 1829–1837* (Stanford: Stanford University Press, 1960), esp. chaps. 3, 4, and 10.

[26] Daniel Webster, "Speech of June 3, 1834," *Writings*, 7:41; for almost identical predictions in other speeches, see Webster's speeches of February 22, March 7, and March 28, 1834, *ibid.*, 6: 272–74 and 7:4, 26.

[27] Bayard Tuckerman, ed., *The Diary of Philip Hone, 1828–1851*, 2 vols. (New York: Dodd, Mead & Co., 1889), 1:95.

[28] Webster to Benjamin G. Wells, April 15, 1834, published in the *New York Daily Advertiser*, April 16, 1834.

[29] *New York American*, April 16, 1834.

editor provided illumination: respect for Daniel Webster "pervades all classes."[30]

Though Webster succeeded in recruiting the support of Whig merchants of New York City for his candidacy, the value of that commitment was diminished by division and defeat later in 1834. Most in the commercial community had agreed that Jackson's removal of the deposits had triggered the economic crisis of 1833-34, but an increasing number came to believe that Nicholas Biddle had prolonged the panic for political purposes, and they brought mounting pressure to bear on the Bank's president to end his curtailments. Aware that the course of the Bank was alienating businessmen, Webster himself urged Biddle to ease up.[31] In July, Biddle capitulated, and the prompt return of prosperity seemed to confirm Democratic claims that the recession had been the Bank's doing all along. When the Whigs of New York sought to expand their power in the congressional and state elections of late 1834, they continued to insist on the unity of all classes. But the end of economic distress removed the earlier source of that unity and forced Whigs to employ more extreme tactics. They accused Democrats of the "wicked design of arraying different divisions of the community against each other"; they drew a parallel to "the worst features of the beginning of the French Revolution."[32] On the eve of the election Webster returned to New York City to contribute his own "incendiary . . . harangue."[33] Webster's partisans hoped such tactics would win in November and expected to use victory as the occasion to bring Webster's name formally before the country.[34] But Whig candidates throughout New York went down to thorough defeat.

Assessing the failure, one Whig journal insisted that the tactics of Webster and the Whigs in 1834 had backfired. Whigs had too closely associated themselves with the Bank of the United States. They had left themselves vulnerable to the "unreasonable prejudice which exists in the minds of the working classes against all monied institutions and

---

[30]*New York Daily Advertiser*, April 17, 1834. Webster fully endorsed the tactics of New York Whig leaders and recommended them to Whigs and merchants elsewhere. Everett to William Plumer, Jr., May 27, 1834, Plumer Family Papers; Samuel Reid to Seward, November 11, 1834, William Henry Seward Papers, University of Rochester, Rochester, N.Y.; Webster to Everett, [January 7, 1835], Edward Everett Papers, MHS.

[31]Govan, *Nicholas Biddle*, pp. 256-60, 272-73. The shift in business opinion is evident from Biddle's correspondence. For Webster's request, see Abbott Lawrence to Webster, [July 1, 1834]; and Webster to Biddle [July 2, 1834]; Biddle Papers, LC.

[32]*New York Journal of Commerce*, October 28, 1834.

[33]*New York Evening Post*, November 5, 1834.

[34]Tuckerman, *The Diary of Philip Hone*, 1:116-17; Van Buren to Jackson, August 7, 1834, *The Correspondence of Andrew Jackson*, ed. John Spencer Bassett, 7 vols. (Washington, D.C.: Carnegie Institute of Washington, 1926-35), 5:279-80.

monied men." Whig editors and politicians had erroneously imagined that "the people were so stupid as to be gulled into the belief" that Jackson alone had brought on the recent panic. Worse yet, they had vainly sought to suppress evidence of economic recovery. The conduct of the Bank and Whig partisans had only exacerbated the natural "envy . . . of the poor towards the rich," and, with the return of prosperity, the laboring classes had taken revenge on their "more affluent" neighbors. Meanwhile, the immoderation of Whig spokesmen had "disgusted a great many conscientious" Whigs; the fury and deceit of party zealots had produced "a remarkable coolness on the part of the best men among us," who elected not to vote in the contest.[35] For more reliable help for his candidacy, Webster would have to try different tactics and other allies.

III

Having no hope of winning an easy nomination from a united party and little more for counting on the Northern business community to secure his cause, Webster relied increasingly on the most potent anti-Democratic political faction in the North, the Anti-Masons. Anti-Masonry as a sentiment sprang from a timeless suspicion of secret organizations. The mystic rites and secret oaths of Masonry made it a natural object of envy and fear to those excluded from the order, and in an egalitarian society the Masons were easily associated with impermissible snobbery and exclusivism. American Masonry became linked to far worse after 1826, when a former New York Mason who had vowed to expose the order was abruptly abducted and was never heard from again. Influential Masons obstructed investigations of the case by the courts of New York, and, when a body was found near the victim's home a year later, the public took it as proof that the Masons had authorized and suppressed murder. The celebrated case launched a political movement to ban Masonry and secret oaths everywhere, and this took firm root among moralistic and Democratic citizens of the North, who were opposed to the brutality and privilege the order represented. In almost every way, Anti-Masonry rehearsed and duplicated the Jacksonian attack on monopoly and special privilege, and, in New York, Pennsylvania, and New England, it competed with Democrats for the allegiance of the voter.[36]

[35] *New York Journal of Commerce*, November 21, 1834.

[36] The standard account of political Anti-Masonry is Charles McCarthy, "The Antimasonic Party," in American Historical Association, *Annual Report, 1901* (Washington, D.C.: Government Printing Office, 1902).

Webster's experience in seeking to claim the Anti-Masons for his cause suggested again his difficulties in establishing himself as the chief spokesman of the North. Webster initially thought there would be little problem in attracting the politically potent Anti-Masons. Already opposed to Jackson in most states, they seemed to have little choice but to align themselves with the Whigs, and Webster expected that his reputation as a patriot and a friend of the Anti-Masonic cause would force the party's leaders eventually to back his candidacy. With the opposition of the North united behind him, the road to the nomination would be clear.

But Webster seriously underestimated the resistance of Anti-Masons to his candidacy. Though most of the party's leaders agreed by 1834 that they could no longer go it alone and must fuse with the Whigs, they were reluctant to attach themselves to Webster.[37] Oriented toward the voters and victory, they shared no commitment to the leadership standards Webster represented, and they regarded the Bank and the exclusivist reputation of Webster's old party, the Federalists, as political millstones. Webster's association with both issues, New York Anti-Mason Samuel P. Lyman told the senator in 1834, stamped him as a loser.[38]

Webster remained optimistic about his chances of winning Anti-Masonic support, and believed that the major difficulty might come from the Anti-Masons of his own state. In Massachusetts, Whigs and Anti-Masons were more rivals of each other than allies against the Jacksonians.[39] Not only was it improbable that Anti-Masons would join Webster's cause by default. It was quite possible that they could upset all his plans and undercut his claim to be a sectional leader by inflicting a defeat on the Whig party of Massachusetts.

The emergence of the Anti-Masons of Massachusetts as a threat to the hegemony of Webster and the Whigs in 1834 had its roots in the political confusion of the previous year. The predecessors of the Whigs in Massachusetts, the National Republicans, had built a strong alliance of former Jeffersonians and Federalists on the personal labors and reputations of three men. The coalition had been cemented together by the popularity of Levi Lincoln, son of Thomas Jefferson's attorney general and governor of Massachusetts from 1823 through 1832; the name and reluctant cooperation of John Quincy Adams; and the influence of

---

[37]Weed to Seward, June 5, July 20, 1833, Seward Papers. James Dunlop to Biddle, April 6, 1834, Biddle Papers, LC.

[38]Samuel P. Lyman to Seward, July 24, 1834, Seward Papers.

[39]Webster to Everett, August 11, 1833, Edward Everett Papers, MHS.

Webster. For a decade, the majority party had overwhelmed all opposition, but Clay's defeat in 1832 and the political uncertainty of 1833 made doubtful the status of the National Republican party in the country and the state. When the mainstay of the coalition in Massachusetts, Governor Levi Lincoln, announced in the spring of 1833 that he would not seek re-election, many feared that the scramble for a successor would bring complete chaos and open the way for a Democratic victory that fall.[40]

In fact, the Democrats were not an immediate danger in 1833. Earlier Jacksonian attacks on Adams and New England, as well as retaliatory appeals to regional patriotism, had temporarily discredited the party. Its organization, devoted largely to the distribution of federal patronage, was feeble, and its leadership was inept. State Supreme Court Justice Marcus Morton lent laconic respectability to the Democratic cause; others, such as David Henshaw, Boston banker and collector for the Port of Boston, seemed little more than spoilsmen. Democrats were in no position to exploit the confusion in the dominant party.[41]

The Anti-Masons were of much more immediate concern to Webster and the nascent Whig party in 1833. Anti-Masonry was respectable among people and in places where the Democratic party of Andrew Jackson was not; and its cause found friends among all those who were frustrated by the one-party politics of Massachusetts. Many who had long burned at the domination of the state's economy and politics by Boston found in Anti-Masonry an outlet for their resentments. Young politicians, such as Edward Everett and Charles Francis Adams, who chafed at the order and pace of promotion within the National Republican party, looked to Anti-Masonry to slake their ambitions.[42] Perhaps most important, the Anti-Masons had the friendship of John Quincy

---

[40] Arthur B. Darling, *Political Changes in Massachusetts, 1824–1848: A Study of Liberal Movements in Politics*, Yale Historical Publications, no. 15 (New Haven: Yale University Press, 1925), pp. 45–54, 106. For a recent discussion of Webster and Anti-Masonry, see Norman D. Brown, *Daniel Webster and the Politics of Availabilty* (Athens: University of Georgia Press, 1969), chap. 5.

[41] Darling, *Political Changes in Massachusetts*, pp. 83, 95–101, 110–114. From 1826 to 1836 no Democratic candidate for governor received more than 31 percent of the vote in Massachusetts. Election statistics appear in the Official Massachusetts Election Return Records, Massachusetts State Archives, Boston. For a thoughtful discussion of Democracy in Massachusetts, see Arthur M. Schlesinger, Jr., *The Age of Jackson* (Boston: Little, Brown & Co., 1945), pp. 144–58.

[42] Everett complained that few men advanced without the sanction of the Boston "coterie," and of his exclusion from the "confidential councils" of the party. Everett to George Bancroft, September 11, 1828, Edward Everett Papers, MHS; Everett to Caleb Cushing, December 9, 1832, Caleb Cushing Papers, LC.

Adams. The former president, who had been re-elected to Congress in 1830, had always been suspicious of State Street, and especially of the ex-Federalist wing of the National Republican coalition. It seemed no coincidence to Adams and others among the disaffected that many of the leaders of the state were Masons, and since 1831 Adams had become increasingly vocal about the Masonic "hydra."[43] Charges that Masons secretly favored one another in business, politics, and even in jury trials seemed convincing to all who believed in 1833 that they were victims of an establishment.[44]

Almost all Massachusetts Anti-Masons in 1833 regarded Webster as a likely ally. Anti-Masonic members of the state legislature had nominated him for president in January, and over the summer the state's leading Anti-Masonic newspaper, the *Boston Advocate*, lauded Webster and his candidacy.[45] Both Everett and John Quincy Adams, who were the leading gubernatorial prospects for the Anti-Masons in the fall elections, expected Webster's aid.[46] Most Anti-Masons judged that Webster, though obviously of the Massachusetts establishment, was also independent of it. They calculated that Webster was eager to fuse the Whig and Anti-Masonic parties as a prelude to fusion throughout the North.[47]

Webster wanted an understanding with the Anti-Masons, but he also wanted supremacy in state politics, and he did not intend to arrange any alliance which would upset Whig hegemony. He was perfectly willing to make concessions to the Anti-Masons as long as they respected Whig control of Massachusetts. The loss of men like Everett and Adams to what Webster regarded as a rival party was unacceptable, and he moved quickly to check the defections. Webster stopped Everett in August with a flat statement that fusion was out of the question and

[43] Adams claimed that 35 of the 63 Boston delegates to the state National Republican Convention of 1833 were Masons. Charles Francis Adams, ed., *Memoirs of John Quincy Adams*, 12 vols. (Philadelphia: J. P. Lippincott & Co., 1876), 9:6, 16 (July 10 and September 26, 1833).

[44] See, for example, Edward Everett to H. Atwell and the Middlesex Antimasonic Committee, June 29, 1833, Edward Everett Letterbooks. This cluster of suspicions is, of course, almost interchangeable with the feelings of Jacksonians about special privilege.

[45] The 1833 endorsement is cited in the *Address to Antimasonic Representatives of Massachusetts* (Boston, 1836), in the pamphlet collection of the Boston Athenaeum, Boston, Mass. See also the *Boston Advocate*, July 24 and September 17, 1833.

[46] Everett to Webster, August 9, 1833, copy, Edward Everett Papers, MHS; Adams, *Memoirs*, 9:6 (July 10, 1833).

[47] Webster apparently encouraged such expectations in his canvass for a new party in 1833, when he made it clear that Anti-Masons of other states could expect an important place in his organization. Norman D. Brown, "Webster-Jackson Movement for a Constitution and Union Party in 1833," *Mid-America*, 66 (July, 1964): 158, 163.

with an intimation that Everett could expect the regular party nomination for governor within two years.[48] Webster failed to check John Quincy Adams, however. The former president did run for governor as the Anti-Masonic candidate and won enough votes to force the choice on the Massachusetts General Court. But, when it seemed likely that the Anti-Masonic legislators would combine with Democrats to prevent a choice, Adams withdrew in late December, and John Davis, the candidate hand-picked by Webster, won the governorship.[49]

Despite Davis' victory, it was clear that Anti-Masons were far from tamed, and in January, 1834, Webster sounded out Adams on concessions to the Anti-Masons. Webster suggested that Massachusetts Masons themselves renounce their general charter. Adams rejected the gesture as inadequate and demanded a bill outlawing Masonic oaths, a full investigation of Masonry, and appointments of prominent Anti-Masons to the governor's council. Promising to do what he could, Webster promptly urged the governor-elect to place one or two Anti-Masons on his council, "for the purpose of manifesting a spirit of Union, & to show that we have no secrets." Webster added that Adams displayed an "*earnest* desire" to reconcile the two parties, and would help do so if the proper gestures were made. "*Cannot the thing be done?*"[50]

In fact, neither Webster nor Davis, both of whom were ready to deal with the Anti-Masons, had full control over the Whigs in the legislature, and they could wring only token concessions from the party. The Whigs decided all contested elections against the Anti-Masonic candidates; they named no Anti-Masons to the governor's council. The state Senate appointed a committee to investigate Masonry, but did not give it power to compel Masons to testify; the General Court went through the charade of banning Masonic oaths by passing a resolution without sanctions. By late February, Adams complained that "every possible thing had been done to fret and exasperate" the Anti-Masons in the legislature, and he washed his hands of further "vain" efforts to reconcile the groups.[51] Unless the Whigs allowed "Masonry utterly, openly, & without qualification to go down," Everett warned in early March, the

---

[48] Webster to Everett, August 11, 1833, Edward Everett Papers, MHS.

[49] Webster urged Everett to persuade Adams to withdraw, but Everett dropped the matter when Adams asked him to put the request in writing. Webster drafted John Davis to run as Adam's opponent. Adams, *Memoirs*, 9:10, 16; Webster to Davis, September 30, 1833, John Davis Papers, American Antiquarian Society, Worcester, Mass.

[50] Webster to Levi Lincoln, January 8, [1834], Levi Lincoln Papers, MHS. Webster sent his suggestions to Davis through Lincoln.

[51] Adams, *Memoirs*, 9:103–04 (February 28, 1834); Everett to Cushing, March 2, 1834, Cushing Papers.

state's dissident Anti-Masonic and Democratic parties would formally unite and take control of the state.[52]

That the dissidents might do just that was evident in February, 1834, when, in response to Webster's request for Massachusetts legislative support of his Bank recharter proposal, Caleb Cushing had to report back that Webster's forces were paralyzed by the Anti-Masons, "who upon all occasions vote with the Jackson party."[53] The alliance of those who opposed the "vast," irresponsible, "hydra-like" exclusivism of Masonry and those opposed to the "monster" Bank monopoly presented a clear danger to Webster's political plans. An effective coalition of Anti-Masons and Democrats could not only throw the Whigs into a minority in Massachusetts but would cripple Webster's hopes of attracting other Northern Anti-Masons.

Hence, in March, Webster redoubled his efforts to disarm Anti-Masonry—but now he turned to Masonry itself. On March 12 he drafted a letter calling for dissolution of the secret order,[54] and simultaneously solicited the help of Massachusetts colleagues to see that his call was well received. He asked Masonic friends to sound out their brethren on the surrender of charters, and preliminary responses indicated that, while Boston would balk, Masons in the interior would consent. By June, Webster's plan was complete. The governor would arrange a better law which banned oaths; at Davis' call, lodges would meet publicly, renounce secrecy, abandon their charters, and open the order to all.[55] As Webster's friends toured eastern and western Massachusetts, winning pledges of support from fellow Masons, Webster negotiated with Anti-Masons to accept his solution.[56] By the summer's end, more than a dozen lodges had surrendered their charters.

The senator's maneuvers did not dispel the frustrations which Anti-Masonry expressed. His use of Masonic friends to make the order appear benign only supported Anti-Masonic claims that a secret system of sympathy did exist among the rulers of Massachusetts. The network allowed them to ask special favors from one another which they denied to outsiders. Anti-Masons wanted that brotherhood of privilege destroyed; they wanted Masons pilloried. Webster's alternative to ostra-

---

[52] Everett to Cushing, March 2, 1834, *ibid.*

[53] Cushing to Webster, February 23, 1834, draft, *ibid.*

[54] Everett to Cushing, March 12, 1834, *ibid.*

[55] George Bliss to Cushing, March 13, 1834; and Everett to Cushing, March 23, 1834; *ibid.* Rufus Choate to Davis, [June 30, 1834]; and Webster to Davis, August 14, 1834; Davis Papers.

[56] Choate to Davis, August 23, 1834; and Cushing to Davis, August 28, 1834; Davis Papers. Choate to Cushing, August 23, 1834, Rufus Choate Papers, New York Public Library, New York, N.Y.

cism, the voluntary abandonment of charters, was unacceptable. Sacrifice of the charters made the Masons seem like martyrs instead of enemies of the people; the opening of the lodges seduced the gullible into the Masonic web.[57]

Yet Webster's tactical concessions to Anti-Masonry did prove successful in preserving Whig hegemony in 1834. Confused, Anti-Masons hesitated even to run a slate of candidates in the Massachusetts fall election,[58] and, when the party chose to compete, it fared badly. Governor John Davis handily won re-election in October, though the Whig majority in the General Court was slim. Whig numbers were sufficient to win a test of strength in early 1835, when, to fill a vacancy in the U.S. Senate, the party beat back a move to name Adams and instead chose John Davis on the first ballot.[59] Still, danger remained. Despite strong support from Webster, Davis won the Senate seat by a majority of one. The Anti-Masonic *Boston Advocate* had all but deserted to the Democrats. And Adams, holding Webster responsible for his loss of the Senate post,[60] could be counted on to seek vengeance.

The threat of a Democratic–Anti-Masonic fusion was checked only for the moment, and Whig control of state politics remained tenuous through 1836. Anti-Masonry continued to wither as a distinct political movement, but Massachusetts Anti-Masons increasingly crossed over to the Democrats instead of joining the Whigs. Webster had contained Anti-Masonry, but he had not made Massachusetts a safe political base.

Yet, by the fall of 1834, even the presidential candidate's minimal achievements were important ones. Outside the state, his efforts to conciliate Anti-Masonry seemed impressive. In Massachusetts, control of the legislature remained in Whig hands, and control of the Whigs fell increasingly to Webster. Momentary control of both the state and the party paved the way for Massachusetts's formal nomination of its senior senator as a candidate for the presidency.

---

[57] For a useful model which helps distinguish between the pragmatic, atomistic organization of the Anti-Masons and the traditional, kinship structure of the Masonic order, see Arthur L. Stinchcombe, "Social Structure and Organizations," in *Handbook of Organizations*, comp. James March (New York: Rand McNally, 1965), p. 149. For thoughts on the conspiratorial bent of the Anti-Masons and other political protest movements, see David Brion Davis, "Some Themes of Counter-Subversion: An Analysis of Anti-Masonic, Anti-Catholic, and Anti-Mormon Literature," *Mississippi Valley Historical Review*, 47 (June, 1960): 205–24.

[58] Darling, *Political Changes in Massachusetts*, p. 123.

[59] *Boston Daily Evening Transcript*, February 6, 1835; *Boston Advocate*, cited in the *Boston Atlas*, August 6, 1835.

[60] Martin B. Duberman, "Charles Francis Adams and the Antimasonic Movement," *Mid-America*, 43 (April, 1961): 114–16, 124.

IV

Webster's leverage in Massachusetts had simply made his nomination there possible. What made a state nomination necessary was the structure of the national party, and what made it imperative in January, 1835, was the appearance of new rivals late in 1834.

The Whig party lacked a formal procedure for choosing its presidential candidate for 1836. Choice by congressional caucus had long been discredited, yet Whig leaders in Washington and in the states had hesitated to embrace the less malleable alternative of a national convention.[61] Though all parties to the 1832 contest had nominally picked their candidates in convention, the Whigs subsequently charged that the system was a Democratic sham to make voters think a pre-picked party candidate was a popular choice. The Whig stance was reinforced by the certainty that a national convention for 1836 would only agree to disagree,[62] yet it also reflected the decentralized structure of the party. Leaders rallied by the Whig summons to men of "independence" could hardly pledge in advance to submit to the choice of a convention. Independent groups gravitating toward the Whigs were equally unwilling at this point to submit to discipline. States'-rights Southerners and Northern Anti-Masons alike felt they lacked sufficient influence to dictate a convention's choice, and neither group felt secure enough locally to risk a choice which they could not later disclaim.[63]

In the end, the Whigs relied on action by state parties and Whig newspapers to select a candidate. Either form of "nomination" was a proto-primary; the favored candidate and his friends then agitated for ratification by other legislatures and presses to built momentum and finally win agreement on their man. There was, of course, a danger of

---

[61]The nature of the origins of, and opposition to, the new nomination procedure, as Richard McCormick suggests, awaits an "adequate study." In *The Second American Party System: Party Formation in the Jacksonian Era* (Chapel Hill: University of North Carolina Press, 1966), McCormick finds strong Whig opposition to the convention system in several Western states. See pp. 341–49. For further discussion of the Whig's fitful movement toward acceptance of a national convention, see Richard P. McCormick, "Political Development and the Second Party System," in *The American Party Systems: Stages of Political Development*, ed. William Nisbet Chambers and Walter Dean Burnham (New York: Oxford University Press, 1967), pp. 104–5. Henry Clay's correspondence, cited below, suggests considerable objection among Southern congressmen to a presidential convention.

[62]E. Malcolm Carroll, *Orgins of the Whig Party* (Durham: Duke University Press, 1925), pp. 444–48; Clay to [unidentified correspondent], July 14, 1835, *The Works of Henry Clay*, 5:394; William Slade to John Bailey, December 30, 1834, MHS.

[63]Clay to Francis T. Brooke, July 20 and August 19, 1835, Henry Clay Papers, Duke University Library, Durham, N.C. Calhoun to Christopher Van Deventer, January 25, 1834; and Calhoun to Lewis S. Coryell, August 19, 1834; in Jameson, "Correspondence of John C. Calhoun," pp. 330, 340. Thurlow Weed to Seward, June 5, 1833, and February 10, 1835, Seward Papers.

multiple nominations and no consensus, but this was the best the Whigs could do, trapped as they were by their decentralized organization and their commitment against a convention. Whigs could and did hope that multiple candidates might prevent a Democratic majority and thus throw the decision to the House of Representatives, where one of the Whigs might acquire the presidency.

No aspirant, under the bandwagon system, could long allow the entry of a rival to go unanswered, lest silence be taken as consent, and, by late 1834, Webster's friends felt compelled to act. In November, Whigs of the Alabama legislature announced for Hugh Lawson White, a Tennessee Democrat who had bolted the party over the removal of the Bank deposits, and, in December, Ohio Whigs put Supreme Court Justice John McLean into the race. White's nomination evoked mixed reaction from Webster. White appealed to those Southerners who were disenchanted with Jackson and reluctant to support a Northerner, Martin Van Buren, as his successor.[64] Webster recognized that the same sectional bias applied to him—he had never supposed "it would be easy to get Southern votes for any Northern man"—but was temporarily satisfied that White's candidacy would strengthen the Whigs by undermining Van Buren in the South. Not until mid-1835 would Webster's spokesman attack White's candidacy. The candidacy of John McLean, a former postmaster general under Adams and Jackson, was far more of a danger because it jeopardized Webster's strategy of being the sole Whig candidate of the North.[65] McLean came from the crucial state of Ohio, was acceptable to many Anti-Masons, and was bland enough to seem to be all things to all men. As Rufus Choate wrote, sufficient "religion, cant, good Jacksonism, mere morals, mediocrity, demagogism, nullification," and a "reputation of useful service in the post-office" made McLean troublesome in the absence of a true "*Whig candidate.*" Choate and others called for immediate counteraction by Massachusetts to put McLean out "like a faltering candle."[66]

The Boston press initiated the call for a nomination by the Whig members of the Massachusetts General Court in mid-December, but, despite unanimous editorial endorsements and Webster's own activity, a nomination proved surprisingly difficult.[67] None openly opposed Web-

---

[64] Carroll, *Origins of the Whig Party*, p. 133; Arthur C. Cole, *The Whig Party in the South* (Washington, D.C.: The American Historical Association, 1914), pp. 39–42.

[65] Webster to Jeremiah Mason, January 1 and February 6, 1835, *Writings*, 16:245–46, 253.

[66] Choate to Everett, January 11, 1835, Edward Everett Papers, MHS.

[67] *Boston Atlas*, December 17, 1834. Webster drafted an article for the *Atlas* calling for his nomination by Massachusetts Whigs. See "The Crisis," December 17, 1834, J. O. Sargent

ster, but many privately doubted that he could win. Some preferred Clay, others thought the Whigs ought to search for a demonstrably popular man, and both groups stalled for time. To end the delay, Webster's Boston sentinel Rufus Choate dispatched an urgent call on January 11 to Edward Everett, who was in Washington, for letters of support from the Massachusetts, Maine, Vermont, and Connecticut congressional delegations. Everett, who did not touch his "pillow . . . till after midnight, laboring in the Cause," hurriedly collected the signatures—apparently even getting a kind word from Clay—and sped them back.[68] The letters arrived on January 16, "safe & *sound*," and Choate used them tellingly to convert the "timid" and the "uninformed."[69] In a crucial maneuver on the eighteenth, Webster's friends shrewdly arranged to put the leading "waverers" on the committee appointed to consider party action—so "they cannot bolt, or get out of the traces, without being noticed." Despite a "shyness, a shirking, a pretending of policy & perhaps some honest doubts, which have delayed & almost defeated the measure," triumph came on the evening of January 21, when the caucus of 315 Whig legislators unanimously nominated Webster for president.[70]

The appeals that accompanied Webster's nomination stressed his orthodoxy, though Whig "orthodoxy" was tailored to fit Webster's credentials. Whiggery and Webster alone stood for the cause of "American patriotism" and constitutional liberty. That cause would be "irretrievably ruined" if the Whigs chose a former Democrat—an obvious reference both to White, who had come to the Senate as a Democratic spokesman from Tennessee, and to McLean, who had served in Jackson's cabinet.[71]

But Webster's friends made it clear that in this contest Webster also stood squarely for the traditional breed of political leader. The issue before the party and the country was whether a great man could become president. Webster alone was a statesman of the old school—an

---

Papers, MHS. See also *Boston Courier*, January 10, 12, 1835; and Cushing to Webster, January 3, 1835, Cushing Papers.

[68] Henry Kinsman to Webster, January 18, 1835, Daniel Webster Papers, New Hampshire Historical Society, Concord (hereafter cited as NHHS). Cushing to Webster, January 9, 1835; and Everett to Cushing, January 9, 1835; Cushing Papers, LC. Choate to Everett, January 11, 1835, Edward Everett Papers, LC.

[69] Choate to Everett, January 16, 1835, Edward Everett Papers, LC.

[70] Kinsman to Webster, January 18, 1835, Webster Papers, NHHS; Winthrop to Everett, January 21, 1835, Edward Everett Papers, MHS; *Boston Courier*, January 22, 1835.

[71] *Boston Courier*, January 23, 1835; "Legislative Nomination of Daniel Webster," Daniel Webster Papers, Houghton Library, Harvard University, Cambridge, Mass.

intellectual man, a man of international stature, a distinguished patriot. He alone was a public man—"a Man of the Country"—who impartially served East and West, North and South.[72] To the crucial question of whether greatness would win votes, Webster's partisans answered yes. While the candidate himself conceded that he lacked a hold on the "imagination" of the people, he claimed to have a firm grip on their "affections." The primary affection was gratitude.[73] Grateful for his defense of the Constitution, proud of his talents, the electorate would reward Webster, just as they had rewarded Washington.

Webster's nomination and appeal carried many with him, but the response to his entry revealed once again the power that the loose Whig organization gave to the nay-sayers. The Massachusetts nomination did stop McLean, who bitterly watched his fortunes melt away in the course of the spring.[74] Yet McLean's failure in the West was not accompanied by Webster's rise. In Maryland, too, stalemate was the outcome. Sentiment for Webster there stopped a budding Clay movement, but the balance of Clay's forces blocked a pledge to Webster.[75] In the rest of the South, Webster was rejected outright. Presses of all persuasions asked only if the Massachusetts senator was safe on the slavery question,[76] and Southern Whig newspapers reiterated their support for former Democrat Hugh Lawson White of Tennessee as their section's first choice for the party candidate. Though initially tolerant of the South's sectional preference, Webster began to worry as he became the butt of charges that his candidacy obstructed the chance of a Whig victory under White's leadership.[77] Webster's partisans grew increas-

---

[72] "Legislative Nomination of Daniel Webster."

[73] Everett drafted a pro-Webster editorial for the *Boston Courier* in August, 1833. In it he asserted that Webster was the only candidate "having any hold upon the imagination of the people." Webster read over the draft and substituted the word "affections" for "imagination." Webster added—perhaps somewhat imaginatively—that he alone was "known, quoted, & admired in Europe, as one of the great before his country." Everett to Editor of *Boston Courier*, [August, 1833], Edward Everett Papers, MHS. Similar themes ran through Joseph Story's "anonymous" article, "Statesmen—Their Rareness and Importance: DANIEL WEBSTER," *The New England Magazine*, 7 (August, 1834): 89-104, and in two articles on Webster in the *North American Review*, 8 (March and July, 1835): 220-28 and 249-51. The latter article asked if it was impossible to "do justice to contemporary worth."

[74] McLean to Salmon P. Chase, February 25, 1835, Salmon P. Chase Papers, HSP; McLean to Samuel Bell, April 27, 1835, Samuel Bell Papers, NHHS; George Chambers to Thomas Ewing, June 11, 1835, Ewing Family Papers, LC.

[75] Everett to Cushing, February 1, 1835, Cushing Papers; Edwin Harriman to Clay, February 8, 1837, Henry Clay Papers, LC.

[76] *Richmond Whig*, n.d., quoted in the *Boston Courier*, May 27, 1835.

[77] *Washington United States Telegraph*, April 11, 18, 20, 1835; Webster to Biddle, May 9, 1835, in *The Correspondence of Nicholas Biddle dealing with National Affairs, 1807-1844*, ed. Reginald McGrane (Boston: Houghton Mifflin Co., 1919), pp. 250-51.

ingly strident in their attacks on the Southern "Whig" candidate. North and South, however, the assaults won only rebuke from Whigs, who were increasingly resigned to a multiple candidacy.[78]

In the crucial task of uniting his own section, Webster made greater headway. Intense lobbying by Webster's friends produced endorsements from Rhode Island, Connecticut, and Maine Whigs, but the party's defeat in the summer and fall elections in all three states badly tarnished Webster's image as the Northern favorite.[79] Many Northern Whig papers spoke well of Webster's candidacy; these included the *United States Gazette* of Philadelphia, the *New York American*, the *Washington National Intelligencer*, the *Columbus Ohio State Journal*, the Anti-Masonic *Pittsburgh Advocate*, and dozens of smaller papers.[80] Yet powerful newspapers held back. The *New York Commercial Advertiser* called the Webster entry "premature"; the *New York Herald* remained silent.

Hostile editors turned against Webster the very claims that were being made for his candidacy. Webster was "too pure a man—of too enlarged views—wedded in his modes of thinking and acting to considerations too lofty to be a successful candidate," lamented Thurlow Weed's *Albany Evening Journal*. The public did not appreciate his talents, judged Weed, and, understandably, Webster could not "stoop to act the politician—to study the art of political strategy—to play the popular man." The *New York Star*, which favored Clay, concurred: "The day has gone by to hope for the success of great intellectual men, who rely on talent, and not on tact,—who are familiar with books, and not with men."[81]

Such damning praise infuriated Webster's backers, as did intimations that these objections could bring about his withdrawal from the contest. To meet the challenges, Webster's backers staged a series of rallies in Massachusetts during the spring of 1835. Webster would "not with-

---

[78] *Boston Courier*, May 28, 1835; *Boston Atlas*, May 19, 1835; Joseph Gales, Jr., to Everett, September 4, 1835, Edward Everett Papers, MHS.

[79] [Richard Haughton] to J. O. Sargent, February 15, 1835, Sargent Papers, MHS; Webster to Everett, May 1, 1835, Edward Everett Papers, MHS; *Boston Atlas*, June 27, 1834; Clay to John Bailhache, September 13, 1835, *The Works of Henry Clay*, 5:400.

[80] Carroll, *Origins of the Whig Party*, pp. 137-40, 143. The *Boston Courier* cited endorsements for Webster from the *Ohio State Journal*, the *New York American*, the *Baltimore Chronicle*, and numerous smaller papers; see the *Courier* for January 6 and 29, October 30, and November 4, 1835. The *Boston Atlas* ran similar announcements on April 30, June 3, 25, 27, and September 22, 1835.

[81] *Albany Evening Journal*, May 29, 1835; *New York Star*, quoted in the *Boston Courier*, May 7, 1835.

draw," faithful Bostonians pledged in Faneuil Hall on May 29. "The whole nation had heard of his eloquence and honesty, of his generosity and patriotism," the assembly declared. Countrymen knew Webster's speeches by heart; they knew that he had "put down Nullification, and thereby saved the Union." "Must not such a man be popular?"[82] Independence Day rallies throughout the state repeated the call for all to back "the first patriot and Stateman of our Country."[83] To quash doubts about Webster's stand on slavery, the senator's friends arranged an August assembly in Faneuil Hall to denounce abolitionism, and the *Boston Atlas* alleged that the abolitionists were backing Van Buren.[84] Meanwhile, Boston papers complained of the silence of leading Whig politicians. If those who claimed that Webster was too sublime "for the common touch . . . *honestly* endeavored to promote his election," they would discover the depth of sentiment that existed for the senator.[85]

For those who opposed Webster, however, there was a distinct danger that he would become the Northern candidate by default. William Henry Seward and Thurlow Weed, the skillful managers of New York's Anti-Masonic party who had come over to the Whigs in 1834, viewed such a prospect as a disaster. Though Seward's conscience reproached him for rejecting Webster—"*too great, too wise, too pure*"—he was convinced that support for the senator would forever taint the Whigs with Federalism and "cast us into a perpetual minority."[86] He and Weed scouted for an alternative.

The two New Yorkers, along with other Whigs, who were reluctant to forfeit the Northern nomination to Webster, found their man in General William Henry Harrison of Ohio. Victor of the Battle of Tippecanoe in the War of 1812, Harrison bore all the marks of a winner. He was a military hero; he came from a critical Western state; he had been removed from a diplomatic sinecure by Jackson without cause; and he possessed, Weed thought, "all the zeal we once had for Anti-Masonry." Equally important, he had no notable political views. Perfectly willing to run Harrison in the North and White in the South, Seward and Weed, along with Anti-Masons in Pennsylvania and Ohio, quickly attached

[82] *Boston Courier*, May 15, 1835.

[83] *Boston Atlas*, May 28, 29, and June 3, 6, 20, 1835; *Boston Courier*, May 30 and June 1, 1835; Webster to Everett, [July 2, 1835], Edward Everett Papers, MHS.

[84] *Boston Atlas*, August 8, 18, 1835.

[85] *Boston Courier*, September 12, 1835.

[86] Weed to Seward, February 10 and March 8, 1835, Seward Papers; Seward to Weed, February 15 and March 15, 1835, Thurlow Weed Papers, University of Rochester, Rochester, N.Y.

themselves to the "Hero of Tippecanoe" and, by mid-1835, looked to him as their Northern savior.[87]

Webster moved to counter disappointment and the new danger by urging Whigs to keep the faith. In speeches throughout New England in the fall of 1835, he warned that, if the Whigs did not battle the cult of personality, no one would. "Man-worship" had already made the Democratic party despotic, and it threatened to infect the nation; there would be no nation left if the Whigs yielded their own standards. "Unlimited, unconstitutional confidence in men" would rule both parties; wisdom and judgment would vanish; blind partisanship would end both liberty and the Union.[88] Such themes were meant to rally the faithful, and in particular to mobilize citizens who supported the Whigs and Anti-Masons because those groups opposed party as a menace to individual conscience. Webster appealed directly to those Americans who rankled at "dictation" from authority. For them, in politics and religion, the individual conscience must be free to rule. Any organization which sought to control freedom of thought was anathema. In his repeated use of the term "man-worship" to characterize the Democrats, Webster sought to portray the party of Jackson as one which no longer allowed latitude for individual judgment. The Democratic party had become the political analogue of the Catholic church and the Masonic order. Only when men were emancipated from the "enslaving prejudices of party" would individuals be "free to act for the best interests of the country."[89]

Yet, to most Americans—indeed, to many Whigs—Webster's fears of "elective monarchy" and loss of individual freedom must have seemed remote. There was little anxiety about the dangers he had forecast.[90] If man-worship was evil, what was the retribution? If men such as Webster

[87]Seward to Weed, February 15, March 15, and June 12, 1835, Weed Papers, University of Rochester; *Albany Evening Journal*, March 10, 1835; George Chambers to Thomas Ewing, June 11, 1835, Ewing Family Papers.

[88]Daniel Webster, "Speech at Bangor, Maine, August 25, 1835"; "Speech at Hallowell, Maine, October 3, 1835"; and "Speech at Boston, October 12, 1835"; *Writings*, 2: 162–64, 13:60, and 2:181–83.

[89]This typical expression of antiparty sentiment can be found in Roland P. Formisano's illuminating discussion of persistent opposition to parties in the Jacksonian era. See Formisano, "Political Character, Antipartyism, and the Second Party System," p. 703.

[90]Foreign observers, such as Alexis de Tocqueville, detected at once what Webster was just beginning to understand about the American voter. Tocqueville found most Americans obsessed with equality and unworried about freedom; only for those already wealthy and secure was liberty a desperate concern. See Alexis de Tocqueville, *Democracy in America*, ed. Phillips Bradley, 2 vols. (New York: Alfred A. Knopf, 1945), 2:99–103, 312.

were out of power, what was the loss? The country was prosperous and at peace; events seemed only to prove the departure from good form profitable and the need for self-designated great men dubious. Webster's increasingly vocal complaints about apathy in the face of mortal dangers suggested that he himself sensed the impotence of his alarms.[91]

Despite the anxious tone of Webster's fall speeches, he and his backers remained confident that they would surmount the challenge from Harrison. They regarded the General as a man whom no right-thinking Whig, properly reminded of his duty, would endorse. While the Anti-Masons were less predictable, here, too, Webster believed he could beat back the Harrison challenge and establish his claim as the favorite of the North.[92]

The decision between Webster and Harrison fell to the Anti-Masons of Pennsylvania. The rival minorities within the party had produced a stalemate, and the deadlock had given inordinate power to groups which could hope to swing crucial votes to the Whigs. Pennsylvania, with its large bloc of electoral votes, was a critical state, and within Pennsylvania the Anti-Masons were the Whigs' only hope. Apparently speaking for his congressional colleagues, Clay reported in July, 1835, that the choice of Pennsylvania Anti-Masons, who were scheduled to convene at Harrisburg in December, 1835, would be the choice of the Whig party. Nothing epitomized the weakness of the Whig organization more than its agreement that a faction of non-Whigs should determine the party's Northern nominee.[93]

Webster's use of all the traditional tactics to win over Pennsylvania Anti-Masons was thorough but unavailing. He had carefully cultivated contacts in the state, and the most responsive of these were gentlemen who had some influence with Anti-Masons.[94] During 1835, Webster established a record on Anti-Masonry that was clearly superior to

---

[91]Webster, "Speech at Hallowell, Maine," and "Speech at Boston," *Writings*, 12:39 and 2:183.

[92]Webster to Everett, April 2 and [November 22], 1835, Edward Everett Papers, MHS; Everett to Nathan Sargent, October 26, 1835, Biddle Papers, LC.

[93]Clay to [unidentifed correspondent], July 14, 1835, *The Works of Henry Clay*, 5:394; Clay to Francis Brooke, July 20, 1835, Henry Clay Papers, Duke; Benjamin W. Leigh to Brooke, August 16, 1835, Henry Clay Papers, LC.

[94]Two of Webster's contacts with Pennsylvania Anti-Masons were Elihu Chauncey of Philadelphia and John B. Wallace of Meadville. The temper of the men is evident from their reflections after the defeat of 1832. "I presume that our partnership with the Anti-Masons has come to an end," Chauncey wrote Wallace, "and that we shall not be again disposed to dabble in such dirty water." Chauncey to Wallace, November 9, 1832, Wallace Papers, vol. 7. Webster's other contacts were Harmar Denny of Pittsburgh and George Chambers.

Harrison's. Earlier that year, Webster's partisans had drawn from Harrison a letter so hostile to Anti-Masonic demands that many thought it would eliminate the General.[95] Subsequently, Webster produced statements which avowed that Masonry was "essentially wrong" in its principles and which affirmed that Webster concurred entirely with the opinions of the Anti-Masonic party.[96] Webster's pledges eventually won the reluctant support of Anti-Masonic leader Thaddeus Stevens,[97] but most party leaders stood by the more popular candidate. They wanted a presidential nominee who would at least bolster them locally; most felt, with Nicholas Biddle, that Webster's election was an "impracticable good for which it was vain to contend."[98] In December, the General won the Pennsylvania endorsement overwhelmingly. Webster's candidacy for 1836 was over.[99]

V

Instead of a year of triumph, then, 1836 was for Webster a year of reappraisal. In the beginning, he was bitter and defiant. Despite the expectation, even among Massachusetts congressmen, that he would withdraw in Harrison's favor, Webster refused.[100] Without him, the senator said after two months of silence, the state party might suffer defeat that fall—and Massachusetts came first.[101] Though probably correct, Webster's claim disguised the fact that almost no circumstances would have led him to withdraw for the sake of the national party in

---

[95] Weed to Seward, October 22 and December 3, 1835, Seward Papers.

[96] Webster to Harmar Denny and Others, November 20, 1835; Webster to John B. Wallace and Others, November 28, 1835; and Webster to William W. Irwin, November 30, 1835; *Writings*, 18:12–14 and 16:259–61. Webster to Everett, [November 22, 1835], Edward Everett Papers, MHS.

[97] Stevens initially refused to support Webster, but reversed himself by the time of the December convention. Thaddeus Stevens to John B. Wallace, October 24, 1835, Wallace Papers, vol. 7; Brown, *Daniel Webster*, p. 140. For additional details on Webster's attempt to win the aid of Pennsylvania Anti-Masons, see *ibid.*, chap. 7.

[98] Biddle to Everett, November 12, 1835, President's Letter Book, no. 5, Biddle Papers, LC.

[99] Cushing to Everett, December 17, 22, 24, 1835, Edward Everett Papers, MHS; H. M. Stuart to Cushing, December 22, 1835, Cushing Papers; Crittenden to James Morehead, December 23, 1835, John Jordan Crittenden Papers, LC.

[100] Crittenden to Morehead, December 23, 1835, Crittenden Papers, LC; Samuel C. Phillips to John Davis, January 3, 1836, Davis Papers; Amos A. Lawrence to Amos Lawrence, January 8, 1836, Amos Lawrence Papers, MHS. Philo C. Fuller to Weed, February 14, 1836, Weed Papers, University of Rochester.

[101] Webster to Henry Kinsman, February 20, 1836, Kinsman Letters, Frederick M. Dearborn Collection, Houghton Library, Harvard University, Cambridge, Mass.; Cushing to T. Parsons, February 27, 1836, Theophilus Parsons, Jr., Papers, Boston Public Library, Boston Mass.; Webster to Kinsman, February 29, 1836, Robert C. Winthrop Papers, MHS.

1836.[102] Since Massachusetts men had "nothing to hope [for], now or at any other time . . . from the South or the West," he wrote privately, "Massachusetts must stand alone."[103] To the public, which had ignored Webster's alarms, the *Boston Courier* seemed to speak for the defeated candidate. In late December it slashed at the "stupid beastliness . . . of the mass of people." The *Courier's* statesman would not fawn to the beast. He would continue to cater only to his "conviction of political rectitude," to listen to no voices but the steady "voice within."[104] Webster's first speech after his setback reflected the same truculent mood. It was "no holiday business," the senator told his colleagues in January, 1836, "to maintain opposition against power and against majorities," to contend for "principles, against popularity." But Webster would fight the inroads of *"man-worship"* to the last; he promptly launched a savage attack on "popularity," the despotic growth of presidential power, the servility of Democrats before party discipline, and the special spinelessness of the "popular branch of the legislature."[105]

Webster's jeremiads to the Senate continued, but within two months his doomsday tone subsided, for he abruptly perceived that the Democrat's day of reckoning was near. By March, 1836, it was apparent that the long-awaited crisis of Jacksonian financial policy was approaching. The dispersal of government funds to state banks had helped produce inflation, and by the spring of 1836 the issues of paper currency and the number of banks were multiplying beyond control. The increase in credit and in expectations had spurred the speculative purchase of Western lands from the government, and the income from exploding land sales had created a surplus in the Treasury. If the sales and the surplus in the Treasury continued to mount, the government's income, added to the state bank depositories, would only spur inflation and speculation further. The Democrats therefore faced painful choices. They could either spend the money, confine its use so that the pet banks

---

[102]Webster's claim also cloaked the fact that Massachusetts Whigs were divided over whether a Webster candidacy in Massachusetts was needed to retain Whig control in the state. Cushing, Everett, Abbott Lawrence, and Webster thought it was; the Massachusetts delegation in Congress had to be persuaded. Only after two months of caucusing did they finally urge Webster, on February 27, to "stick fast." Everett to Davis, January 30, 1836, Edward Everett Letterbooks; memorandum on the Massachusetts caucus, February 10, 1836, Lincoln Papers; Parsons to Cushing, Februry 22, [1836], Cushing Papers; Cushing to Parsons, February 27, 1836, Parsons Papers.

[103]Webster to Davis, April 7, 1836, Davis Papers.

[104]*Boston Courier*, December 16, 1835.

[105]Daniel Webster, "Speech of January 14, 1836," *Writings*, 7:222–23, 227–29.

could not create more credit, or curtail deposits by curbing government income.[106] Though Webster personally favored distribution of the surplus revenue to the states as an emergency remedy, he now doubted that any solution would prevent financial crisis. He expected the administration to try all expedients, and he welcomed them all. "Let them go on. Let them add to the catalogue" of "schemes, projects, and reckless experiments." "Go on, gentlemen," he told Democrats of the Senate, "and let us see the upshot of your experimental policy."[107]

But Webster sensed further that the Whigs would profit in a remarkable way from the coming Democratic dilemma. He correctly judged that the administration, already opposed to spending for internal improvements, chronically unable to regulate the depository banks, and reluctant to distribute the surplus, would eventually opt to reduce government income. That meant curbing land sales through tighter credit. Since the means for tightening credit were crude without a national bank, in practice the policy would exclude paper currency and allow only gold and silver as payments for Western land. Those who had counted on paper credit, those whom Democrats had won with promises of increased opportunity, would be antagonized. The future promised that those who stood for credit, those who stood for the Democratic promise of easy cash, those who stood for opportunity, would be the Whigs. With clarity, Webster saw that the yearning for credit was as much a bond among Americans, as much a basis for national community among all classes and all sections, as was love of the Union. In a way that public men, their projects, and their eloquence never could, steam, enterprise, and the markets they generated were uniting the nation. The hopes of enterprise, the hopes of union, depended on credit.[108]

Though Webster grew more confident that vindication was near, his style had yet to unbend. That he would have to consider a new public style became clear in the Harrison campaign of 1836. For, in the Whig

---

[106] Reginald C. McGrane, *The Panic of 1837: Some Financial Problems of the Jacksonian Era* (Chicago: University of Chicago Press, 1924), chaps. 2–5; Bray Hammond, *Banks and Politics in America from the Revolution to the Civil War* (Princeton: Princeton University Press, 1957), chaps. 12, 15.

[107] Daniel Webster, "Speech of April 23, 1836," and "Speech of May 31, 1836," *Writings,* 7:240–43, 254–55, 257.

[108] *Ibid.,* pp. 239, 262–64. For a full synthesis of Webster's views on credit, steam, and enterprise, see his lecture "Diffusion of Useful Knowledge, Boston, November 11, 1836," *ibid.,* 13:66, 74–77. See also Robert Lincoln Carey, *Daniel Webster as an Economist* (New York: Columbia University Press, 1929), pp. 79–105.

appeals of that year, it was not Harrison's stature or achievements but the General's "plain, unostentatious manner" which warranted his claim to the presidency.[109] Some Whig claims were made for Harrison's genius in war, and others emphasized his talents in peace; efforts were even made to link him with Washington and other notables of the early Republic.[110] But most Whig editors lauded the General's homely personal virtues—his integrity, rusticity, honesty, purity, poverty, and simplicity.[111] Indeed, obviously liberated, the Whig press of 1836 made the General over in the image of Jackson in 1828. Like Jackson, like Cincinnatus, Harrison had "returned to the plough" after the War of 1812. Like the "farmer of Tennessee," Harrison had become the "farmer of North Bend." As with Jackson, the soil had endowed Harrison with a "calmness of mind," a "spirit of manliness," a power like the forest. And, with the untutored wisdom of the forest, Harrison would yet, claimed none other than Nicholas Biddle, heal and save the country. From whom? From that "prig ruffled shirt gallant," that aristocrat, Martin Van Buren, who had grown rich and effete in politics and European courts while Harrison had tilled the soil in poverty. The script for the future seemed complete when the *Philadelphia National Gazette*, long a friend of Webster, proclaimed in August, 1836, that only common sense was needed in a president, and that the honesty of Harrison and the decadence of Van Buren made the "true democrats . . . the Whigs."[112]

As a popular hero to compare with Harrison or Jackson, Webster had far to go in 1836. In his demeanor as a public man, he epitomized Tocqueville's description of the rich in politics. "They are very ready to do good to the people, but . . . at arms length; they think that is sufficient, but they are mistaken." Only slowly did the rich realize that

---

[109] *Washington National Intelligencer*, August 26, 1836.

[110] *Ibid.*, August 17, 20, and September 29, 1836.

[111] See, for example, the *Portland Advertiser* (Maine), September 15, 1836; the *Ohio State Journal*, February 26, June 3, and August 19, 1836; the *Indiana Palladium*, September 17, 1836; and *The National Gazette* of Philadelphia, August 25, 1836.

[112] For a discussion of the appeals made for Jackson, see John William Ward, *Andrew Jackson: Symbol for an Age* (New York: Oxford University Press, 1955), pp. 41–43. For use of the same imagery by Harrison partisans in 1836, see the *Washington National Intelligencer*, June 3 and August 20, 29, 1836; the *Cincinnati Advertiser*, August 24, 1836; the report of the Young Men's Convention at Harrisburg in the *Ohio State Journal*, June 3, 1836; *The National Gazette* of Philadelphia, August 3, 25, and September 10, 1836. Biddle's remarks were reported in the *Washington National Intelligencer*, October 19, 1836. For a discussion of the Whigs' use of similar themes in the campaign of 1840, see Robert Gray Gunderson, *The Log Cabin Campaign* (Lexington: University of Kentucky Press, 1957), pp. 7–9, 74–77.

democrats were attracted more by "manner than by benefits conferred," more by "affability," "simplicity," and "even want of polish" than by legislation.[113]

By mid-1836, at least one of Webster's partisans had decided that the statesman must be humanized, and he wrote an anonymous pamphlet which described the frontier virtues of Daniel Webster. After properly praising Webster's fitness, the pamphleteer asserted that Webster's real majesty lay in his simplicity. He was born on the "frontier" of New Hampshire. His father was a "pioneer" and a "farmer always," who rose from penury by dint of thrift and hard work. Amid these "hardships and privations," Webster was reared; on the "democratic benches" of New England's free schools, Webster was educated.[114] In short, Webster had the presidential pedigree for the age of Jackson. No man of his origins could be an aristocrat.

The hero himself, however, only inched toward blending old and new appeals. Though a bid for the friendship of the West seemed an obvious time to call in the colloquial, Webster, as he endorsed internal improvements during Senate debate in May, continued to speak of the duty of "statesmen," "enlightened self-interest," and the particular interest of New England in seeing "*our* commerce floating on these Western rivers." Even when he added that he would support Western interests though other New Englanders opposed them—which in fact Webster did—his style was leaden. When it came to the interest of the Western "producer," Webster was as "Western a man . . . as he among them who is the most Western." There "are no Alleghenies in my politics."[115]

Hints of what Webster had learned and would have to learn from failure emerged by the end of 1836. Forced to go outside the Whig congressional coalition to win party support for his ambitions, he had gone to Northern opposition leaders and to the country solely as a patriot and a statesman. His claims were impressive but not winning; his colleagues had succumbed to the standard of "popularity." After 1836, with his own party now infected, Webster would have to come to terms with the new standards, or at least with the new style. To ease

---

[113]Tocqueville, *Democracy in America*, 2:111-12.

[114]*Daniel Webster* (February, 1836), in the pamphlet collection of the Essex Institute, Salem, Mass.

[115]Daniel Webster, "Speech of May 25, 1836," *Writings*, 7:250-51. For Webster's farsighted and often politically risky concern for the West, see Peter J. Parish's incisive "Daniel Webster, New England, and the West," *Journal of American History*, 54 (December, 1967): 524-49.

the change, Webster had Harrison's precedent, but more important, he had a renewed confidence that those to whom he could appeal included an ever-increasing number of citizens. Those ready to promise that government could and would underwrite the enterprise of the country would tap a vast constituency. With his faith in the fundamental community of interests of Americans renewed, Webster prepared to accommodate popular tastes.

IV

THE DISPENSABLE MEN

B ETWEEN 1837 AND 1839 the Whig party changed. From a loose
federation of personalities and state organizations, it became a
political organization dedicated to victory. It adopted a procedure for selecting a single presidential candidate, chose its nominee
solely on the basis of his ability to win, became competitive in every
state, and found a strategy which brought success. Discipline did not
come easily to the Whig club of proud and independent men; total
commitment to victory was not an abrupt decision but a process. Leader, symbol, and victim of that process was Daniel Webster.

For the Whigs the legacy of 1836 was mixed. On the bright side there
was their remarkable showing in the recent election. Despite the fact
that they had run multiple candidates and that several states had fallen
to the Democrats virtually by default, the divided party had cut the
Democratic margin of victory from 57 percent under Jackson to 51
percent under Van Buren. "How easy it would have been to have defeated him!" marveled New York's Thurlow Weed.[1] Financial recession, which began in the final weeks of 1836, further buoyed up Whig
hopes for the future.

---

[1] Eugene H. Roseboom, *A Short History of Presidential Elections* (New York: Macmillan,
1967), pp. 45, 50; Weed to Seward, November 30, 1836, William Henry Seward Papers, University of Rochester, Rochester, N.Y.

Yet the party's improved position against the Democrats seemed only to weaken it internally, as chronic strife over presidential candidates intensified. The scent of success merely strengthened the claims of the leading rivals—Webster, Harrison, and Clay—for the party's support. Clay believed he had generously stepped aside in 1836, that others had failed, and that now he was entitled to another chance at the White House. Harrison felt that his superior showing in 1836 made it clear that he could win in 1840 if he were the only Whig entry. Webster, bitterly certain that Clay's neutrality had cheated him of a real run for the presidency in 1836 and determined to prove himself as popular as Harrison, also felt that he could win if he was the party's sole nominee.[2] Such tangled, intractable, and jealous ambitions constituted the darker legacy of 1836, which the Whigs had to control if they were to unite in 1840.

I

The threat of party fratricide was finally checked through the Whigs' adoption of the national nominating convention.[3] The convention would allow men to pledge themselves to an assembly's decision rather than to a candidate, and so would facilitate cooperation in state and local contests among men of different presidential preferences. It fell to Webster to trigger the process which would lead to the party's acceptance of a nominating convention, for he was first of the rivals to renew his quest for the presidency.

As a first step toward the White House, Webster decided in January, 1837, to resign from the Senate. Seeking the blessings of his friends in Massachusetts, he assured them that he wished to leave Washington not out of disgust or discouragement—"though there is much here to disgust one"—but "to get some little time for" his "own affairs." He envisaged the move more as a leave of absence than as a permanent departure, and hoped that the state legislature would reappoint him

---

[2]Henry Clay to [unidentified correspondent], July 14, 1835, *The Works of Henry Clay, Comprising His Life, Correspondence, and Speeches,* ed. Calvin Colton, 10 vols. (New York: G. P. Putnam's Sons, 1904), 5:392-95 (hereafter cited as *The Works of Henry Clay*); Webster to Jeremiah Mason, February 1, 1835, *The Writings and Speeches of Daniel Webster,* ed. J. W. McIntyre, 18 vols. (Boston: Little, Brown & Co., 1903), 17:251 (hereafter cited as *Writings*); Webster to Hiram Ketchum, January 28, 1837, Daniel Webster Papers, Dartmouth College, Hanover, N.H.

[3]Professor Richard P. McCormick discusses the spread of the convention system in his essay, "Political Development and the Second Party System," in *The American Party Systems: Stages of Political Development,* ed. William Nisbet Chambers and Walter Dean Burnham (New York: Oxford University Press, 1967), pp. 90-116.

when his seat came up again in 1839. Meanwhile, he wanted time—time to see his own country, time for travel abroad.[4]

Webster's real goal was not leisure, however; it was financial independence. He had engaged in unabashed speculation in Western lands throughout 1836. Now he needed time to arrange investments so "as to be able to live, without pursuing much longer" his profession. Good fortune would release him from debts to the Bank of the United States and to protariff friends in Massachusetts.[5]

Resignation would also unshackle him in politics. Wearied by the demands of persistent opposition to the Jacksonians, he wanted respite from the daily pressure to commit himself on every issue. Two years would illuminate the new president's policy on old economic disputes about the currency and the tariff; time would also reveal Van Buren's less predictable response to a novel problem, the posture of the American government toward the new Republic of Texas. American settlers in the Mexican territory of Texas had rebelled in 1836 and had successfully established their independence. Many Texans and Americans then sought prompt annexation of Texas to the Union. But obstacles to immediate annexation abounded. Mexico still claimed Texas and threatened war if the United States incorporated the territory. More important, Texas permitted slavery. Hence, annexation proposals posed explosive questions. Should the government strengthen and expand the institution of slavery? Should the country tamper with the existing sectional balance of free and slave states? From retirement Webster could cautiously witness the unfolding of presidential policy and of popular sentiment on issues old and new—and, to the candidate, knowledge of public opinion was increasingly important. While "we may be sure," Webster wrote a friend, that Van Buren's course "will not be such as you & I are likely to approve, it may be more or less acceptable, or unacceptable, to the Country."[6]

Finally, Webster desperately needed to leave Washington to escape the shadow of Henry Clay. If he remained in the capital, under the daily tutelage of the party's undisputed parliamentary commander, Webster sensed he would find it more difficult than ever to be his own

---

[4]Webster to Winthrop, January 27 and February 15, 1837, *Writings*, 18:23, 27.

[5]*Ibid.*; Webster to Everett, January 31, 1837, Edward Everett Papers, Massachusetts Historical Society, Boston (hereafter cited as MHS).

[6]Webster to Ketchum, January 28, 1837, Webster Papers, Dartmouth; Webster to Winthrop, February 15, 1837, Robert C. Winthrop Papers, MHS. For Van Buren's stand on the Texas question, see James C. Curtis, *The Fox at Bay: Martin Van Buren and the Presidency, 1837-1841* (Lexington: University of Kentucky Press, 1970), chap. 8.

man and to assert his claims to the presidency. He intended no delay in asserting those claims. Only a month after Van Buren's victory, Webster called for an immediate launching of his candidacy. The first step must come in New York, he asserted, for he rightly perceived that Harrison's strength in the West would compel both of his rivals to anchor their candidacies in the Middle Atlantic and New England states. In the "great Central States," Webster judged, New York and Pennsylvania were the keystones. Whatever "candidate is agreed on in these States, will receive the support of the party."[7] Since Pennsylvania was a bastion of Harrison support, New York would be the major battleground. A "first, decisive, & *determined* step," Webster urged in late January, should begin immediately among the Whigs of New York City.[8]

Webster singled out New York City partly because he had loyal friends there, whose attachment he had cultivated with much success during the Bank crisis. Most belonged to a select group of lawyers, merchants, and financiers whom one politician called the "good society" Whigs. They shared Webster's tastes, admired his talents, enjoyed his company, and endorsed his politics. They generally concurred with aristocrat Philip Hone that "the very thought (wild and hopeless as it is) of having Daniel Webster President . . . should make the heart of any American leap in its busom and cause him to dream of the days of George Washington." For Webster's partisans his candidacy was a symbol of restoration—restoration of the era when a "grateful people" did "honor to distinguished merit."[9] Webster's friends had money and virtual control over three major Whig papers in the city.

But a deeper logic led Webster to focus on the city, as it would later lead Clay. The leaders of the Whig party in New York were upstate Whigs, William Henry Seward and Thurlow Weed, who believed that neither Webster nor Clay had a chance for the presidency and bluntly told Webster so. Partisans of Harrison, both felt the senators were so loaded with liabilities that they would cripple the Whig cause in New York if nominated. Webster, a former Federalist, would invite a revival of charges of aristocracy; Clay, a Mason, would alienate the thousands of former Anti-Masons who composed a large segment of the state party. Both, as former "Bank men," would jeopardize efforts, just beginning to succeed, to liberate the Whigs from identification with the

---

[7]Webster to Ketchum, January 28, 1837, Webster Papers, Dartmouth.

[8]*Ibid.*

[9]Seward to Weed, April 10, 1837, Thurlow Weed Papers, University of Rochester, Rochester, N.Y.; Bayard Tuckerman, ed., *The Diary of Philip Hone, 1828–1851*, 2 vols. (New York: Dodd, Mead & Co., 1889), 1:237; *New York Journal of Commerce*, May 31, 1838.

Bank.[10] Since supporting either man seemed suicidal to the upstate leaders, Webster naturally relied on his friends in New York City. Webster hinted to those allies that New York Whigs could use his pending resignation to initiate the movement on his behalf. Nothing could be more proper than a testimonial to the departing defender of the Constitution. Following his hint, Webster's New York backers made plans for a mighty demonstration to prove that "fairly brought out before the people, he will command the strongest vote of any man in the opposition."[11] But Webster's Massachusetts supporters—some fearful that a new senatorial election would expose and perhaps divide the tenuous Whig majority in the Massachusetts General Court, some reluctant to relinquish their spokesman at the capital—persuaded Webster to postpone, and eventually to abandon, resigning. For the senator's New York backers, however, a pending resignation was as good as an actual one, and they went ahead with their plans for a reception and public speech in mid-March.

The March 15 reception and morning parade proved dramatically that Webster could draw a crowd, and the senator's performance that night in a speech to 6000 partisans at Niblo's Saloon was equally impressive.[12] Advised in advance of what the city's finest wished to hear, Webster threw caution aside. Deliberately sectional, he warned that Northerners must bar further tariff change and must resist donation of the public lands to the West. With him, Northerners must resist the call for the annexation of newly independent Texas. They must fight "anything that shall extend the slavery of the African race on this continent," for extension not only would upset the balance between free and slave states but would assist abolitionism, which was already intruding dangerously into Northern politics. Purposely orthodox, Webster exhorted his Whig audience to battle on against executive tyranny. "There are men, in all ages, who . . . mean to govern well," but they mean to govern. "They promise to be kind masters; but they mean to be masters." The cardinal usurpation by the executive, the destruction of the national bank, now convulsed the economy. Present spasms were just the beginning, for the executive remained obdurate. Whigs

[10]Weed to Francis Granger, December 24, 1837, Francis Granger Papers, Library of Congress, Washington, D.C. (hereafter cited as LC); Harriet A. Weed, ed., *Autobiography of Thurlow Weed* (Boston: Houghton, Mifflin & Co., 1883), p. 431; Glyndon G. Van Deusen, *William Henry Seward* (New York: Oxford University Press, 1967), p. 61. Of both Webster and Clay, Seward wrote: It " 'is not a question of who [sic] we would prefer, but whom we can elect.' "

[11]Ketchum to Luther Bradish, March 3, 1837, Luther Bradish Papers, New York Historical Society, New York, N.Y. (hereafter cited as NYHS).

[12]*New York Commercial Advertiser*, as reported in the *Boston Daily Evening Transcript*, March 17, 1837.

must seek to regain control of the currency from the executive and return it to Congress. Webster reserved his final plea for the wealthy and the wise of New York. "Whigs of New York! You cannot shrink from your public duties; you cannot obscure yourselves"; you cannot "bury your talent."[13]

Webster's message was clear: Northern Whigs could trust only one of their own. With panic around the corner and sectional clash possible, it would be foolish to go with Harrison, a man of few known views, or with Clay, a known compromiser of Northern interests.[14]

Yet Webster knew that orthodoxy alone did not make a presidential aspirant available, and he recited the expected truths in an unexpected tone. "You are for the Constitution of the country; so am I," he declared in short, stump-style, whiplash sentences. "You are for equal laws, for the equal rights of all men . . . and so am I," he proclaimed, borrowing a slogan from the radical Equal-Rights faction of New York's Democrats.[15] Though his friend, William Kent, thought Webster looked "fat" and marked by "age and high living" that weekend, to the evening crowd, which repeatedly punctuated his three-hour speech with applause, he was clever, confident, and effective. They came to hear an orator; they heard a candidate.[16]

II

After a celebration of the speech by his friends in New York, Webster returned to Boston and prepared for a tour of the West. He left in May as a candidate in search of support; en route he found the strategy and appeals which promised to carry the Whigs to victory in 1840.

Just before Webster crossed the Alleghenies, on a trip that would take him to Harrisburg, Pittsburgh, Lexington, Frankfort, Louisville,

---

[13]Daniel Webster, "Speech at Niblo's Saloon, March 15, 1837," *Writings*, 2:194–230; see esp. pp. 194, 206–11, 226–30.

[14]Marie Kathryn Hochmuth, W. Norwood Brigance, and Donald Bryant, eds., *A History and Criticism of American Public Address*, 3 vols. (New York: Longman's Green & Co., 1943–55), 2:721–24. Brigance notes the differences in the speech as summarized by the reporter the next day and as modified for publication by Webster a month later. The original address is yet more sectional and orthodox than the public version. Clearly Webster tailored the message to the audience.

[15]Webster was not so crude as to demean Clay outright. Indeed, in the reporter's version of the address there was praise for the Kentuckian. Nonetheless, the gist of the speech, with its reaffirmation of a high protective tariff and its underlying sectional belligerence, was anti-Clay. That Webster referred to Clay's recent bill on the public lands as the "lucky hit" of a great mind seems more than coincidence. *Ibid.*

[16]William Kent to Moss Kent, March 19, 1837, James Kent Papers, LC.

Cincinnati, Saint Louis, Chicago, and Buffalo, the first of a series of financial tremors rocked New York City. Firms failed, banks suspended payments of specie, and, as Webster moved West, so did the shock waves of panic.

Spreading depression provided Webster with a dramatic, if grim, setting; he spoke with the anger and rebuke of a prophet vindicated. He and others had forecast from the first that destruction of the Bank would bring calamity. Slandered as aristocrats for their defense of a national bank, they had borne the smears in "silent contempt."[17] Now the Whigs' hour had come. "The experiment has exploded," he declared in Wheeling, Virginia. "That bubble, which so many of us have all along regarded as the offspring of conceit, presumption, and political quackery, has burst." All had been foretold.[18]

In fact, though Webster had predicted for three years that disaster was just around the corner, the panic of 1837 came for reasons very different from those he had expected. Webster thought in 1834 that the end of the national bank, and of its financial stewardship, would spawn a crisis of confidence. Commercial men would hoard money, and the economy would stagnate. Instead, after a brief period of contraction, inflation became the rule. High prices for crops and goods encouraged migration to the Northwest and Southwest. Anticipating migration, speculators—Webster among them—raced to buy lands for resale later, or invested in the canals which would carry the flood of immigrants and goods. All prices rose, and with higher prices the demand for credit also rose.[19] Though, in actuality, most of the credit was supplied by an influx of foreign silver and by massive British investments, Jackson's fiscal policy—contrary to the expectations of Webster and of Jackson himself—also contributed to meeting the demand. With the Bank of the United States no longer empowered or inclined to check inflation, Jackson found no substitute devices to control the multiplication of banks or bank credit. Whether any controls on credit could have succeeded is dubious, but the fact was that the Jackson administration's dispersal of government funds to selected state banks abetted the expansion of the currency. Moreover, since the government accepted

---

[17] Daniel Webster, "Speech at Rochester, July 20, 1837," *Writings*, 13:93.

[18] Daniel Webster, "Speech at Wheeling, Va., May 17, 1837," and "Speech at Madison, Ind., June 1, 1837," *ibid.*, 2:235, 259.

[19] Douglass C. North, *The Economic Growth of the United States, 1790-1860* (Englewood Cliffs, N.J.: Prentice-Hall, 1961), pp. 198-200; Reginald C. McGrane, *The Panic of 1837; Some Financial Problems of the Jacksonian Era* (Chicago: University of Chicago Press, 1924), pp. 1-69, 91-117; Bray Hammond, *Banks and Politics in America from the Revolution to the Civil War* (Princeton: Princeton University Press, 1957), pp. 452-57.

paper money in payment for Western lands, it found itself further encouraging issues of bank paper for speculative purposes. Disdainful of profits made through speculation, and apprehensive that unchecked speculation would bring only economic collapse, Jackson finally acted to curb the boom. In July, 1836, he issued the Specie Circular, an executive order which required that all future payments for Western lands be made in gold or silver. Jackson's action, and the simultaneous steps taken by the Bank of England to curtail the outflow of British capital to the United States, abruptly tightened the supply of credit, ended the economic euphoria that had sustained the boom, and set the stage for the financial contraction and panic of 1837.[20]

Webster had seen the entrepreneurial possibilities of Jackson's banking policy belatedly and had cast his lot with the new energies making for expansion. He had placed all his hopes for financial independence on Western expansion, and had borrowed thousands to buy acres in Wisconsin, Michigan, Illinois, and Tennessee. He had staked his hopes on the hopes of others; through their common enterprise he would make his fortune. Webster's tour of the West only confirmed his judgment that Jackson's bank policy had massively stimulated the enterprise of the country and had involved thousands more Western townsmen and farmers in a market economy.[21]

To Webster, the danger of the Specie Circular was that it threatened to choke off the easy credit which had encouraged the stunning growth of the West. Hence, while Webster contended that Jackson's irresponsible "experiments" with the currency had brought on the depression, ironically the Whig leader was forced to insist that the government could not now retreat from Jackson's expansionist fiscal policy. The administration could not now ignore the expectations and commitments its policy had spawned. With or without a national bank, the government must be an agent of expansion and a guarantor of credit. At minimum, Webster demanded that the administration revoke the Specie Circular and so relieve the pressure for gold and silver which had palsied credit. Beyond that, the government must reassume, not abandon, its responsibility for creating a stable paper currency.[22]

---

[20]Peter Temin, *The Jacksonian Economy* (New York: W. W. Norton & Co., 1969), chaps. 4 and 5.

[21]Daniel Webster, speeches in Madison, Ind., and Saint Louis, June, 1837, *Writings*, 2:251-53 and 13:79-80. For an analysis of Webster and the West which also suggests that Webster's investments and tour deepened his already enlightened concern for that part of the country, see Peter J. Parish, "Daniel Webster, New England, and the West," *Journal of American History*, 54 (December, 1967): 524-49, esp. p. 531.

[22]Daniel Webster, speeches in Wheeling, Madison, and Rochester, May 17, June 1, and July 20, 1837, *Writings*, 2:234-35, 238, 240, and 13:90-92, 96-97.

Webster believed that the entrepreneurs who had profited from the expansion of credit would recoil from the crude stability of deflation. Out of economic kinship and political necessity, Webster sought the political allegiance of those Jacksonians who favored easy credit. The central issue of the day, he told Western listeners in June, 1837, was new. It was not a national bank; it was the larger matter of whether the national government had a duty to regulate the currency. If the administration abandoned regulation, it would abandon the enterprising citizen, for regulation of the currency was directly connected to the extent of credit in the economy. A sound currency meant credit, that magic agency which determined whether men could exploit the providential abundance of the land: the rich prairies, the mines of lead and iron, the restless energies of the people. Credit also determined whether a man or his children could rise to higher stations in life. Indeed, to take credit away harmed not the rich but the poor. "It is the industrious, working part of the community, men whose hands have grown hard by holding the plow and pulling the car, men who depend on their daily labor and their daily pay," who face "beggary and starvation" when commerce is palsied. Why the "present distress? Why?" Webster asked at Saint Louis. In a country never more prosperous, "we cannot pay our debts with money."[23]

Van Buren's persistence through the spring and early summer of 1837 in his decision to maintain the Specie Circular and in his refusal otherwise to regulate the currency, led Webster more than ever to strike at what he saw as the fatal weakness of the Democratic party. Van Buren had abandoned not only currency regulation, but the principles of Andrew Jackson as well. Jackson had erred, but he had abandoned neither the currency nor the people. Good Jacksonians, the Whig oracle warned, must save the faith; they must not let the Old Hero's successor disguise new departures with old names. For one, Webster judged that the eyes "of the whole people seemed to be opened, and they begin to look for themselves. We are not so much under the influence of party names as we have been; nor does individual authority go for as much as it has done. . . . It appears to me, fellow citizens, that we have reached a new era."[24]

---

[23] Daniel Webster, "Speech at Rochester, July 20, 1837," *Writings*, 12:99; *idem*, speeches in Madison, Saint Louis, and Rochester, June, 1837, and July 20, 1837, *ibid.*, 2:256–57 and 12:83, 86–87, 97–98.

[24] Webster, "Speech at Rochester," *ibid.*, 13:99. A year later Webster reiterated this point in a speech at Boston on July 24, 1838. "We ought to address ourselves . . . to the candid and intelligent of all parties," he told Bostonians. It "is a new question," and the "great mass of the people of any party, is not committed to it." *Ibid.*, 13:278–79.

Struck by his new affinity for the common man, and instructed by the lessons of the Harrison campaign, the farther West Webster traveled, the more humble he became. "What am I, my fellow countrymen?" he asked his listeners at Saint Louis. You "all know: I am a plain man. I never set up for anything. . . . I am a farmer, and on the yellow sands of the east, many a time have I tilled my father's field, and followed my father's plough." Again, at Rochester, he was simply one "plain Republican" speaking the thoughts of his heart to others. Those thoughts came increasingly in he argot of the West. "All are broke," he snapped at Saint Louis. Old "Uncle Sam growls sullenly on, and pays 'nobody nothing.' " At the beginning of his tour, the senator called his audiences "gentlemen"; at the end, he called them "fellow citizens."

III

In terms of strategy and style, Webster's political instinct was unerring. Van Buren did indeed stand by the Specie Circular and deflation, stating in September to an emergency session of Congress that measures for relief were "not within the constitutional province of the General Government." His sole constitutional duty, Van Buren declared, was to secure the government's funds. To that end he proposed the creation of a new deposit system, independent of the state banks, to receive, hold, and disburse national revenue—an "independent treasury."[25]

Webster's claims notwithstanding, Van Buren's decision to establish an independent treasury was quite consistent with the goals of his predecesor. The separation of bank and state jibed perfectly with the Jacksonian view of what made for effective democracy. Democracy was majority rule, and the sole agent of the national majority in Washington was the executive. But sometimes the executive was unable to control a function of government from the capital; it could not supervise internal improvements, and now it could not control the banks. Rather than let that control fall into the hands of bargaining minorities, the executive was bound to return control of internal improvements and the banks to the local level, where state or local governments, more responsible to majority will, could make policy decisions. Efforts at federal control of the currency through the "pet banks," coinage legislation, and pressure for better state laws had foundered. Too many Democrats, Silas Wright

[25] James D. Richardson, comp., *A Compilation of the Messages and Papers of the Presidents, 1789–1905*, 11 vols. (Washington, D.C.: Bureau of National Literature and Art, 1907), 3:344–45.

later reflected, had resisted controls or had openly favored inflation and speculation. The machinery needed for effective power over the currency would make the government itself a monster and would tempt the corrupt to seek its control. "You cannot make a democrat out of a bank director," concluded Churchill C. Cambreleng. "Sick to the heart of banks and bank morals," the administration chose to sever its connections with the banks.[26]

Despite Van Buren's underlying fidelity to the Jacksonian creed—a fidelity made all the more necessary by his lack of personal magnetism—Democrats swiftly divided over the suspicion of banks and credit which was implicit in the president's policy. To Democrats who believed that banks were vital for enterprise and that some government supervision was needed for a stable currency, Webster's charges were telling. These men believed Van Buren had capitulated to the radical, hard-money wing of the party. He had betrayed the "old" democracy. The Whigs now stood where Jackson had been—for enterprise, opportunity, and credit. Webster's party would keep the promises of Jackson's policies. It was this theme of keeping the Jacksonian faith that Webster perfected in the summer of 1837, when he labeled Van Buren's policies, present and anticipated, "un-American."[27]

IV

Despite his prescience, Webster returned from the West in 1837 a defeated man. His financial hopes remained unfulfilled, and, more important, his political hopes had been jolted. The candidate's friends had tried to establish a political base in New York City while the senator was gone but had failed. Their failure had ended all chance of making New York Webster's political base.

As word filtered back to the East of the enthusiastic throngs which greeted Webster wherever he toured, Webster's friends in New York City moved to put his name formally before the country.[28] Satisfied by mid-June that the time was ripe, Hiram Ketchum, leader of the Webster forces in the city, announced a public meeting of the Whigs of New York to make a nomination late that month.

---

[26]Wright to Van Buren, June 4, 1837; [William Gouge] to [Van Buren], March 19, 1837; and Cambreleng to Van Buren, November 18, 1837; Martin Van Buren Papers, LC. Levi Woodbury to George Bancroft, November 12, 1839, George Bancroft Papers, MHS, reprinted in Frank Otto Gatell, "Spoils of the Bank War: Political Bias in the Selection of Pet Banks," *American Historical Review*, 70 (October, 1964): 58.

[27]Richard N. Current, *Daniel Webster and the Rise of National Conservatism* (Boston: Little, Brown & Co., 1955), pp. 102–7.

[28]Ketchum to Cushing, [May, 1837], Caleb Cushing Papers, LC; *New York American*, May 17 and 22, 1837.

Not all New York Whigs were ready to endorse Webster, however, and the call for a meeting brought heated protests from Clay's partisans in the city. Matthew L. Davis, watchdog for Clay's interest in New York, challenged Ketchum at a private meeting of Whigs called to prepare for the nomination. He pointedly labeled the Webster movement "high handed, imprudent, and dictatorial," worthy of the arch-Federalist "champions of the black cockade in 1798."[29] James Watson Webb, editor of the *New York Courier* and the *New York Enquirer*, also objected to the nomination of Webster. The implicit threat of Clay's backers publicly to disclaim the assembly forced Webster's friends to compromise. They would meet and "recommend" Webster to the country, but they would not nominate him. Rather, the meeting would call on other Whig groups to avoid iron-clad commitments and to support a national convention to pick a candidate. Future Whig assemblies might properly extol their favorites, but they would avoid making pledges to individuals and would bind themselves to the choice of the convention.[30]

With its purpose thus altered, the New York meeting took place on June 28, with neither group fully satisfied. Though Ketchum was pleased with the "great and enthusiastic" demonstration that "Mr. Webster is the favorite of the people of this City," he was also angry. A "powerful band of selfish politicans in our ranks," he told Cushing, had tried to keep Webster's name from the people and had succeeded in dulling the impact of the city's endorsement.[31]

The Clay faction did act to choke the spread of the Webster movement. Not as numerous as the former Federalists and original opponents of Jackson who comprised Webster's New York supporters, Clay's friends made up in zeal and political skill what they lacked in numbers. Composed of many recent defectors from the Democratic ranks and warmly attracted to Clay as a man, they brought from their former party dexterity in political management and a distinct dislike of Federalists.[32] Clay's New York managers promptly dispatched orders to friends in Upstate New York to block any efforts to support the Webster "recommendation." Meanwhile, Clay's partisans in the city

[29]Men of the 1770s wore a black cockade on their hats as a mark of support for the American Revolution. In the late 1790s, when many veterans of the Revolution endorsed the Alien and Sedition acts, the black cockade took on a new meaning and "became a malodorous symbol of malevolent repression." David Hackett Fischer, *The Revolution of American Conservatism: The Federalist Party in the Era of Jeffersonian Democracy* (New York: Harper & Row, 1965), p. 34.

[30]Matthew L. Davis to Clay, July 12, 1837, Thomas Jefferson Clay Papers, LC; *New York Evening Post*, June 29 and July 17, 1837.

[31]Ketchum to Cushing, July 1, 1837, Cushing Papers.

[32]*New York Evening Post*, July 24, 1837.

agreed to insist that, at all similar Whig assemblies in the future, no resolution should pass without unanimous consent. Spurred by danger, they organized their own ward committees and a committee of correspondence. By mid-July, Davis assured Clay that "all is well," and, indeed, that "good is coming out of evil."[33]

Upstate Whigs, who controlled the machinery of the state party, were relieved that Clay's partisans had defeated Webster. "The New York affair is even *more* abortive than we anticipated," Weed told Seward on July 8. "It utterly extinguished Mr. W." Weed thought the timing of Webster's New York endorsement was both bad and decisive. The candidate had borne himself "so nobly in the West" that but for "this folly . . . he would have come home a strong man."[34]

The growing desperation of Ketchum's efforts in the summer of 1837 to capitalize on the New York endorsement confirmed Weed's judgment that Webster was blocked. By August 5, Ketchum admitted that Webster's opponents seemed to control the machinery of the party, with those "powerful in arranging and controlling the proceedings of the preliminary meetings of the people" able to jam all efforts. Ketchum stepped up activity to exploit the "means we possess to secure a nomination"—namely, the Whig presses and money. He exhorted that "activity, perserverance, and boldness" would yet make Webster president and he reiterated that Webster was still "the most popular man in the nation." Anxiously he commissioned articles to counter the multiplying charges of Webster's supposed liabilities. The New Englander's national views balanced off his Eastern origins; the "offense of federalism, if it ever was an offense, is forgiven, is out-lawed." Ketchum further suggested that Eastern newspapers begin to stress Webster's views on slavery and on the annexation of Texas, volatile issues on which Clay was most vulnerable north of the Potomac.[35]

But Ketchum had to acknowledge failure. By the end of August, even Webster confessed that the New York movement had been a mistake. Though Ketchum urged friends to continue to seek "all proper occasions to *talk him up*," it was with more hope than conviction that he added: "I do not despair that profuse exertions will yet make our friend the candidate of the Whig party."[36] Webster had been checked.

---

[33]Davis to Clay, July 12, 1837, Thomas Jefferson Clay Papers; *New York Evening Post*, July 17, 24, 1837.

[34]Weed to Seward, July 8, 1837, copy, Weed Papers, University of Rochester.

[35]*New York Evening Post*, July 8, 1837; Ketchum to Cushing, August 5, 8, and September 15, 1837, Cushing Papers.

[36]Weed to Seward, September 1, 1837, Seward Papers; Ketchum to Cushing, September 15, 1837, Cushing Papers.

V

The Webster movement had "ruined the Candidate," judged Thurlow Weed, but it had decisively impressed on the Whigs "the stern necessity for a National Convention."[37] Despite the manifest inadequacy of the multiple candidacy of 1836, resistance lingered to a convention whose choice all delegates were pledged to accept in advance. The greatest objection came from Southern Whigs. Too few and too poorly disciplined before 1836 to use state conventions themselves, they had labeled the device as a Democratic fraud.[38] With some justice they charged that, under the cover of a convention, Democrats offered the public a preselected candidate as the common man's choice. For these Southerners, reversal was awkward. As important as Southern embarrassment were the suspicions of both Harrison and Clay that a convention would cheat them. Harrison saw Clay's superior access to congressmen as giving him unfair influence over the choice of delegates. Clay feared in part that Southern Whigs, if adamant, might boycott the proposed convention and deprive him of their indispensable delegate support; he preferred nomination by a congressional caucus.[39]

But followers of both men judged that premature rivalry was more dangerous than future plots, and, when a collision between Clay and Webster seemed likely after Webster's Western canvass and the New York movement, party managers, editors, and congressmen swiftly concurred in the need for delay. A national convention was an obvious means to postpone a clash. Harrison's backers, who met in Columbus, Ohio, on July 7 to rally for the General, accepted the call for a convention over the doubts of their favorite. Rejection would have implied disloyalty to the Whigs and doubt about the popularity of their candidate.[40] Caucusing in Washington in the fall of 1837, Whig congressmen informally agreed to press their state parties to endorse the procedure. Southern Whigs were given time to get over their "repugnance" to the device; for others, the main issue became the date of the assembly.[41]

---

[37]Weed to Willis Hall, July 28, 1837, Daniel Ullman Collection, NYHS.

[38]M. L. Davis to Willis Hall, October 13, 1837, Daniel Ullman Collection; Clay to Peter Porter, January 5, 1838, Peter B. Porter Papers, Buffalo Historical Society, Buffalo, N.Y.

[39]Clay to Peter Porter, January 5, 1838, Porter Papers. William Henry Harrison to Silas M. Stilwell, July 12, 1837; and Harrison to William Ayres, October 1, 1838; William Henry Harrison Papers, LC; Glyndon G. Van Deusen, *Henry Clay* (Boston: Little, Brown & Co., 1937), pp. 322–23.

[40]Weed to Willis Hall, July 28, 1837, Daniel Ullman Collection; *Ohio State Journal*, July 7, 1837; *Cincinnati Gazette*, July 11, 1837; E. Malcolm Carroll, *Origins of the Whig Party* (Durham: Duke University Press, 1925), pp. 156–58.

[41]M. L. Davis to Hall, October 13, 1837, Daniel Ullman Collection.

Clay belatedly acquiesced to a national convention, confident that he would be its choice.[42] Events in the summer and fall of 1837 only strengthened his confidence. Depression devastated the Democrats, and, throughout the fall, in state after state, the Whigs were victorious. The voters seemed ready for a true Whig president, and, with Webster an unelectable Whig and Harrison a dubious one, Clay seemed the man. Those who still thought victory would require groveling to the Democrats, Clay brushed aside. Recession had made all the converts the Whigs needed, and penitent ones at that.[43]

Clay had no illusions, however, that a convention would postpone strife over the nomination. It was obvious that suspension of his activities would only give faltering opponents time to regroup or unite. He was, of course, aware of the danger of premature action. The most conspicuous candidate was also the most vulnerable, and at different times Clay had the serious problem of overeager lieutenants. Yet the Kentuckian sensed that, if the depression abated, Whig confidence might ebb, and he decided to strike for pledges at high tide. As various Whig groups met in the spring of 1838 to approve a convention, Clay's backers sought to get them to couple their consent to the national assembly with an endorsement of Clay. To those who said that pledges violated the spirit of harmony, Clay countered that the way to end division was to settle on a man as soon as possible.[44]

VI

Clay's instincts were exactly right; one way or another he had to wrap things up in 1838. When the economy gradually revived that year, voters demonstrated how fickle their conversion to Whiggery had been. Whig election losses in 1839 made obvious to all what had become clear to Webster in 1837; Whigs would have to woo Democrats in order to win. Failing to achieve sufficient commitments to his candidacy in 1838, Clay watched helplessly in 1839 as the leadership of the party shifted from those who were gifted at governing to the popular candidates and professional managers who were adept at winning.

Webster helped to hasten this transfer of control. He worked with the professional managers to thwart Clay's hopes for an early convention and to frustrate Clay's drive for delegate pledges in 1838. Timing was a point of *"the greatest importance,"* Webster wrote the editor of

---

[42] Clay to G. D. Prentice, August 15, 1837, Thomas Jefferson Clay Papers.
[43] *Ibid.*
[44] Clay to Peter B. Porter, December 24, 1837, January 5, 1838, Porter Papers.

the *Boston Atlas* in February, 1838. In approving a convention, the Whigs of Massachusetts must insist "by all means" that it be held no earlier than the fall of 1839. Webster's friends in New York made the same demand, arguing that an earlier choice would demoralize friends of defeated candidates and would weaken the party in state elections.[45] It was difficult to counter such arguments. Harrison's forces did not try; still reluctant to bind themselves to a convention, they participated little in the debate about its date. Clay, unable to be too insistent about the time without seeming uncertain of his strength, agreed to leave the decision to his congressional colleagues. Among congressional Whigs, Webster's reasoning about the dangers of an early convention prevailed, and they agreed in April to call a national Whig assembly to meet at Harrisburg, Pennsylvania, in December, 1839.[46]

Webster similarly opposed preconvention pledges and vigorously battled for an assembly that would permit maximum freedom of action to its delegates. The proposed "convention . . . must be free, & deliberative, its members acting upon their convictions of the preferences of their constituents" at the time they met. When a group of Rhode Island Whigs endorsed Clay, Webster admonished his backers to blast the move. "It is high time for our friends to awake," he bristled. If "there are to be Committees, & Meetings, & Caucuses, & Commitments, in favor of a candidate," he warned after similar action in Philadelphia, "what will the convention do? It will have no power of deliberation whatever."[47]

By mid-1838 the relatively uncoordinated Clay drive for delegates was stalemated. Only in Rhode Island and Kentucky had Clay succeeded in winning commitments. In Ohio, Maryland, and Maine he had failed. Above all, he had failed to win the endorsement of the Whigs of New York, and there, too, Webster had assisted in the work of obstruction. Clay was convinced that if the Whigs of New York State gave him their blessings, the recommendation would "settle absolutely the question" of the party's candidate.[48] In fact, the assumption by both Webster and Clay that a New York recommendation would have determined

---

[45] Webster to Richard Haughton, February 23, 1838, Webster Papers, Dartmouth; Winthrop to Everett, [February 25, 1838], Edward Everett Papers, MHS.

[46] Winthrop to Everett, [February 25, 1838], Edward Everett Papers, MHS; Clay to Brooke, April 14, 1838, *The Works of Henry Clay*, 5:426–27; Clay to Porter, April 15, 1838, Misc. Papers, Clay File, Buffalo Historical Society; *Washington National Intelligencer*, April 20, 1838; Carroll, *Origins of the Whig Party*, p. 161.

[47] Webster to [Winthrop], February 7, 24, 1838, Winthrop Papers; Webster to Richard Haughton, February 23, 1838, Webster Papers, Dartmouth.

[48] Clay to Porter, December 24, 1837 and January 5, 1838, Porter Papers.

the nominee was open to question. A New York endorsement might equally have divided the party anew. Harrison's backers were more wedded to their candidate than to any party at his point; the hope that they could capture the Whig nomination led them to affect more fidelity than they felt. The loss of New York might have forced their acquiescence, but it might also have triggered their defection. Whatever the merits of Clay's strategy, he found—as Webster had before him—that he could not win the aid of Seward and Weed.[49]

By May, 1838, Clay could wait no longer for the upstate leaders to come around, and he chose to try Webster's strategy of the year before—to prod the Whigs of New York State by rallying the Whigs of New York City. Now it was Webster's friends who joined with upstate Whigs to block Clay. When the Kentuckian's backers held a meeting in the city to endorse Clay, the pro-Webster press promptly labeled the endorsement premature, and Seward and Weed muted the response outside the city. The effort at stalemate succeeded, a confidant reported to Clay, "but too well."[50]

Meanwhile, the parliamentary leader of the Whigs faced an equally gloomy situation in Congress. On the surface, the Congress of 1837-38 had achieved all the Whig goals. It had rescinded Van Buren's Specie Circular and had blocked passage of the president's bill for an "Independent Treasury," which would handle government revenue without the agency of state banks. But defecting Democrats had provided the Whigs the margin of success on these antiadministration votes: there was little reason for comfort about the future on the part of the minority party.

Less discomfiting, perhaps, was John C. Calhoun's decision in September, 1837, to cut his ties with the Whigs and return to the Democrats. Calhoun immediately proceeded to make life miserable for leaders of both parties. The states'-rights senator supported the Independent Treasury and gladly endorsed its implicit denial of federal power over the currency. He temporarily forced the Democrats into reluctant endorsement of an amendment to confine the transactions of the government to gold and silver. Exaggerating his own influence, the South Carolinian believed he had the administration at his mercy.[51]

---

[49]Porter to Clay, February 16, 1839, Peter B. Porter Folder, New York State Library, Albany; Clay to Porter, April 15, 1838, Misc. Papers, Clay File, Buffalo Historical Society.

[50]Weed to Granger, May 29, 1838, Miscellaneous Thurlow Weed Papers, New York State Library; Porter to Clay, May 25, 1838, Porter Papers.

[51]Charles M. Wiltse, *John C. Calhoun*, 3 vols. (Indianapolis and New York: The Bobbs-Merrill Co., 1944-51), 2:342-52; Calhoun to S. D. Ingham, December 18, 1836, John C.

Calhoun wasted no time in seeking to strengthen the Democratic commitment to states'-rights and to the protection of slavery. Increased antislavery agitation in the North had prompted a flood of petitions to Congress. Calhoun sought to force the Senate to guarantee the interests of the South. In December, 1837, he offered six resolutions designed to obstruct any "intermeddling" with slavery. Four resolutions, reaffirming the principle of state control over "domestic institutions" and defining slavery as a peculiar institution of the South, passed with little difficulty. The Senate refused to concede, however, that congressional interference with slavery in the territories or in the District of Columbia would constitute "a direct and dangerous attack" on slavery in the South, and it approved a milder resolve labeling such interference a "just cause for alarm." Tabled altogether was Calhoun's final demand that the Senate censure those who employed antislavery arguments to oppose admission of new states or territories to the Union.[52]

Calhoun's resolves prompted replies from Webster and Clay. Both senators repeated their stands against annexation and for the right of petition; both also reiterated their view that the federal government had no right to interfere with slavery where it existed. For the moment, their position was satisfactory in the North and acceptable in most of the South; even Calhoun complained that Southerners ignored the danger abolitionism represented.[53] But public emotions about abolition, expansion, and Southern rights were volatile imponderables. How long either senator could pursue the traditional strategy of retaining the support of his own section while groping for that of others was increasingly uncertain.

VII

Clay, in particular, sensed that, unless Webster withdrew, he faced new threats in maintaining an effective candidacy. The immediate difficulty remained New York. There, Webster's candidacy provided a sincere alternative for some, but an excuse for those who were yet afraid openly to oppose Clay or to support Harrison. Still uncritically

---

Calhoun Papers, South Caroliniana Collection, University of South Carolina Library, Columbia; Curtis, *Martin Van Buren*, pp. 99–104.

[52] For Calhoun's resolves, see Wiltse, *John C. Calhoun*, 2:371. For his hopes that existing parties would polarize around his resolutions, see Calhoun to J. R. Mulvany, December 28, 1837, John R. Mulvany Papers, Duke University Library, Durham, N.C. The best analysis of the Senate debate over Calhoun's resolutions can be found in Curtis, *Martin Van Buren*, pp. 117–19.

[53] Calhoun to W. C. Preston, June 1837, photostatic copy, John C. Calhoun Papers, LC.

certain that, with Webster out, New York and the country would swing to him, Clay moved to eliminate Webster from the race.

Clay took the battle to oust Webster directly to his Senate colleague. He implored Webster personally in June, 1838, that withdrawal would be "best for him and for the common cause," and hinted that magnanimity now would be remembered generously later. Politely rebuffed, Clay then turned to Webster's associates in Massachusetts. Knowing that many were eager for Webster to abandon the contest, Clay sought through Harrison Gray Otis, former mayor of Boston and a close friend of Webster, to put pressure on the senator at home. After correctly praising Webster's talents, Clay got to the point: it was "perfectly manifest that he cannot be elected President at the next election." By staying in the contest, Webster only exacerbated party division and stood between Clay and success. "If he retired, the feelings of the North, now stifled, would burst forth, and Genl. H's friends would perceive the utter hopelessness of his remaining in the field." The "whole matter would be finally settled" within six months of Webster's withdrawal.[54] Clay did not hide that his object was to end the stalemate in New York City. Collisions had already occurred there between Clay and Webster partisans; "the inevitable consequence of our present respective positions" would only increase "with the progress of time and the natural zeal of ardent friends." Webster had "no bad advisers in Massachusetts; but . . . it is otherwise in the City of N.Y."[55] Clay invited Otis to show his letter to Abbott Lawrence, Senator John Davis, and other friends.

As Clay well knew, Lawrence, Davis, Otis, and others among Webster's associates were exceedingly embarrassed at his staying in the race. Eager to board the Clay bandwagon and hostile to Harrison as an interloper and a political nonentity, Lawrence and Supreme Court Justice Joseph Story had in May pressed Webster to withdraw, but had failed. Even Webster's lieutenants were growing skittish and grumbled at his seemingly futile tenacity. Otis feared that Webster would "keep the party in an attitude of perplexity and danger," and might even promote Harrison rather than withdraw to aid Clay.[56]

Helplessly, Otis had to report to Clay at the end of July that their senator seemed doggedly determined to remain a candidate that politics and honor compelled all his friends to follow until he freed them. With restrained anger Clay replied that Massachusetts erred; now only a mira-

---

[54] Clay to Otis, July 7 and June 26, 1838, Harrison Gray Otis Papers, MHS.

[55] *Ibid.*

[56] Everett to Winthrop, May 21, 1838, Winthrop Papers; Winthrop to Everett, [June 30, 1838], Edward Everett Papers, MHS; Otis to George Harrison, July 20, 1838, Otis Papers.

cle could halt the feud between their friends in New York City.[57] Clay apparently never considered the possibility that a Webster withdrawal in Massachusetts, like the Webster defeat in New York, might work to benefit Harrison rather than himself.

Clay did not have to wait for renewal of the feud, for September marked the start of a winter of reversals. The first came on September 14, when the *Boston Atlas*, long regarded as a Webster paper, abruptly dropped Webster's candidacy and endorsed Harrison. Giving as its reason a recent Whig defeat in Maine, the *Atlas* declared that "we in New England have been long enough calling upon the mountain to come to us." Popularity, however ignoble a standard, was essential for a presidential candidate; Clay and Webster lacked it, and Harrison had it. If Massachusetts did have to sacrifice Webster, it should do so for a man "in truth available."[58]

Webster's supporters were relieved by the *Atlas* turnabout. "I am inclined to think that it will excite no murmurs at Marshfield," Robert Winthrop commented after a talk with the *Atlas* editor. Though Edward Everett thought the article was indiscreet in discounting Webster's popularity—"when will he ever be more popular?"—he nonetheless suspected that Webster approved the piece. Patently relieved, Everett added: "After this sally I think the W. flag must be considered as struck."[59] The pro-Harrison *Philadelphia Gazette* was likewise encouraged by the *Atlas* defection and expressed the hope that other Whig journals, especially the New York papers which had stubbornly clung to Webster, would now exhibit similar "liberality."[60]

Clay burned. "I am mortified—shocked—disgusted with the course of some men." In every respect, the *Atlas* article was galling. Ill-timed, it came just before the New York and Pennsylvania state elections, "pregnant with the fate of the Whig cause!" Malicious, it implied that Clay's "alleged want of popularity" had some "connection with our defeat in Maine," and that the defeat was a portent of the future. While "unwilling to believe that Mr. Webster has counselled or acquiesced" in the course of the *Atlas*, Clay insisted that only an explicit disavowal from him could check the inevitable conclusion that "his views and wishes have not been overlooked."[61]

No word came from Marshfield. In fact, since January, Webster had moved steadily toward Harrison. Astonished in December, 1837, at the

---

[57]Clay to Otis, September 1, 1838, Otis Papers.

[58]*Boston Atlas*, September 14, 15, 1838.

[59]Winthrop to Everett, [September 14, 1838], Edward Everett Papers, MHS; Everett to Winthrop, September 17, 1838, Winthrop Papers.

[60]*Philadelphia National Gazette*, quoted in the *Boston Atlas*, September 21, 1838.

[61]Clay to Otis, September 24, 1838, Otis Papers.

suggestion that the General was the strongest candidate,[62] by February, 1838, Webster seemed to agree. The movements of "Mr. Clay's friends, intended to operate agt. me, have only the effect . . . of strengthening Genl. H."; the "great depths below cry out for somebody else. It will always be so, in [Clay's] case."[63] Caleb Cushing, almost certainly on Webster's orders, sounded out the Massachusetts General Court in February on sentiment for Harrison if Webster withdrew.[64] Finding that the majority would accept Harrison, but preferred Clay, Webster remained in the contest. By June he privately intimated to Everett that he had stayed only to keep the door open for Harrison.[65] Though not responsible for the *Atlas* article, which was as dubious about his availability as about Clay's, Webster issued no protest when the paper dropped him for Harrison, and he made only private disclaimers when the *Atlas* continued to disparage Clay throughout the fall.

VIII

Had the *Atlas* attack on Clay as the "darling of the aristocratic Whigs" and "*not the choice* of the democracy of the Whig party" been an isolated sortie, the Kentuckian might have paid it no heed, but the setbacks spread. During the summer and fall of 1838 the severity of the depression began to abate; Whigs won in New York but lost elections elsewhere; defeats in New Jersey, Delaware, Pennsylvania, and Maryland made Whig editors wonder in print whether the party could go with a candidate of celebrated and controversial political views.[66] Clay's enemies linked him to each Whig defeat—even to that in Harrison's Ohio. Though the nettled candidate complained that "nothing could be more unfounded or absurd" than to blame him for every reversal, the denigration continued, and by the year's end Clay admitted that his friends were discouraged.[67]

For Clay, the work of the spoilers finally began to tell. By January, 1839, with few pledged delegates to show for all the optimism of the past year, Clay maneuvered from growing weakness. Once more he looked to New York, but negotiations in February with Weed and

[62] Weed to Granger, December 24, 1837, Granger Papers.

[63] Webster to Ketchum, February 18, [1838], Webster Papers, Dartmouth.

[64] Joseph T. Adams to Cushing, February 22, 1838, Cushing Papers; Clay to Otis, September 24, 1838, Otis Papers.

[65] Everett to Winthrop, June 8, 1838, Winthrop Papers.

[66] *Ohio State Journal and Register*, November 6, 1838; *Portland Advertiser* (Maine), December 24, 1839.

[67] Clay to Otis, November 14, 1838, Otis Papers; Clay to Porter, December 27, 1838, Porter Papers.

Seward, the newly elected Whig governor, proved futile.[68] In Washington, meanwhile, Webster effectively used each fresh disappointment to snipe at Clay. Throughout the spring, Clay reported that Webster spoke "very kindly but very despondingly of my pretentions" and labored for Harrison, "not very openly but very earnestly."[69]

Clay's report was accurate but incomplete. Webster was certain the Kentuckian would fail and did work for Harrison—but, like many others, he increasingly doubted the chance that any Whig could win. If the party could be saved, only unity and the Whig General could do it;[70] Webster's salvos at Clay were based on political judgment as well as personal enmity. Personal gloom over his finances, however, increasingly removed Webster from the politics of 1839. Acres of unsaleable Western lands were all he had to show for thousands borrowed since 1835. Obligated to the Bank of the United States alone for $93,000, Webster turned entirely to the goal of unburdening himself from crushing debts. Hoping to sell his lands abroad, he left in June for England, where he had minimal success. Only after his departure did he finally authorize the withdrawal of his candidacy and free Massachusetts to support whomever it wished. By then, Webster's delay had done its work; Massachusetts delegates voted for Harrison at the convention.[71]

Meanwhile, the Whig leaders of New York had produced a new candidate. Party setbacks in the West had reflected badly on Harrison as well as Clay,[72] and, with a convention deadlock increasingly likely, Seward and Weed readied Winfield Scott as a compromise choice.[73] General Scott was stationed in western New York State, as the leader of troops charged with quieting the Canadian frontier. Popular and eager, Scott was certain to help the party in New York, and his Virginia birth seemed to make him eligible in the South. Successfully, Weed labored to win a majority of the New York delegation to Scott's cause. National success could bring control of the White House to the young brokers from New York.[74]

---

[68] Porter to Clay, February 16, 1839, Porter Folder, New York State Library.

[69] Clay to Otis, March 22, 1839, Otis Papers; Clay to Porter, February 24, 1839, Porter Papers.

[70] Webster to Jaudon, March 29, 1839, Daniel Webster Folder, NYHS.

[71] Abbott Lawrence to Thomas W. Ward, April 26, 1839, Thomas W. Ward Papers, MHS; Webster to J. P. Healey, June 12, 1839. Daniel Webster Papers, George F. Hoar Collection, MHS.

[72] Van Deusen, *Henry Clay*, pp. 327–28; *Onondaga Standard*, n.d. cited in the *Albany Argus*, August 14, 1839.

[73] Weed to Seward, August 10, 15, 1839; and John C. Spencer to Seward, August 18, 1839; Seward Papers, University of Rochester.

[74] Granger to Weed, December 1, 1839, *ibid.*; Carroll, *Origins of the Whig Party* pp. 161–63; Robert Gray Gunderson, *The Log Cabin Campaign* (Lexington: University of Kentucky Press, 1957), pp. 52–63.

IX

Yet it was not simply the name of the Whig nominee that remained uncertain in 1839. Far more unsettling was the fact that Whig prospects for success were less certain than ever. The weakness of the Whigs went deeper than election reversals. The unpredictable behavior of the economy had undercut earlier Whig arguments that the panic had been the inexorable result of Democratic experiments with the currency. In the dark days of 1837, events seemed to bear out the Whig explanation of the disaster, but gradual recovery in 1838 buoyed the Democratic view that the business cycle—rather than government error—had brought on the panic. The return of prosperity reinforced the Democrats' claim that a natural revival of business, rather than a new national bank or any other government remedy, would bring recovery.

More devastating still to the Whig reading of the cause and cure of the panic of 1837 was a second and more severe depression that blighted the economy in 1839. Credit again atrophied, many banks suspended payments, and millions suffered once more from the ensuing economic dislocation.[75] The discontinuity of the two depressions voided the sequence of experiment-to-collapse which underlay the earlier Whig analysis. The explanation for the failure of 1839 seemed to lie deeper than Jackson's veto of the Bank seven years before. More radical views gained currency; new accounts placed the blame on selfish corporations and foreign capitalists. Bankers and other purveyors of easy credit had duped the people; their promises of easy riches had brought only widespread ruin.

No one sensed the new, radical mood of the electorate more promptly than Martin Van Buren. Though he continued to advocate an independent treasury as the proper solution to the country's economic ills, with the onset of the second depression he defended the measure on new and unprecedented grounds. In 1837 Van Buren had insisted that the government had no constitutional power or duty to provide economic relief; banking was a matter for local control. In 1839 he declared that the federal government must use its powers to bring overbanking and overtrading under restraint. He promised that his proposals would be the spearhead for a far-reaching reform of the "system of paper credit." The divorce of bank and state would deny private banks the use of public funds to underwrite their "extravagance." The confinement of government business to gold and silver payments would help curb the "excessive issue" of paper money.[76]

---

[75] Temin, *The Jacksonian Economy*, Chap. 5.
[76] Curtis, *Martin Van Buren*, pp. 142–48.

Regardless of who would win the right to be the Whigs' standard-bearer in 1840, then, the forces relentlessly at work in 1839 pressed the party toward greater caution. No longer would Webster and other Whigs make bold about the beneficence of banks and credit. The fluctuations of the economy, as well as the vicissitudes of the voters, quashed the confidence and outspokenness of 1837 and 1838. It was an anxious party that mulled over its candidate for the contest of 1840—a party not simply uncertain of its hold on the electorate, but no longer sure of the cause or remedy for economic distress.

X

The national convention which met at Harrisburg on December 5 belonged to a new breed of Whigs. Powerful local kingmakers and skillful tacticians, they looked pre-eminently to success—local as well as national—as the standard for picking a nominee. Thurlow Weed and John Spencer of New York, Charles Penrose and Thaddeus Stevens of Pennsylvania—former Anti-Masons all—had a high attachment to victory and none at all to the personal leadership of Clay and Webster, long central to the Whig coalition. Under their guidance the convention adopted procedures which gave strength to the anti-Clay forces. Enforcement of a unit rule wiped out Clay minorities in the New York, Pennsylvania, and Ohio delegations. Public debate on the candidates was ruled out; a secret "Grand Committee" of state representatives discussed the nominees.[77] These devices maximized public amity and private bargaining and hurt the sentimental favorite from Kentucky.

Availability, not sentiment, was the guide of the managers and the majority of delegates. They rebuffed a belated Clay effort to rescind secrecy and the unit rule, and on the first two ballots demonstrated that they could deadlock the convention and deny Clay a majority.[78] Clay's 103 votes on the first ballot were as close as he came to the 128 needed for victory. Though in control, the anti-Clay forces were divided over favorites and now had to choose between Harrison and Scott. Just when it seemed that Virginia might defect from Clay to Scott and trigger a rush to the "compromise candidate," Thaddeus Stevens frightened the Southerners by "dropping" a letter from Scott designed to reassure Northern abolitionists of his acceptability. Virginia held, and with no prospect of a Southern switch to Scott, four Northern states—including New York—shifted to Harrison and gave him the nomination.[79]

[77]Gunderson, *The Log Cabin Campaign*, pp. 57-62; Van Deusen, *Henry Clay*, pp. 332-33.

[78]Van Deusen, *Henry Clay*, pp. 332-33.

[79]*Ibid.* For a summary of the convention proceedings, see Richard C. Bain, *Convention Decisions and Voting Records* (Washington, D.C.: The Brookings Institution, 1960), pp. 24-27.

Clay's backers abided by the decision. As a testimonial to their leader, however, they refused to add any obvious Clay partisan to the ticket. Thus, they made way for John Tyler, representative, though scarcely leader, of the states'-rights Virginia party, itself hardly representative of Southern Whigs, to become the Whig nominee for vice-president.

Though in Boston when the convention finally met, Webster had helped to make its outcome possible. Clay's delegate total would have surpassed the 128 votes needed for nomination had he won the support of the 31 delegates from Massachusetts, Maine, and New Hampshire. Unlike New York and Pennsylvania, these were states where anti-Clay sentiment was slight and Webster influence great. From the first ballot, however, all three went with Harrison. They created and sustained the deadlock which the Ohioan's nomination finally resolved.[80]

So it was that the Whig party in the winter of 1839 relieved its old guard of command. The traditional leaders, Clay and Webster, were victims of one another and of the structure of their party. Both had the influence to say no to the other's aspirations, but neither alone had the power to secure his own.

In a different sense, both men were victims of timing. Webster's presidential chances, always marginal, peaked and perished early. Insofar as circumstance might have favored any former Federalist New Englander for president, it did so in the summer of 1837. But the opportunity that depression and a triumphant campaign tour offered was squandered by the New York City movement before the candidate's success was evident. Clay's defeat also was a consequence of timing. The depression of 1837 made him the front runner, but economic revival and Democratic resurgence in 1838 toppled him from favor. Recovery discredited the Kentuckian, his basic strategy of relying on Whigs and penitent Democrats for success, and, indeed, the Whig view of the cause of the depression.

Yet the misfortunes and deadlock of Webster and Clay galvanized the making of a new Whig party, a party hungry for victory and organized to get it. The party's power had gradually become decentralized, and, by the time of the convention, it had devolved to men who were professional at winning elections. At least at this moment in American politics, that structural change made the party more responsive to the electorate the managers so desperately wanted to woo.

The most authoritative account of the proceedings of the Whig convention is the *Niles' Register*, December 14, 1839.

[80]Gunderson, *The Log Cabin Campaign*, p. 60.

William Henry Harrison was a part of that responsiveness. In many ways he was more Whiggish than the Whig founders; his view of executive tyranny and total congressional rule verged on a caricature of the defensive Whig philosophy that evolved in the 1830s. But his basic appeal was to the disappointed of Jackson's America. Webster, too, had stood for those thwarted entrepreneurial hopes in 1837, not simply out of despair, but out of his involvement in them. In 1839, however, the Whig party recognized what Webster had sensed in 1837. It was not enough for a candidate to say to his countrymen, "you all know what I am: I am a plain man." He had visibly, palpably, to be of the same estate. In the Harrison, the Whig party, and the Daniel Webster of 1840, message and medium would merge victoriously.

V

HUZZAH!

I N 1840 THE WHIG PARTY stooped to conquer. Unable to win with an
established Whig leader, the party chose a surrogate Andrew Jackson as its presidential nominee. Unable to find a unifying issue,
despite experiments with fitness, a national bank, and executive usurpation, the party strayed farther and farther from a candid statement of
its goals and finally abandoned the quest. The convention that nominated William Henry Harrison issued no platform. Without issues, the
substance of the Whig campaign became style, song, and hysteria. "If
huzzahing and meetings can make a president of the United States,"
declared the *New York Evening Post*, "the Whigs will do it."[1] That
they did it reflected to contemporary Democrats and to subsequent
historians discredit on the Whigs and portents for the future.[2]

Daniel Webster became one of the great performers in the Whig show
of 1840. With ever-increasing skill, he adapted himself to the varied
audiences of his campaign itinerary. With flair and apparent fervor, he
also accommodated himself to the style of the stump. Weeping, shout-

---

[1]*New York Evening Post*, March 2, 1840.

[2]Richard N. Current, *Daniel Webster and the Rise of National Conservatism* (Boston: Little,
Brown & Co., 1955), pp. 113-14; Arthur M. Schlesinger, Jr., *The Age of Jackson* (Boston:
Little, Brown & Co., 1945), pp. 289, 293.

ing, and bantering with his audiences, Webster eulogized humility, called his enemies liars, and challenged detractors to fistfights. In the words of one biographer, the Whig philosopher became "the Whig rabble-rouser."[3]

Yet to isolate the instances in which Webster manifestly played the demagogue obscures the continuing ambivalence, felt by Webster and other established Whig chieftains, toward the Whig effort of 1840. The senator from Massachusetts was among those who were most troubled by the tone of the Whig campaign. In private he lamented the demagogic drift of his party and in public he often struggled to argue the issues. Given a choice, men like Webster and Clay almost certainly would have scorned the songs and slogans that came to dominate the Whig campaign for more respectable forms of persuasion.

But the campaign did not belong to older Whig leaders like Webster. Democrats who labeled Webster and other Whigs as "old aristocrats," and younger Whigs who met such charges in kind, set the guidelines for 1840. If Webster often yielded to the tactics of his comrades or the taunts of his enemies, he nevertheless struggled more than most Whigs in 1840 to meld winning appeal with intelligible argument.

I

Webster had little to do with the early organization and tone of the Whig canvass, though both were to affect him profoundly. Hitherto the founding personalities of the party had, as candidates, set the tone and loosely scrutinized the efforts of the presidential campaign. But the Harrison nomination had removed their authority and, in a deeper sense, rejected their styles. Harrison, however, did not take up the reins. For much of the campaign he was deliberately silent, and even after he spoke he did not presume to lead.

Control of the Whig effort of 1840 instead dispersed to the editors and professional managers who had been instrumental in Harrison's nomination. Bent on winning, unconstrained by values about proper public decorum or respect for the enemy, the new breed of partisan professionals conducted a campaign which Webster watched and finally joined with deep misgivings.

Already there was a tacit understanding among these men that unprecedented "political tact" must guide the Whigs in 1840. Certain questions "will not stand the test of discussion," the editor of the *Ohio*

---

[3]Robert Gray Gunderson, *The Log Cabin Campaign* (Lexington: University of Kentucky Press, 1957), pp. 176-82; Current, *The Rise of National Conservatism*, pp. 113-14.

State Journal warned his party. "This is plain talking," he added, but there were some objects for which "silence is a much more efficient agent than argument." Muting the issues, Whig managers exhorted organization: "Each man must be a committee."[4]

The Whig editors, in particular, were emancipated by Harrison's nomination. They had shown four years earlier what they could do when unfettered by issues. Eulogizing Harrison in 1836, they had appropriated Democratic imagery without restraint, and, by the end of that year, the General had become the Whigs' Andrew Jackson. The once staid and issue-bound Whig press was more than eager to return to the arsenal of themes, slogans, and stories it had assembled in 1836. The fact that one could say little else about the General save that he was the humble hero of Tippecanoe made almost certain an escalating use and exchange of homilies about Harrison and smears against Van Buren; and local editors and managers met with no check. The presidential candidate was silent. The campaign "executive committee" in Washington confined itself to the distribution of handbills and pamphlets. The offended among the Whigs muttered privately to one another.[5]

Given the structure of the Harrison campaign and the temper of its many managers, it was no surprise that the "log cabin" became the symbol, "hard cider" the beverage, and humility the theme of the Whig drive. A Democratic newspaper inadvertently gave the opposition their symbol and spirit when it ridiculed the choice of Harrison. The *Baltimore Republican* recommended that disappointed Clay men give the General a "barrel of hard cider," settle a "pension of two thousand a year on him . . . and my word for it, he will sit the remainder of his years in his log cabin."[6] The sneer was perfect for the Whigs. It energized the whole cluster of themes party editors had built about Harrison in 1836 and gave correspondents a chance to outmatch each other in an outrage at Democratic snobbishness. Yet the Democratic newspaper's faux pas has more meaning than historians usually accord it. The suggestion that hard cider and a pension could buy off Harrison implied that he was among the intemperate poor for whom whiskey and welfare—and not respectability—were life's only promising possibilities. The point was not that the Whig candidate was too simple to be

---

[4] *Portland Advertiser* (Maine), December 24, 1839; *Columbus Ohio State Journal and Register*, November 6, 1838, and October 25 and December 10, 1839.

[5] Gunderson, *The Log Cabin Campaign*, pp. 148–60; Clay to William Browne, July 31, 1840, John Jordan Crittenden Papers, Duke University Library, Durham, N.C.; Webster to Winthrop, August 10, 1840, Robert C. Winthrop Papers, Massachusetts Historical Society, Boston (hereafter cited as MHS).

[6] *Baltimore Republican*, December 11, 1839.

president. What disqualified Harrison was that he was a failure and a dependent, déclassé among the middle-class respectables who made up the bulk of the Whig party. Whigs immediately understood the main thrust of the remarks and their first replies exploited the deprecation of Harrison's poverty. Only Democrats scorned "the nomination of a poor man for President." Only Democrats measured a man by his "plunder." "What say ye, Farmers and Mechanics?"[7] It was another month before Whigs shifted their emphasis to the editorial's incidental jibe at Harrison's "log cabin."

As Senators Webster and Clay watched silently from Washington, local Whig partisans took the initiative in exploiting the log cabin boon. Two wealthy Pennsylvania Whigs hit on the idea of making a cabin the official symbol of Whig posters and handbills.[8] Others began building real cabins throughout the towns and countryside.

Spontaneous in its origin, cabin construction spread and proved to be a stroke of electioneering genius. "Cabin-raising" became a pseudo event, the cause for a rally, and the enticement to come hear an uncelebrated speaker. Even though it usually occurred in the center of a village, the rustic ritual drew hundreds from the surrounding countryside. In crowded wagons and carriages, farmers flocked to town with the requisite logs and expertise. Many joined the Whig parade, holding high homemade banners. In azure, crimson, and sunset gold, the banners blazoned "BACKSETTLERS for OLD TIP" and "HARRISON, the People's Sober Second Thought."[9] The cabin-building itself leagued the brawn of city and country and allowed the town Whigs to prove their manual skill or good intentions. Barbecue and cider usually convinced the audience to stay for the speakers of the day, who were frequently relieved by Whig songmasters. The cabin thus provided the Whigs with a chance to impress their message through the most effective media.[10]

Taking advantage of the country's advances in transportation and the enormously quickened interest in politics, Whigs initiated mass rallies of unprecedented size.[11] Speakers confronting audiences of milling

[7] *Harrisburg Telegraph*, December 26, 1839; *New York Whig*, cited in Gunderson, *The Log Cabin Campaign*, p. 75.

[8] Gunderson, *The Log Cabin Campaign*, pp. 75–76; Schlesinger, *The Age of Jackson*, pp. 290–91.

[9] *Albany Evening Journal*, June 4, 1840; *Portland Advertiser*, June 12, 1840.

[10] Richard Rose, *Influencing Voters: A Study of Campaign Rationality* (New York: St. Martin's Press, 1967), pp. 159–60. My thinking for this chapter has been stimulated by Mr. Rose's effort to set up and test a model for measuring the influence of issues and media techniques on voters. See his overview, *ibid.*, chap. 1.

[11] Of course, this was not the first use of mass meetings, songs, symbols, barbecues, and lies in an American political campaign. Feting the voters was a regular part of politics in colonial

thousands instead of the usual hundreds faced special demands. The size, diversity, and attention span of the groups virtually dictated a heavy emphasis on wit, banter, and homely stories. Emotional appeals were at a premium, and entertainment was indispensable. It is little wonder that songs, sloganeering, and short speeches often dominated a Whig campaign day, or that when speakers like Webster finally took to the hustings they behaved more like celebrities than senators.[12]

II

Despite reservations about the tone and tactics of the Whig campaign, Webster adapted himself to its demands and played the role of Whig campaigner with growing skill. He came to accept the "rage for conventions," and between May and October spoke at dozens of meetings. From one meeting to the next, he demonstrated an ever-greater ability to tailor a speech to the audience at hand. Yet, even as Webster turned increasingly to the homily and sarcasm which thrilled mass audiences, even as he incorporated into his speeches the simplified themes and log cabin imagery developed by others, he struggled to press issues.

Of course, electioneering tours and the style that large and heterogeneous audiences required were not new to Webster, for he himself had boldly become a plain republican farmer as he canvassed West in the summer of 1837. Yet he was hardly prepared for the Whig tactics of 1840. Webster understood electioneering to be a way to reach and reason with men otherwise indifferent to politics, or, more likely, men deceived by partisan newspapers. Rightly or wrongly, he saw tours as the only way to overcome a Democratic stranglehold on the press.[13] The mass meetings of 1840 struck him as something else again. Almost all "splendid show," they scarcely afforded the chance to "compare notes" with citizens, most of whom could not hear the speaker.[14]

Virginia and recurred with new intensity and spurts of tactical innovation in the Jefferson and Jackson years. Still, the Whigs' refinement of politics as drama was exceptional. Richard P. McCormick, *The Second American Party System: Party Formation in the Jacksonian Era* (Chapel Hill: University of North Carolina Press, 1966), pp. 349-50.

[12]*Portland Advertiser*, June 12, 1840; Clay to William Browne, July 31, 1840, Crittenden Papers, Duke.

[13]Daniel Webster, "Speech at Worcester, October 12, 1832," *The Writings and Speeches of Daniel Webster*, ed. J. W. McIntyre, 18 vols. (Boston: Little, Brown & Co., 1903), 2:24, 114-15 (hereafter cited as *Writings*); James Watson Webb to Clay, September 29, 1837, Henry Clay Papers, Library of Congress, Washington, D.C. (hereafter cited as LC); *Washington Madisonian*, October 2, 1840.

[14]Webster to Winthrop, August 10, 1840, Winthrop Papers; Daniel Webster, "Speech at Boston, September 10, 1844," *Writings*, 13:158.

Likewise, Webster had sensed in 1837 that a simple manner and a homely idiom were needed to get a candidate's message across to new and perhaps suspicious audiences. But the style of plainness was the medium for ideas, not their replacement, and Webster occasionally rebelled in 1840 against the abject homage to humility. Even as he celebrated his own birth near—though, alas, not in—a log cabin, he denied as preposterous the notion that birth in a log cabin uniquely qualified a man for the presidency.[15] As early as February, Webster lamented that the people were being "cajoled & humbugged." Both parties were playing so many "poor popular contrivances off against one another" that, whatever the outcome, the public mind would be irretrievably warped from "right principles."[16]

Yet, as wary as Webster was about the devices used to generate Whig fever, by early spring he also shared the spreading confidence that his party would at last savor victory,[17] and his first campaign speeches were quite in the heady spirit of the canvass.

Long on fervor, short on substance, Webster's talks to the Whig "festivals" at Baltimore and Alexandria in May and June celebrated Whig unity. Making the best of the absence of a party platform, he declared that Whigs no longer operated by a calculus of personal or sectional interest. "Common feelings" and sentiments, a "true patriotic American heart," had brought together the 50,000 Whigs at Baltimore and the 15,000 at Alexandria. No Democrats would tear asunder the fraternity these feelings had created. "I ask," said Webster to the Southern Whigs with him on the podium at Alexandria, whether Whigs of the North have feelings any different from your own? "No! No!" they chorused back, and Webster sat down amid a frenzied ovation.[18]

Webster did not hesitate to cite the "excitement" generated by the Whigs as proof that a "popular revolution" had already been achieved. Whigs were on, and all should join, the winning bandwagon. Webster denied that the innumerable Whig meetings were "gotten up" by party effort. "I say . . . no effort can keep" the meetings down. His repeated and widely quoted use of the phrases "the times are extraordinary" and the "breeze says change"[19] drew fire from Democrats. The senator,

---

[15] Daniel Webster, "Speech at Saratoga, August 19, 1840," *Writings*, 3:29.

[16] Webster to Everett, February 16, 1840, Edward Everett Papers, MHS.

[17] Webster to [Francis P. Healy], January 31, 1840, Daniel Webster Papers, MHS.

[18] Daniel Webster, "Speech at Baltimore, May 4, 1840," and "Speech at Alexandria, June 11, 1840," *Writings*, 13:108-13.

[19] Daniel Webster, speeches in Baltimore, Saratoga, and Patchogue, May-September, 1840, *ibid.*, pp. 5-6, 108-9; and 3:6, 115.

they charged, sought to herd the people into a change.[20] Whether or not Webster calculated that many would go with the crowd on election day, he did blatantly ask audiences to ignore familiar arguments, to defy the hold of habit, and to witness instead the unexampled ferment of the country. "Independent" men should yield to their impulses, follow their feelings, surrender to the current of change.[21]

When Webster returned to New England in July, he yielded still further to the emotionalism promoted by the Whigs. His section was already caught up in the tactics of the day when the senator took to the stump. After a trip to western Massachusetts, he canvassed north to New Hampshire. New Hampshire votes were few, but he wanted his native state, which had become the Union's staunchest Democratic borough, to head the "glorious Whig procession." To dash once and for all the innuendos that he was an aristocrat, he insisted on camping out with the other Green Mountain Boys at the Whig festival at Keene.[22]

Even as Webster outdid himself as a roving celebrity, even as he won plaudits for his conspicuous public humility, he privately continued to worry that Whig tactics had obscured the purpose of the "popular revolution." Indeed, by mid-summer, all three of the nominal leaders of the Whig party had begun to chafe at the roles the campaign had prescribed for them. Whig editors and managers were relatively impervious to Democratic barbs that the Whigs were running a campaign without issues or courage,[23] but Clay, Harrison, and Webster proved more sensitive. Campaigns without issues—and public men as platform personalitites—had not been their style in the past, and each felt that his character compelled a response to the Democrats' taunts. Whether winning actually required argument was irrelevant; integrity did.[24] With varying degrees of political care, each leader broke the bonds of silence and safety and took a stand.

Clay led the way in July, and as always was programmatic. Ignoring counsel to be silent, he set out his view of the optimum Whig platform at Hanover, Virginia. Duly noting that he spoke only for himself, Clay forthwith itemized a single presidential term, a curb on the president's

---

[20]Speech of Benjamin F. Butler in New Brunswick, N.J., October 8, 1840, *New York Evening Post*, October 15, 1840.

[21]*Writings*, 13:108 and 3:34.

[22]Gunderson, *The Log Cabin Campaign*, pp. 179–80.

[23]*New York Evening Post*, March 10, 25, April 17, and June 9, 17, 1840; *Baltimore Republican*, September 17, 1840.

[24]Clay to William Browne, July 31, 1840, Crittenden Papers, Duke; Webster to Winthrop, August 10, 1840, Winthrop Papers; Harrison to Clay, August 6, 1840, Henry Clay Papers, LC.

veto, and a national bank as measures he would see the Whigs enact.[25] Had Clay been the candidate, his speech might have done considerable harm, eager as the Democrats were to revive the bank as the central issue of the contest. But he was not the nominee, and the candidate himself proved more skillful.

Like Clay, Harrison also had been advised not to speak out in 1840 and for months had fobbed off pressures with the statement that all his views were well known. A committee of three spokesmen had responded to campaign interrogations and had monotonously referred all questioners to the candidate's past statements. But Harrison's silence had its perils. Democrats claimed it masked onimous views on abolitionism and a national bank and taunted Harrison as the candidate in a "cage" and as "General Mum." Rankled, Harrison took to the stump in July.[26]

The General's speeches from July to the end of the contest were remarkable blends of Whig orthodoxy and campaign obfuscation. Harrison would leave all decisions up to the Congress. He would serve only one term. He would not use the spoils system or abuse the veto. As to the bank, well, he opposed it unless there was no alternative. Basically, however, it did not matter where the president stood on a bank. The important thing was where the people stood, and they would express their choice through their proper agent, the Congress.[27]

Though Webster had not been under any injunction to remain silent, it was not until mid-summer that he reacted against Democratic taunts and Whig tactics. His doubts and concerns surfaced in early August when Massachusetts Whigs asked him to address a mass meeting on Bunker Hill planned for September. Knowing that enthusiasts meant for the rally to eclipse in size and splendor any yet held, he voiced his concern about the value of such tactics. A mass rally, with its plans for a great "procession and parade," might "gratify the love of splendid show, but would it get us any votes? I think not." If anything, Webster wrote Boston congressman Robert C. Winthrop on August 10, the pro-

---

[25]Clay to Clayton, May 19, 1840, John M. Clayton Papers, LC; Richard P. Marvin to Seward, July 13, 1840, William Henry Seward Papers, University of Rochester, Rochester, N.Y.; Glyndon G. Van Deusen, *Henry Clay* (Boston: Little, Brown & Co., 1937), pp. 335-36.

[26]*Ohio State Journal*, December 27, 1839; Harrison to [unidentified correspondent], May 13, 1840, William Henry Harrison Papers, LC; Gunderson, *The Log Cabin Campaign*, pp. 163-64. Harrison resentfully noted that Democrats sought to depict him as "entirely decrepit & imbecile." The "best means of obviating the effects of this story" was to go on tour. Harrison to Clay, August 6, 1840, Henry Clay Papers, LC.

[27]Harrison's speeches were reported in full in the *New York Evening Post* of July 1 and September 23, 1840.

posed meeting would spur the opposition to greater exertions. But Webster's objections were more fundamental. There was no way to reason with an audience of 100,000. Nine-tenths of them could hear nothing from the platform. In addition, Webster found something "in what is proposed too near approaching joy and festivity." The expected air of "celebration" belied the senator's private view of the solemn purpose of the campaign: "We are beseeching the people to relieve us from unbearable distress." Webster, who had already spoken to half a dozen "festivals" where he certainly could not be heard, refused to address the expected throng. He agreed to draft a set of sober resolutions to be distributed to the crowd and consented to "preside" over the meeting. But, if the arrangements committee wanted the resolves read, someone else must do it.[28]

Webster's qualms about the Boston rally made it apparent that, despite his earlier speeches and despite his seeming willingness to embrace the new political style at Baltimore and Alexandria, the senator had not wholeheartedly accepted the new order of things. He certainly did not yet understand the role of the huzzahing and mass meetings in gaining the new voters vital to success. In his view, it was still the Democrat who had to be converted, and preferably by rational argument. While he mulled over the essentials of what became a "Declaration of Whig Principles" for the Bunker Hill assembly of September 10, Webster found an earlier opportunity to set out the issues of the campaign. He was to visit Saratoga, New York, summer resort for New York City's finest, within a week of his August 10 letter to Winthrop. With the forum to himself for the first time in the campaign, Webster was determined to make the most of the occasion, to get to the "right principles" involved in the contest of 1840.

Webster's address at Saratoga revealed, however, that right principles in 1840 would not be the same as the truths of two years before. In 1838, and indeed throughout the 1830s, Webster had boldly defended banks and credit as the mechanisms of mobility in American society. The depression of 1839 had shaken his certainty and had led the Democrats to advance a radically different view: credit was not the cure for depression but its very cause. Contraction was not the lamentable result of distress but its only remedy. In 1840, Webster abandoned the defense of credit and attacked Democratic deflation instead.

Democrats insisted that the depression of 1839 was no more than a general fall in prices, and argued that the deflation was both unavoid-

---

[28] Webster to Winthrop, August 10, 1840, Winthrop Papers.

able and healthy. Prices had become "bloated" in the 1830s, largely because of an oversupply of money and credit. High wages had followed high prices, but wages too had soared because of inflation. Massive state expenditures for internal improvements, and heavy European credits to finance state projects, had created this "deceptive" prosperity. In 1839, foreign investment fell drastically, and British capitalists called in their debts. Unable to meet these demands, banks suspended payments altogether, and states defaulted on their loans. Prices and wages, artificially inflated by the influx of foreign captial and by state spending, fell back to more natural levels. Democrats insisted that wages and prices had fallen in proportion; deflation had not brought unemployment or privation. Hence, the issue of 1840 was not, as the Whigs argued, one of relief. The issue was retrenchment. Could any act of the government have prevented deflation? Democrats said no, insisting that the federal government could never have more than a "trivial" impact on the international flow of capital. Should the government combat deflation? Democrats argued no, insisting that it was time for the country to abandon an economy of "fluctuation and change," risk and ruin, and return to the pursuit of "constant employment" and modest but steady rewards.[29]

The Democratic analysis of the depression of 1839 was remarkably accurate,[30] and in 1840 Webster and other Whigs rarely chose to challenge it directly. No longer confident that unlimited credit was a boon or that a national bank was a panacea, Webster shifted his ground and focused on the implications of enduring deflation rather than on its necessity. Democrats, Webster argued at Saratoga and in subsequent campaign speeches, advocated a radical new policy for the United States: "the reduction of the price of labor." The administration claimed that it was seeking to promote "the interests of the poor," yet it was precisely the "honest and industrious mechanic" whom deflation "crushed to the earth." What Democrats forgot in their "mad" defense of deflation was that *"American labor"* was unique—"it is *not* European labor"—and that high wages had made the difference. At high wages the American worker could have a comfortable home, educate his children, and rise easily above the condition of a "day-laborer."

---

[29] For an excellent statement of the Democratic explanation of the distress, see the speech made by James Buchanan in the Senate on March 3, 1840, as reported in the *Niles Register*, March 21, 1840. For Webster's summary and attempted rebuttal of the Democratic analysis, see his Senate remarks of April 1, 1840, as reported in *ibid.*, April 11, 1840.

[30] The Democratic analysis is almost entirely supported by Peter Temin's revisionist interpretation of the financial crises of the late 1830s. See his *The Jacksonian Economy* (New York: W. W. Norton & Co., 1969), chap. 5, esp. pp. 153-59, 164, 166-67.

Economic stagnation devastated his hopes. At high prices, no American farmer had to walk to church with his family in a "jacket *two years old.*" Retrenchment meant privation. Webster proclaimed the Democratic prospect repugnant. "Away with this plan for humbling and degrading the free, intelligent, well-educated, and well-paid laborer of the United States to the level of the almost brute laborer of Europe!"[31]

Vivid in his tribute to American labor, impassioned in his account of shattered hopes, Webster was considerably more cautious in his analysis of the panic. The fault, he believed, lay with "the disordered state of the circulation," though this was "not a perfectly obvious truth." The remedy was a stable money supply, and, in particular, a paper currency that had an *"odor of nationality"* about it. Only the national government could supply such a currency. Webster declared that the government must devise "some means, I say not what, of raising the whole currency to the level of gold and silver." Perhaps a new national bank could do the job; perhaps men could come up with some other approach. But to Webster it seemed "indisputably true that the currency should, in some degree, or in some portion of it, be *nationalized* in its character."[32]

Webster was far less evasive when he turned to the matter of why current Democratic leaders defended deflation and refused responsibility for control of the currency. "Why, my friends, these gentlemen are party-mad." Faced with a bankrupt policy and a beleagered country, they had refused to admit error and had declared the crisis cathartic. Casting about for scapegoats, they had resorted to increasingly inflammatory rhetoric and had in turn attracted to the party radicals "of extreme opinions" who "assailed" even "the rights of property" and inheritance. Webster warned that the "cry against credit, against industry, against labor, against a man's right to leave his own earnings to his own children" constituted an alien "new democracy." True Jacksonians should repudiate the party zealots who "forget that they are American citizens." Whigs stood for the "deliberative age of the government," when men of "self-respect, decorum, and dignity" put country before party—the "old pure school of democracy."[33]

---

[31] Webster, "Speech at Saratoga," *Writings*, 3:5, 23-27; *idem*, speech in the Senate, April 1, 1840, as reported in the *Niles Register*, April 11, 1840. For a later restatement of the same themes, see Daniel Webster, "Speech at Patchogue, N.Y., September 22, 1840," *Writings*, 13:122-24, 127.

[32] Webster, "Speech at Saratoga," *Writings*, 3:6-8; *idem*, "Speech on Wall Street, September 28, 1840," *ibid.*, p. 59.

[33] Daniel Webster, speeches of August 19 and September 22, 1840; and "A Declaration of Whig Principles and Purposes, Boston, September 10, 1840," *ibid.*, pp. 35, 46-47; and 13:123.

That Van Buren had abandoned the principles of the Democratic party under Jackson was in fact false. That he had permitted the reversal of the inflationary consequences of Jackson's fiscal policies was in large measure true. By 1840, Van Buren and other Democrats believed that the country was at a crossroads. An economy which encouraged boom and speculation invited social disaster. High-flying prosperity made more men wage-earners, and inevitable depression made more wage-earners poor.[34] Increasingly, Democrats advocated a stable economy over a heady one. Hence, Van Buren's fiscal policy was not, as Webster charged, "un-American." Rather, it was designed to preserve an older America. The president sought to constrict the widening net of the market economy, to limit the ranks of those lured by its glittering promises, and to minimize the number pauperized by its unavoidable falls.

III

Though Webster twice more spoke to the issues of the campaign, once in Boston and again in New York City,[35] he increasingly regressed to the role of "rabble-rouser." Not merely the desire to win forced him again to play the demagogue. In the waning months of the campaign, the very right of Webster to speak of and to his democratic countrymen came under attack. Democrats charged that, even if the country needed saving, Webster and his party were unfit for the task. They were aristocrats. They lacked the credentials to serve democracy. Spurred by such attacks, Webster became determined the demonstrate his democratic pedigree once and for all.

Democrats belatedly awoke to an awareness that the rhetoric and display of the Whigs might successfully delude the public. Early in the campaign, administration leaders had dismissed the possibility that their partisans would be gulled by Whig clap-trap about love for the people. Only gradually did they acknowledge that the Whig claim to be more democratic than the Democrats and the Whig panacea of a "change of men" might make inroads on the party's natural majority. Finally counterattacking on the right issue, they challenged the assertion that

[34] [William Gouge] to [Van Buren], March 19, 1837; [Memorandum of Van Buren to his Cabinet], [March], 1837; and Silas Wright to Van Buren, June 4, 1837; Martin Van Buren Papers, LC; James D. Richardson, comp., *A Compilation of the Messages and Papers of the Presidents, 1789–1905*, 11 vols. (Washington, D.C.: Bureau of National Literature and Art, 1907), 3:144–45.

[35] Webster, "A Declaration of Whig Principles and Purposes"; and *idem*, "Speech on Wall Street,"; *Writings*, 3:37–52, 53–113.

"modern Whigs" were different from old Federalists and aristocrats. The president instructed his partisans to stress that the Whigs stood where they had always stood: for monarchy, for England, for a national bank, for a national debt, and for monopoly and privilege.[36] The "god-like Daniel,"[37] the last prominent Federalist among the Whigs, increasingly became a target for such Democratic attacks. Well aware of the mounting assaults on him as the aristocratic exemplar of an unchanged Whiggery, a goaded Senator Webster abruptly abandoned his reservations about Whig tactics. Determined conclusively to establish his claims as a democratic American, he accepted a request to speak in Democratic downstate New York on his return to Washington.[38] Word of his visit spread, and New York Democratic leaders Silas Wright and Benjamin Butler arranged a parallel speaking tour, which followed Webster's by a day. A confrontation was in the making.

When a Long Island crowd gathered to hear Webster on September 23 at Patchogue, New York, the aroused senator wasted no time on windy preliminaries. The issue of 1840 had become aristocracy, he said at once. Two Democrats would come by the next day and warn, "Don't believe Webster, that old aristocrat." Many in the crowd before him would probably heed the warning. But he had come before them to prove the charges false. "The man that says I am an aristocrat—is a liar!" he thundered. Opponents who would not meet him with arguments must meet him with fists.[39]

Then, as he had done at Saratoga, Webster transposed the issue. The real question was whether those speaking for the Democratic party were democratic. Citing issue after issue, Webster repeated: "Is that Democratic? Is that Democratic?"[40]

Webster's Patchogue speech firmly established him among the most effective of the new campaigners[41]—and Webster himself apparently began to find his changed style congenial. Certainly he was equally direct and electric when he spoke two weeks later in Richmond. Demo-

---

[36]Martin Van Buren, "Thoughts on the Approaching Election in New York," n.d., Van Buren Papers, LC.

[37]Benjamin F. Butler, speech at Tammany Hall, September 24, 1840, as reported in the *New York Evening Post*, September 29, 1840. Butler's use of the phrase was sarcastic.

[38]Azariah C. Flagg to Van Buren, September 24, 1840, Van Buren Papers, LC.

[39]*Writings*, 13:115, 118.

[40]*Ibid.*, pp. 118-21.

[41]The day after his speech, rumors spread that Webster had begged off a debate with Democratic Senator Silas Wright, who was scheduled to speak at Patchogue the next day. Webster publicly challenged him to a stump debate. Declining, Wright noted that he saw no reason to inflict Webster on an audience convened to hear a Democrat, and declared that, in any case, he had no time to debate him. *Niles National Register*, October 3, 1840.

crats charged that he and Northern Whigs were abolitionists, that the South would perish if it put a Whig in the White House. Webster was there to deny the calumny. "I hold that Congress is absolutely precluded from interfering in any manner, direct or indirect," with slavery. "Repeat! Repeat!" shouted his audience. "Well, I repeat it . . . tell it to all your friends." The crowd interrupted him with cries of "We will! We will!" "Tell it, I say, that, standing here in the Capitol of Virginia, beneath an October sun, in the midst of this assemblage, before the entire country . . . I say there is no power . . . in the Congress . . . to interfere . . . with the institutions of the South."[42]

Webster's stumping counterattacks outraged Democrats. "Mr. Webster exhibits himself as . . . an out and out Democrat," fumed Benjamin Butler to a Tammany Hall audience. He "lashed himself into a towering passion" at Patchogue and affirmed that the man calling him an aristocrat was a liar and a coward. Was it a "vulgar demagogue," a "brawler from the kennels—that [employed] this language?" No! It was "Daniel Webster, of Boston, distinguished at the bar, thrice distinguished in the Senate, the educated, accomplished, refined Mr. Webster—the orator and the statesman . . . 'the Godlike man!' " who spoke such "miserable stuff." Butler was not so fearful of Webster's fists that he would suppress the truth: Webster *was* "an aristocrat."[43]

But Butler worried less over Webster's appropriation of the name "democrat" that he did over Webster's appeal to his countrymen's material instincts. Whigs had made headway in fixing on the Democrats the onus of the party of economic stagnation. Citizens were inflamed to "quit their occupations and their firesides," to "band themselves into clubs and associations," to devote "all their energies to the overthrow of the present Administration, in order to get 'better times' in the mart and the exchange." The voters failed to see the dangers of fluctuation and failure in an economy geared to "money-getting and money-spending." More fundamentally, men seemed unaware of the immorality of the Whig vision of America. "What are the people, the American people—the young men of America—what are they taught" by Whig appeals? Butler exploded. What but the "false—the pernicious—the fatal doctrine, that the interests of trade and other pecuniary interests are the highest interests of the nation—that nothing is to be esteemed so valuable as money—and that profit-profit-profit is the 'be all and the end all' of the social state?" "How low, how grovelling, how

[42] *Writings*, 3:93-94.
[43] Butler, speech at Tammany Hall, *New York Evening Post*, September 29, 1840.

unsuited to a free people, how demoralizing are these appeals!" he thundered.[44]

Before such appeals, however, Butler sensed that the Democrats were vulnerable because their fiscal policies had failed to contain, and indeed had spurred, the relentless advance of the new world of the market economy. They were vulnerable because moralistic Democratic views of labor, credit, and opportunity itself were outmoded by that world.[45] If Webster did not comprehend the new world fully, and indeed was insensitive to its darker side, he understood at least one decisive point—its irrevocability. The market economy was a world he welcomed and believed mortals could control. Webster and the Whigs articulated, defended, and celebrated that world in 1840.[46] Though Butler promised his audience that the people would spurn the party which treated them "as if their hearts were in their pockets, and their souls the willing slaves of beastly appetite and grovelling avarice!" his stridency suggested he knew that the Whigs of 1840 had hit on a fundamental truth about acquisitive Americans.[47]

IV

Butler's forebodings proved correct. On election day Van Buren was repudiated and Harrison and the Whigs triumphed. Harrison received 53 percent of the popular vote, and Whigs carried most of New England, much of the South, all of the Middle Atlantic states, and much of the West. If their majorities were rarely overwhelming, they were nearly everywhere comfortable, and Whig strategists could well afford a moment to savor the triumph that had been so long in coming.

To the Democrats now fell the unaccustomed agony of post-mortems. All conceded that the party's liabilities in the 1840 campaign

---

[44] Benjamin F. Butler, speech in New Brunswick, N.J., October 8, 1840, as reported in *ibid.*, October 14, 1840.

[45] Louis Hartz, *The Liberal Tradition in America: An Interpretation of American Political Thought since the Revolution* (New York: Harcourt, Brace & Co., 1955), pp. 89–128; Marvin Meyers, *The Jacksonian Persuasion: Politics & Belief* (Stanford: Stanford University Press, 1957), pp. 3–57, 135–41; Karl Polanyi, *The Great Transformation: The Political and Economic Origins of Our Time* (Boston: Beacon Press, 1957), chaps. 5–6; Douglas T. Miller, *Jacksonian Aristocracy: Class and Democracy in New York, 1830–1860* (New York: Oxford University Press, 1967), pp. 54–55, 128–54.

[46] *Albany Evening Journal*, August 25, 1840. Political entrepreneur Thurlow Weed urged that the Whig cause was particularly that of "Young Men. It is the cause of Progress—of Improvement—of Enterprise—of Ambition. Its Principles are the Steps by which Young Men can alone climb the rugged and difficult ascents of human life." Those principles would elevate men of intelligence and industry from "obscurity . . . poverty toil and privation" to "worldly excitements" and "ultimate success."

[47] Butler, speech in New Brunswick, *New York Evening Post*, October 14, 1840; Hartz, *The Liberal Tradition in America*, pp. 89–142.

were substantial. Burdened by a depression, weighted by a lackluster leader, and hamstrung with the accumulated discontents of twelve years in power, the party was vulnerable. Even if the Whigs had run an entirely fair and candid contest, the impulse for change was great, and thousands were ready to try any alternative.[48]

Nonetheless, most Democrats believed their party had been undone by deceit. If the Whigs had manfully avowed Whig programs—support for a national bank or a high tariff or federal aid for internal improvements—the public would have rendered its customary verdict on consolidation and special privilege. But the Whig campaign, with its plastic candidate and its deafening cacaphony of song and slogans, deliberately thwarted a rational choice.[49]

Democratic explanations of their defeat were only partly correct. In retrospect, it was almost certainly the inseparable combination of discontent, the depression, and superior Whig tactics that decided the outcome of 1840. The Whig sweep of the elections of 1837 demonstrated the sensitivity of the electorate to economic currents, and, if anything, the panic of 1839 was more severe and widespread.[50] Yet the depression alone did not win for the Whigs. By mid-campaign, the economy showed spotty signs of improvement, and Webster had to explain in June, in a letter widely reprinted by Whig editors, that the symptoms of health were due solely to confidence in a Whig victory.[51] The slight upturn in the economy, and the belated but strong campaign response by the Democrats,[52] almost certainly made a Whig victory precarious. Decisively, the Whig campaign kept the discontent alive and salient through the summer and fall.[53]

[48]*New York Evening Post*, November 21, 1840.

[49]*Ibid.*, November 11, 1840; Jackson to Van Buren, November 24, 1840, Van Buren Papers, LC; *Ohio Democrat*, November 14, 1840.

[50]Walter Buckingham Smith and Arthur Harrison Cole, *Fluctuations in American Business, 1790-1860*, Harvard Economic Studies, no. 50 (Cambridge, Mass.: Harvard University Press, 1935), pp. 59-69.

[51]Webster's letter of June, 1840, was reprinted in the *Albany Evening Journal*, August 28, 1840. Webster acknowledged some signs of improvement, but denied a general recovery. "Are prices rising? Is produce higher? Is exchange more favorable? Are the farmers, the graziers, and the wool-growers getting rich again? Do the hat makers, shoemakers, carriage makers, the furniture makers, and other mechanics of New England begin to collect their Southern and Western debts? . . . to receive fresh orders?" Profits would return only after a change in leadership.

[52]Despite the Whig victory, William Henry Seward marveled at "the mighty energy and power that remained with our opponents. Nothing could have enabled us to triumph over it [*sic*] but the enthusiasm they in their folly called forth for General Harrison." Seward to Levi Hubbell, November 10, 1840, William Henry Seward Papers, University of Rochester, Rochester, N.Y.

[53]See Angus Campbell, "Surge and Decline: A Study in Electoral Change," in Angus Campbell, Phillip E. Converse, Warren E. Miller, and Donald E. Stokes, *Elections and the Political Order* (New York: John Wiley & Sons, 1966), pp. 40-51.

Equally important to the Whigs' success was the unprecedented "excitement" generated by their campaign. New voters were indispensable to overcome the normal Democratic majority, and the cider, songs, celebrities, and Whig camp meetings, along with Democratic countermeasures, brought the people out by the thousands. Never had the seasoned politicians of the generation seen such an "excitement & uproar among the people. It is sort of Popular Insurrection," gloried Whig John Jordan Crittenden. Anxious Democrats concurred; it seemed "as though every man, woman and child, preferred politics to any thing else." The outpouring worked to the Whigs' advantage.[54] In the atmosphere of anxiety about prices and wages and dreams of riches ahead, many old, and thousands of new voters responded to the Whig call to restore virtue and prosperity to a troubled republic—to replace the corrupt in power with honest William Henry Harrison. The Democratic *New York Evening Post* had spoofed in March of 1840 that, if "noise and boasting can make a President of the United States, if a party can elect their candidate by hard huzzahing and hallooing, . . . then Harrison is our next President to a certainty."[55] Unwittingly, the *Post* had been right. The frenzied campaign was indispensable to Whig success.

V

Yet, to contend that the Whig campaign denied the voters a rational choice and that the Whigs won only because of their substantive silence is another matter.

Admittedly, the Whigs of 1840 were cautious on issues. They proposed not to change Democratic goals but somehow to achieve them. They attacked depression, but proposed "better times" rather than specific remedies. They offered less a program than a classic campaign formula: vote the ins out. The Whigs avoided issues belabored by the

---

[54]Crittenden to Webster, October 27, 1840, Daniel Webster Papers, LC; Samuel Medary to Van Buren, August 15, 1840, Van Buren Papers, LC; James Buchanan to Van Buren, October 25, 1840, *ibid.*; John Chadwick to John P. Hale, September 16, 1840, John P. Hale Papers, New Hampshire Historical Society, Concord. My conclusions about the election of 1840 are speculative. Analysis of who the new voters were and why they voted as they did awaits a full-scale study of that election. I base my views on the conclusions reached about more recent voting behavior in Campbell *et al.*, *Elections and the Political Order*. The authors stress the importance of new voters in overturning the party in power and the role of "excitement" in generating new voters. They argue further that, in times of general discontent with the party in power, a majority of the new voters will vote for the party challenging the incumbent. See *ibid.*, pp. 40–51 and chaps. 3, 4, and 8. Richard P. McCormick analyzes the unprecedented leap in voter turnout in 1840 in his "New Perspectives on Jacksonian Politics," *American Historical Review*, 65 (January, 1960): 288–301.

[55]*New York Evening Post*, March 2, 1840.

Democrats. They denied plans to assume the debts of states which had overinvested in internal improvements. They said little about the tariff, save to pledge fealty to the Compromise of 1833.[56] Though the three most prominent Whig leaders spoke about a national bank, each endorsed it as a last resort, and most Whig campaigners smothered the issue with silence. The reasons for prudence were obvious. As Webster observed candidly in an October speech to Virginia Whigs, "while in the presence of a common enemy, who is armed to the teeth against us both . . . does he imagine that . . . we shall be carrying on our family controversies?" Whig divisions "are not . . . the topic of discussion today."[57]

Yet, for those voters who wished to listen, the Whig formula for "better times" was ever present. Whigs insisted that it was Democratic policy which had twice afflicted the country with depression. Whigs argued that Democratic remedies, designed mainly to minimize the debts of the government, offered no relief to the people. Whigs demanded that the government accept the challenge to restore prosperity and regulate a national currency. What little the Whigs left to inference, the Democrats made explicit. Shrilly, universally, incessantly, they warned that a Whig victory would bring a new national bank.

---

[56]The exception was Webster's solitary Senate statement in January, 1840, that the mounting federal debt and the glutted state of the foreign cotton and wheat markets might compel moderate men to reconsider the value of a high tariff. Webster suggested the need for more cotton-consuming wage-earners. Webster's remarks in debate with Calhoun on March 3, 1840, were reported in the *Niles National Register*, March 14, 1840.

[57]Daniel Webster, "Speech in Richmond, October 5, 1840," *Writings*, 3:84.

VI

HIGH TIDE

FROM THE MOMENT OF VICTORY, the central problem for president-
elect Harrison and for the Whig party was the rivalry of Webster
and Clay. For both men, looking ahead to the presidential contest
of 1844, time and trust had run out. Disappointment and mutual be-
trayals had poisoned their personal relationship, and, even had good
will prevailed, age inclined neither Webster, fifty-eight, nor Clay, sixty-
three, to defer his presidential hopes any longer. What little patience
Clay had demonstrated in years past was gone by 1840. So, too, was his
faith that the party which he had helped to found would do him
justice. In their stead was suspicion, resentment, and a consuming determination to bring the party back under his control and to see himself in
the presidency. Wounded and bitter, the Clay of 1841 trusted only himself. His outburst upon hearing of his defeat at Harrisburg, recalled later
by a witness, was as much a credo for the future as a comment on
defeat: "If there were two Henry Clays, one would make the other
President."[1] If Webster's quest for control proved less compulsive, his
goal was equally to guide events to his favor. Whig appointments and
the Whig program became points of contention in the rivals' struggle for
mastery of the party.

[1] Henry A. Wise, *Seven Decades of the Union* (Philadelphia: J. B. Lippincott & Co., 1872),
pp. 170-72.

I

Neither Webster nor Clay lost time in seeking to manipulate the president-elect. Clay maneuvered Harrison, scheduled to visit Kentucky on "private business" in November, into a reluctant rendezvous at Lexington, and skillfully used their meeting and mutual toasts to squelch rumors of a rift between them. Despite the show of fraternity, little of substance was transacted. Harrison offered Clay his choice of cabinet posts, Clay, as expected, declined, preferring to stay in the Senate. Just when Clay thought the two were about to get down to matters of policy and patronage, they were interrupted, and never got back to serious topics. The General's smiling silence on appointments and issues and Clay's lurking suspicion that "artful men" would seek to "foster . . . jealousy" between them did not leave Clay wholly at ease. Still, Clay was pleased for the time. Harrison had given him assurances of the "most ardent attachment," and the president-elect had leaked word that John Jordon Crittenden, Clay's trusted ally and fellow senator from Kentucky, would be invited into the cabinet. The meeting made exactly the impression Clay had wished—that Harrison had assigned to him all but the scepter of leadership.[2]

Returning from Kentucky, Harrison then offered Webster his choice of cabinet posts, singling out especially the State and Treasury departments, and on December 11 Webster accepted the office of Secretary of State. For more than the all-too-true reason he offered Harrison—that for "the daily details of the treasury, the matters of account . . . I do not think myself . . . particularly well qualified"—Webster found the State Department more congenial than the Treasury. Experience suggested and fact confirmed that Clay would demand leadership in Whig financial measures,[3] whereas Harrison's inexperience and Clay's preoccupation would give Webster a free hand in foreign policy. In the Department of State Webster could concentrate especially on improving Anglo-American relations, which he had come to feel were as vital to the revival of credit and enterprise as any Whig legislation. Those relations had nearly deteriorated into war in 1839 during a dispute over the boundary of Maine and Canada. Webster knew that no new British

---

[2]George Rawlings Poage, *Henry Clay and the Whig Party* (Chapel Hill: University of North Carolina Press, 1936), pp. 15-19; Clay to John M. Clayton, December 17, 1840, John M. Clayton Papers, Library of Congress, Washington, D.C. (hereafter cited as LC).

[3]Harrison to Webster, December 1, 1840; and Webster to Harrison, December 11, 1840; *The Writings and Speeches of Daniel Webster*, ed. J. W. McIntyre, 18 vols. (Boston: Little, Brown & Co. 1903), 18:91, 93-94 (hereafter cited as *Writings*). Webster noted in his letter of acceptance to Harrison that "the duty of originating important measures" of revenue and finance "properly belongs to Congress."

credit would flow to the United States so long as conflict was possible, and he meant to preside over the prompt restoration of amity and British investments.[4]

But Webster accepted the State Department post for another reason. He knew that most Whigs regarded the entire cabinet, rather than the president alone, as the executive branch of the government, and that they considered the secretary of state the "premier" of the cabinet. Webster immediately sought to establish his status and, like Clay, to use Harrison. Taking advantage of Harrison's invitation to suggest other eligibles for the cabinet, he announced his opinion that the cabinet, however composed, should operate as a unit. That unit would consti- tute the executive; in its decisions the president would have one vote, and the president would abide by the cabinet's judgments. Harrison apparently let this view pass until he saw Webster in February, when he rejected it flatly.[5] Meanwhile, the president-elect thanked Webster for his suggestions of possible cabinet colleagues, but on December 27 closed the correspondence by stating that he had decided to postpone further decisions until he reached Washington.[6]

Harrison had thus fended off both men for the moment, but renewed pressures would come. Clay, of course, wished no impediments to re- gaining control of the party he had lost at Harrisburg, and wanted, at least, Harrison's acquiescence in the legislative plans he was beginning to write and talk about in Washington. But Webster, insofar as he sought the White House, needed far more than benevolent neutrality. If ever he was to match Clay's power in the party, if ever he was to offset Clay's authority as Whig congressional leader, he would need a bal- ancing force—and that could come only from the president.

Webster's dependence on the president stemmed less from Clay's strength than from his own weakness in the Whig party. The senator's appointment to the highest cabinet position, and the public approval it elicited, belied Webster's fragile standing among his peers. Clay made no secret of the reluctance with which he endorsed Webster's claims to a post in the cabinet.[7] Less interested parties also doubted the wisdom of

---

[4]Webster to Daniel B. Ogden, March 11, 1839; Daniel Webster, "Suggestions to Joel R. Poinsett on the Northwestern Boundary, March 9, 1839"; Webster to Samuel Rogers, February 10, 1840; and Webster to Edward Everett, February 2, 1841; *ibid.*, 16:304-5, 119-22; 18:75, 99-100.

[5]Leonard D. White, *The Jacksonians: A Study in Administrative History, 1829-1861* (New York: Macmillan, 1954), pp. 47-48, 93.

[6]Webster to Harrison, December 11, 1840; and Harrison to Webster, December 27, 1840; *Writings*, 18:93-97.

[7]Clay to Porter, December 8, 1840, Peter B. Porter Papers, Buffalo Historical Society, Buffalo, N.Y.; Clay to Clayton, December 17, 1840, Clayton Papers.

putting Webster in a high place, or of identifying the new administration with him in a conspicuous way. Even close friends, from whom Webster might have expected support, held back endorsement or privately disapproved of his taking the post.[8]

Though part of the reason for this widespread disfavor was the obvious danger of appointing a former Federalist to the highest place in the first Whig cabinet, there was a more insidious basis for apprehension. Increasingly, men of his own party expressed doubts about the moral fiber and reliability of the Massachusetts senator. Most knew that Webster was deeply in debt, and it was no secret that for a second time his wealthy Massachusetts and New York friends had collected a large sum to extricate him from ruin. Fear that Webster's debts to the United States Bank and to the British banking house of Baring Brothers might compromise him, or that their disclosure would compromise the party, further weakened confidence in Webster. Even Edward Curtis of New York, whom Webster regarded as a trusted ally and whom he was to propose for the post of collector of the Port of New York, privately disclosed that he thought Webster had no credit whatsoever with the Whig party.[9]

But anxiety over Webster's appointment rose mostly from fear of opening so early the contest for Harrison's successor. Friends of party peace, as well as friends of Clay, feared that Webster would stop at nothing to turn back the Kentuckians, that Clay in turn would stop at nothing to quench his own ambition, and that the result—if both had equal power—would be fratricide. In the Senate, Webster might be controlled. In the cabinet, with daily access to the president and a strong voice in policy and patronage decisions, he could make trouble. Uncertainty about the mental and physical strength of the sixty-eight-year-old president-elect only fed the fears of Webster's potential for mischief.

Opposition to Webster, however, took the form of private lament rather than open revolt. From Clay on down, all knew that a cabinet offer had to be made, and all sensed correctly that Webster would probably accept it. But in his quest for power the new secretary of state would have to cope with the fact that, especially in Congress, many

---

[8] Amos Lawrence to Amos A. Lawrence, June 29, 1840, Amos A. Lawrence Papers, Massachusetts Historical Society, Boston (hereafter cited as MHS); *Boston Courier*, September 29, 1842.

[9] The *New York Evening Post* exposed Webster's legendary debts on September 5, 1840. During the campaign Webster had to deny that the had accepted a thousand dollars from the Barings to favor assumption of state debts. For Curtis' appraisal, see Clay to Peter B. Porter, February 7, 1841, Porter Papers.

Whigs were wary of him. If Webster wished to advance, he would have to win over—or overpower—that opposition. Once more, for Webster, the shortest and only road to the White House was through the White House.

II

Webster made steady progress in winning Harrison's favor. His success came less because of his own skill than beause of the mutual petulance of Clay and Harrison.

The cabinet became the first point of contention between the president-elect and Clay, and the first instance of Webster's advancement by default. There was little reason for the cabinet to be a source of friction, for, though Webster played an important role in its formation, as finally composed, the Cabinet belonged to neither rival. By and large the men in it were independent, cordial among themselves, and determined to work harmoniously for a happy administration. But Clay found cause for grievance. Though Harrison had named Clay's protégé, Crittenden, attorney general, two of Clay's other dependables, Senator John M. Clayton of Delaware and Nathan Sargeant of Philadelphia, had been overlooked. Webster had blocked Clayton's appointment to the Treasury by suggesting that Thomas Ewing of Ohio, previously slated for postmaster general, be shifted to the Treasury slot. Webster, Ewing, and Crittenden had then agreed that the postmaster general must be a New Yorker and had concurred on Francis Granger, whom Clay had earlier endorsed for one of the cabinet posts.[10] Harrison then made John Bell of Tennessee his secretary of war and left the remaining slot, secretary of the navy, up to the Southern congressmen.

Despite the fact that every member of the cabinet, with the exception of Webster, was personally cordial to Clay, that none was dominated by Webster, and that the unnamed member was to be a Southerner, Clay felt slighted. On the evening of February 11 he intervened to secure the remaining open position, that of secretary of the navy, for his friend Clayton. His interview with Harrison was "stormy" and confirmed the worst fears of each about the intentions of the other. Harrison, sensitive to campaign charges and capital rumors that he was the mere tool of the Kentuckian, refused to buckle. Clay, convinced that the weak president-elect had indeed been poisoned against him,

---

[10]Clay to Clayton, February 12, 1841, Clayton Papers. Clay chose Granger as the least hostile of prominent New York Whigs. Christopher Morgan to Seward, January 10, 1841, William Henry Seward Papers, University of Rochester, Rochester, N.Y.

grew adamant. Clay's insistence finally goaded Harrison into reminding the senator that he, not Clay, had been elected president—and Clay sulked off with a self-inflicted sense of defeat.[11]

Webster and his fellow cabinet members had already discovered that it did not pay to press the president-elect directly. Harrison had refused to accept any cabinet alterations in the turgid inaugural address—replete with allusions to Greece and Rome—he had composed en route to Washington. Only gentle or indirect pressure persuaded him to relent on some passages, and, after hours of nudging and negotiation one evening, Webster reported that he had succeeded in killing "*seventeen Roman proconsuls* as dead as smelts."[12] Webster apparently also won a paragraph or two on the evils of partisanship, but little else. Insofar as it was within his power, Harrison clearly meant to be his own man.

But a second dispute between Harrison and Clay—this time over patronage—propelled the aged General toward looking more and more to Webster for support and counsel. Webster, Seward, and Weed all favored the appointment of Edward Curtis, a shrewd political tactician, to the crucial post of collector of the Port of New York.[13] Clay regarded the choice of Curtis to the most important patronage-dispensing post in the East as a direct threat to his interests. He correctly blamed Curtis, along with Weed, Seward, and Webster, for his defeat at Harrisburg.[14] Originally, he also believed Curtis to be a devoted partisan of Webster. In fact, Curtis' devotion to Webster was as fickle as the main chance, but an attempt to allay Clay's fears only confirmed Clay's judgment that Curtis was a scoundrel and steeled his determination to see Curtis denied the post. The result was another heated and damaging exchange with Harrison. Though Webster's wishes were known, he shrewdly stayed aloof from the dispute and allowed it to be decided by his cabinet colleagues, who rendered a verdict for Curtis in mid-March.[15] Clay emerged further estranged from Harrison, and the presi-

[11]Clay to Clayton, September 12, 1841, Clayton Papers; Poage, *Henry Clay*, pp. 20–21; Glyndon G. Van Deusen, *Henry Clay* (Boston: Little, Brown & Co., 1937), p. 338. Webster was delighted with Clay's outburst. Richard M. Blatchford to Seward, February 22, 1841, Seward Papers.

[12]William C. Preston to Benjamin W. Leigh, February 20, 21, 1841, Benjamin W. Leigh Papers, Alderman Library, University of Virginia, Charlottesville; *New York Herald*, March 4, 1841. Webster's statement is cited in Claude Moore Fuess, *Daniel Webster*, 2 vols. (Boston: Little, Brown & Co., 1930), 2:91.

[13]Seward to Christopher Morgan, January 3, 1841, Seward Papers.

[14]R. M. Blatchford to Seward, December 22, 23, 1840, and February 8, 1841, *ibid.*; William L. Marcy to Prosper M. Wetmore, February 6, 1841, William L. Marcy Papers, LC.

[15]Clay to Porter, February 7, 1841, Porter MSS., Papers; Curtis to Weed, [March] 28, [1841], Thurlow Weed Papers, University of Rochester, Rochester, N.Y.

dent further attached to Webster, who had shown he would loyally abide by the decision of his chief.

III

Clay's showdown with the president over Curtis' appointment represented a change in tactics. Hitherto Clay had suppressed his contempt for the General, tempered their encounters, and virtually abstained from patronage requests which might be construed as demands.[16] By March, Clay knew that Harrison's control over the patronage and Webster's apparent sway with the president were hardly unmixed blessings to either Webster or Harrison. It was obvious to all in Washington in the weeks after Harrison's arrival that there were far more claimants for office than the executive could ever please. Added to the faithful who had suffered with the Whigs through a decade of defeat were the new cadres who had helped the party attain victory. Office-seekers swarmed to the capital in droves—they even banded into clubs—and bedeviled congressmen, cabinet members, and the president from dawn to dusk.[17] Fully aware of Harrison's sensitivity to pressure, Clay shrewdly informed supplicants that delicacy and Harrison's inexplicable coolness compelled him to confine his role solely to opposing bad appointments. Hence, when a friend did win a place, Clay got the credit for some secret intervention; when friends failed, Clay was absolved from blame, which fell to the malign influence of Webster. Clay's forbearance removed points of further friction between himself and the president and isolated Webster and Harrison from all the disappointed, who found themselves linked to Clay as fellow martyrs.

What had forced Clay to reconsider his stance, and what had led him to intercede with Harrison against Curtis in early March, was a new danger. Since the election Clay and most other Whigs had assumed that the almost-bankrupt condition of the Treasury and the fiscal straits of the country would compel the president to call an emergency session of Congress in the spring of 1841.[18] He had counted on that session to give him all the opportunity he needed to reassert his authority in the party. By March, however, it appeared that Harrison, with Webster's

---

[16]Clay to Porter, February 7, 1841, Porter Papers; Marcy to Wetmore, January 27, 1841, Marcy Papers.

[17]*New York Herald*, February 2, 25, and March 3, 4, 1841.

[18]Morgan to Seward, January 23, 1841, Seward Papers; Crittenden to Robert P. Letcher, January 25, 30, 1841, John Jordan Crittenden Papers, Duke University Library, Durham, N.C.; Clay to Porter, February 7, 1841 Porter Papers.

strong endorsement, might decline to call a special session.[19] Clay and other congressional Whigs would be forced to return home until the next regular convening of Congress, in December, leaving Webster, the Cabinet, and the flocks of editors and managers in the capital to determine all Whig appointments and perhaps even to devise Whig programs. If Curtis was at all typical of the appointments, then there was far more menace than Clay had first thought in placating Harrison by allowing him a free hand in patronage matters. There was, in fact, the danger that the new breed of party managers which had already thwarted Clay once might become sufficiently entrenched in the executive branch and in the party to deny him again.[20]

But the prospect of delay appalled Clay for reasons beyond the personal danger to himself. Clay saw delay as a mortal threat to the Whig party. He had hoped to use the special session to restore the creedal integrity of the Whigs. Almost every act since his return to Washington in December, 1840, for the lame-duck session of Congress, in one way or another bore on the need for an emergency meeting of the new, Whig-dominated Congress, which would otherwise not convene until December, 1841. In daily speeches to the Senate, Clay had sought to impose his meaning on the Whig victory. The voters had "utterly repudiated" the sub-treasury, and Clay even called on Democrats to help the Whigs repeal it. The electorate had furthermore licensed the victors to do whatever was needed to end the hard times. Clay's persistent, if sometimes bullying, tactics had their effect, and by early 1841 most Whigs agreed that the party "*must act*" or risk "disappointing the high hopes & feelings of the people."[21] A caucus of Whig congressmen in early February agreed to recommend to the president an emergency session which would establish a national bank, pass a general bankruptcy law, legislate a new issue of Treasury bonds to replenish the coffers of the government, and pass a land bill providing for the distribution of future surplus revenues. Only one or two Whigs at the caucus demurred from its call for a special session.[22]

---

[19]Webster expressed opposition at a Whig caucus in early February and reiterated it thereafter. *New York Herald*, February 3, 1841; R. M. Blatchford to Seward, February 22, 1841, Seward Papers. On March 5 the *New York Herald* reported Harrison's firm opposition to a special session.

[20]William L. Marcy, the shrewd New Yorker who coined the phrase "To the victors belong the spoils," observed after several conversations with Clay in February, 1841: "I think Mr. C. must look about him or the rogues will cheat him. To guard against such a contingency he ought to take care of his out-posts." Marcy to Wetmore, February 21, 1841, Marcy Papers.

[21]Crittenden to Letcher, January 30, 1841, Crittenden Papers, Duke.

[22]*New York Herald*, February 3, 1841.

Webster was among the minority of Whigs who hoped the party could avoid a special session.[23] Though by February, 1841, the issue of personal power influenced his judgment, initially he disputed Clay's haste for other reasons.

Webster seemed to share the views of some Whigs that convening the new, Whig-controlled Congress in April or May would only expose and harden unsettled Whig differences about a party program. President Van Buren's "panic session," Webster recalled, had savagely rent his party in 1837, and the Whigs of 1841 were no less divided than the Democrats of 1837 over a remedy for the depression. Not only were there disagreements between states'-rights Southerners and their Northern comrades over the constitutionality of a national bank. Easterners were divided over the practicality of a bank. What many regarded as the "reckless" conduct of the Bank of the United States after 1834 had made mercantile and financial magnates wary of establishing a new bank with comparable power for evil.[24]

Indeed, Webster's own views of the proper remedy for depression and on the role of a national bank had changed. Euphoric in 1837 over a bank which would lavish credit on Western enterprise, Webster had regressed to a more conservative view after his catastrophic failure at land speculation in 1839. As early as February, 1840, he confessed he was "coming to the opinion fast, that new modes of [currency] regulation must be adopted in both [England and the United States] . . . , or else these frequent contractions and expansions of the paper circulation will compel us to give it up, and go back to gold or iron, or the Lord knows what."[25] Webster no longer wanted the kind of bank sought by credit-hungry Whigs of the West and South.

Hopeful that the mere defeat of the "anticredit, antisocial" Democrats would help restore business confidence, Webster, like his friend Edward Everett, seemed to fear that mere revival of the old Whig program and heady credit would spur a new Democratic attack and future economic collapse. The Whigs would create little stability by passing

[23] *Ibid.*

[24] Thomas Payne Govan, *Nicholas Biddle: Nationalist and Public Banker, 1786–1844* (Chicago: University of Chicago Press, 1959), pp. 326–31, 367–69; Davis to Webster, April 23, 1841, Daniel Webster Papers, LC.

[25] Webster to Samuel Rogers, February 10, 1840, *Writings*, 18:75. In a speech to the Massachusetts legislature on his return from England in 1840, Webster stated similar views. He endorsed the "creation of a national institution," but not one "precisely like the old national banks, for circumstances were changed." The bank should be one of "issue rather than deposit, not acting for profits, but solely for the regulation of the currency." A contemporary report of Webster's "Remarks" of January, 1840, was published in the *Portland Advertiser* (Maine), January 10, 1840. The revised version of this talk, published in *Writings*, 2:293–307, deals only with the topic of British agriculture.

economic legislation which would invite "some Jackson yet unborn, some Benton of a future age," to assault it with the rhetoric of "unconstitutionality" and "danger to the liberties of the people" which had "gulled majorities in the past."[26] Webster's purpose in seeking postponement of a special session of Congress, then, was only partly to secure his influence with Harrison by evicting Clay from the capital.[27] Webster's goal also seemed to include the creation of Whig laws which would stick—laws which would so satisfy the nation's needs as to be immune to future partisan attack.

Clay doubted that harmony would ever come to the Whigs, or prosperity to the country, unless immediate action was taken. He was determined to strike while victory was fresh and while the country's financial crisis was indisputable.[28] Confident of his ability to use the unique circumstances to force Whigs to act together, he brushed aside worries that a special session might only explode the myth of Whig unity, so tenuously maintained during the campaign. Conditions in early 1841 seemed to compel even the most recalcitrant to support Clay's call for a new national bank and land distribution[29]—proposals designed to revive the credit of the country. Even if the depression dragged on over the summer, delay would betray the Whigs' campaign call for action and would allow doubts and doubters time to thrive. Divisions—between strict and broad constructionists, between Northern Whigs content with the East's regional systems of currency control and Southern and Western Whigs desperate for the credit and currency a national bank made possible—would again immobilize the Whig coalition.[30] They and their parliamentary commander, as Democrats had freely predicted, would

[26] Everett to C. A. Davis, June 28, 1839, Letterbook copy, Edward Everett Papers, MHS.

[27] R. M. Blatchford to Seward, February 22, 1841, Seward Papers. Blatchford reported that Webster hoped a special session "may be avoided"—and exulted that "Webster's influence is paramount."

[28] Crittenden almost certainly reflected Clay's views when he wrote from Washington on January 30 that the Whigs "*must act*. The people expect it, and are entitled to expect it. The fears that some entertain of an extra session, are visionary. The real danger is in *inaction*." Crittenden to Letcher, January 30, 1841, Crittenden Papers, Duke. Clay to Porter, February 7, 1841, Porter Papers.

[29] These were listed as two of the major items for which the Whig caucus of early February agreed to press. *New York Herald*, February 3, 1841.

[30] The Suffolk System of Massachusetts and the Safety Fund System of New York allowed major city banks to regulate the currency in the East. Eastern bankers grew restive when the Bank of the United States, after the expiration of its national charter, increasingly committed its funds to underwriting speculation in Southern cotton and Western lands. The same Bank ventures, however, won much support in the latter regions, which came to regard a national bank as the most efficient conduit of Eastern capital for the credit-poor South and West. For a sample of Eastern preoccupation with currency stability, see John Davis to Webster, April 23, 1841, Webster Papers, LC. For the Bank's Southern and Western activities after 1836, see Govan, *Nicholas Biddle*, pp. 296–375 *passim*.

prove themselves to be as impotent in power as out.[31] If the Whig party was ever to conquer its factionalism, gain internal discipline, and regain public integrity, the time was at hand.[32] At issue to Clay was whether the centrifugal forces which had plagued the coalition since 1834, which had forced it to abandon the items of its platform one by one, and which had triumphed in the Harrison nomination and the 1840 campaign, could be conquered.

In March, however, all signs indicated that the president would refuse to call Congress into special session.[33] If Harrison had been open-minded on the matter when he came to Washington, the pressure from Clay and the internal disputes of the Whigs had dampened the president's zeal. He acknowledged that he was not a leader, yet he was reluctant to be a pawn.[34] He enjoyed the frivolities of capital life and seemed amused at being president; Whig pressure to get on with the job only wedded him further to his presidential pleasures, "to crack his joke—to indulge his good feelings—to pat the cheeks of pretty girls."[35] Increasingly, Harrison yearned for repose, and Webster, who felt every day that his influence with the president was growing, encouraged the aged hero's desire. Repose and delay became the theme of papers known to have the confidence of the secretary of state.[36]

Since Harrison could not deny the wishes of the Whig caucus on the grounds of personal lassitude, Webster found for him a plausible reason for waiting until November. The legislature of Tennessee had not yet chosen its senators and was not scheduled to do so before new state elections in August, when Whigs hoped to win the elections and select the new senators. An earlier meeting of Congress would allow the current Democratic legislature to convene a special session and send two Democrats to Washington. The Tennessee issue provided the president with the excuse he sought, and, when the cabinet deadlocked on the

---

[31] *New York Evening Post*, n.d., as quoted in *Niles National Register*, November 28, 1840.

[32] See Clay to Harrison, March 13, 1841, cited in Poage, *Henry Clay*, p. 30.

[33] *New York Herald*, March 5, 1841.

[34] Harrison acknowledged that he had only a "moderate share of talent" as a leader in a letter to Silas M. Stillwell, July 12, 1837, photostatic copy, William Henry Harrison Papers, LC. His insecurity as the nominal head of the Whigs was manifest in a letter to Clay during the campaign, in which he insisted that any meeting between them "must appear to be accidental." Harrison to Clay, June 21, 1840, Henry Clay Papers, LC.

[35] Harrison's behavior was reported by the Washington correspondent of the *New York Herald*, February 25, 1841. Van Buren and Marcy also observed that the General seemed to prefer battlefield reminiscences and saucy jokes to the duties of office. *Ibid.*, March 1, 1841; Marcy to Wetmore, March 17, 1841, Marcy Papers.

[36] R. M. Blatchford to Seward, February 22, 1841, Seward Papers; *New York Commercial Advertiser*, March 2, 1841.

question on March 11, Harrison cast the deciding vote against a special session.[37]

With so much at stake, and with the lame-duck session of Congress coming to a close on March 15, Clay once more challenged Harrison. He wrote the president on March 13. "Will you excuse me," he began,

for suggesting the propriety of a definite decision about an Extra Session, and of announcing the fact? There is much speculation and uncertainty about it, in circles [sic] and among members of Congress. Time is rapidly passing away, and members of your Cabinet have, it is alleged, added to the uncertainty. . . .

. . . I have never doubted for a moment about [a special session] since Novr. In my deliberate opinion, the good of the Country and the honor and interest of the party demand it.

Clay "respectfully" enclosed a draft of the proclamation Harrison might issue "stating the grounds for the convocation," and informed Harrison that he would "be most happy to learn [the president's] final decision" by dinner.

Harrison replied in kind. "My dear friend. You use the privilege of a friend to lecture me and I take the same liberty with you. You are too impetuous. Much as I rely on your judgment there are others whom I must consult and in many cases to determine [sic] adversely to your suggestion." There was no "difference of opinion" as to the propriety or the timing of a special session except for "The situation in Tennessee." The cabinet had discussed the question that morning and would settle the matter on Monday, the fifteenth. Harrison closed his note by suggesting that future discussions between the men continue to take place by letter.[38]

"And it has come to this!" fumed Clay that night. "I am civilly but virtually requested not to visit the White House—not to see the President personally, but hereafter only to communicate with him in writing."[39]

Through no merit of his own, however, Clay got his special session. The cabinet vote of early March against the meeting had been preliminary, and Harrison had directed Secretary of the Treasury Thomas Ewing to judge whether the expected revenues of the government would enable it to carry on until November. Ewing reported on March

[37] Poage, *Henry Clay*, pp. 28–29; *New York Herald*, March 5, 1841.

[38] Clay to Harrison, March 13, 1841; and Harrison to Clay, March 13, 1841; cited in Poage, *Henry Clay*, pp. 30–31.

[39] Clay's reaction was recorded by a newspaper correspondent who found him in his room that night. See *ibid.*, p. 30.

15 that the government would be bankrupt within a few months, and his verdict decided the issue.[40] On March 15 the president issued a call for an emergency session of the new Congress to convene on May 31.

Webster acceded, but he and his followers remained ebullient. The collectorship of New York seemed to be theirs, and, though Clay had gained the extra session of Congress, the Kentuckian had exhausted the president's good will. Webster seemed to have a clear field for making the most of Harrison's favor.

Precisely what the president's favor was worth in April, 1841, was open to question. Harrison's vacillation had alienated as many Whigs as had Clay's impetuosity, and, if anything, the president commanded less respect among Whigs after a month in office than he had before he assumed it. The power of patronage was substantial, but neither Harrison nor Webster had yet fully experienced its prickly problems. Offices undistributed kept many on a tether, but, once expended, patronage left behind legions of disaffected.[41] Moreover, Harrison had shown an increasing inclination, despite his initial reluctance, to leave matters to his cabinet—including the distribution of offices—and, hence, Webster's influence with the president by no means assured him of control of the patronage. Even if he had been able to gain such control, Webster was, as Calhoun observed, temperamentally "not proscriptive,"[42] and might well have left too many Democrats in office to suit most Whigs. On decisions of policy, Webster's effectiveness promised to be greater, since at least two cabinet members and the president had sided with him in the dispute over the emergency session. But the policies the president's commitment to the sovereignty of Congress[43] would allow the executive to initiate, or even review, were open to question. Certainly Webster was in a better position to influence his party as secretary of state than as the senator from Massachusetts. Whether he was in a decisive position was doubtful.

Such questions were soon rendered irrelevant. On April 1, Harrison abruptly took ill with pneumonia. His strength sapped by the demands of the presidency, the sixty-eight-year-old general worsened rapidly. On April 4, one month after taking office, he died.

[40] Edward Curtis to Weed, March 11, 1841, Weed Papers; R. M. Blatchford to Biddle, March 16, 1841, Nicholas Biddle Papers, LC.

[41] The administration had just begun to sample discontent. See the *New York Herald*, March 3, 1841; Edward Curtis to Weed, March 11, 1841, Weed Papers; and Thaddeus Stevens to Webster, March 27, 1841, Webster Papers, LC.

[42] Calhoun to Virgil Maxcy, February 19, 1841, Galloway-Maxcy-Markoe Papers, LC.

[43] William Henry Harrison, "Inaugural Address, March 4, 1841," in *A Compilation of the Messages and Papers of the Presidents, 1789–1905*, comp. James D. Richardson, 11 vols. (Washington, D.C.: Bureau of National Literature and Art, 1907), 4:9–11, 13–14.

VII

THE ROAD TO DISRUPTION

H ARRISON'S DEATH and the succession of states'-rights Whig John
Tyler added a new and ominous dimension to the internal strife
of the Whig party. Despite the deepening quarrel between Webster and Clay, the two leaders shared important views. Both men were
nationalists, both accepted the world of commerce, both concurred on
the lineaments of Whig legislation. But the elevation of Tyler augured
danger to the entire Whig program. The fifty-one-year-old Virginia planter, one of the last and most rigid spokesmen of the atrophied faction
of states'-rights Whigs, stood opposed to the promotional bent and
national energy the Whigs represented. However anachronistic his
phobias were in the Whig party of 1841, the presidency invested them
with chilling potency. Tyler, a former Democrat, had the power to
wreck the Whig program and all the ambitions staked on its success.

Though John Tyler had neither the wish nor the instinct to destroy
the Whig party—quite the opposite—the Whigs repeatedly miscalculated
his resolve. Error compounded error, positions hardened, and Tyler's
initial disposition to meet his comrades halfway gave way to deepening
mistrust.

Almost from the first, Webster sensed the danger of a split between
the Whigs and the president and he struggled to ward off a schism.
Unlike most Whigs, Webster consistently saw an understanding with
Tyler as perfectly possible and Whig division as a needless calamity.
Unlike most Whigs, Webster never thought of a specific party program

161

or presidential submission to party discipline as being vital to the Whigs' survival. On the contrary, to Webster it seemed clear that there would be no Whig program, no relief for the country, and very little party to preserve if the president and the Whigs did not work together.

In fact, in the tortured months to come, compromise between John Tyler and the Whig party was repeatedly possible. At a number of junctures, the good will and cool temper Webster espoused might have kept the party united and gained it a respectable legislative program. Gentlemanly conciliation, however, was no longer the means by which the Whig party held itself together, and Webster's effort to stop the drift toward disruption starkly revealed the anachronism of his tactics and the limits of his authority.

I

At the moment Tyler took office, few anticipated a party schism or calculated its consequences. On the contrary, many Whigs, especially Clay's supporters, were cheered by Tyler's succession. Clay and Tyler, despite differences over such issues as the national bank, had remained on cordial personal terms, and there seemed little likelihood that Tyler would ever bar Clay from the White House as Harrison had in March.[1] Webster seemed clearly the loser from the change of presidents. The Virginian had been among those most apprehensive of Webster's appointment to the cabinet, and Tyler's intimate friends rejoiced that fate had ended Webster's influence in the White House.[2] The secretary of state himself found Tyler remote and uncommunicative in the first weeks of his presidency.[3]

But Tyler's ties to his party and to Clay were far more precarious than his surface amiability suggested. Indeed, the new president's position in April, 1841, was singularly unenviable. Vice-president only because no other "Clay man" could be found to accept the slot on the ticket with Harrison in 1839, the first man to succeed to the White

---

[1] Clay to John L. Lawrence, April 13, 1841, Miscellaneous Clay Papers, Alderman Library, University of Virginia, Charlottesville. Clay thought Tyler able and "amiable." "I believe—I should rather say, I hope that he will interpose no obstacle to the success of the Whig measures, including a Bank of the U.S."

[2] Tyler to Thomas W. Gilmer, January 7, 1841, John Tyler Papers, Library of Congress, Washington, D.C. (hereafter cited as LC). After Tyler's accession, his friends uniformly celebrated Webster's expected eclipse. W. B. Hodgson to William C. Rives, April 4, 1841; and Thomas Allen to Rives, May 8, 1841; William C. Rives Papers, LC.

[3] Richard M. Blatchford to Seward, April 13, 1841, William Henry Seward Papers, University of Rochester, Rochester, N.Y.; Webster to John Davis, April 16, 1841, John Davis Papers, American Antiquarian Society, Worcester, Mass.

House because of the death of a president, Tyler's status as a Whig and his prerogatives as president both were in doubt.[4] Scrupulous to a fault in defense of states'-rights, committed totally to the strict construction of the Constitution, he had gone on record against a national bank in 1819. Suddenly he presided over a party dedicated to that bank's creation. Ambition or self-doubt might have led another man to compromise. But Tyler had made a career of consistency and had found security and independence in his dogmas. Without compromise. Tyler's alternatives were dishonor or use of the veto power against his own party—a party which stood committed against executive tyranny.

Tyler was a Whig, but a Whig of an era that was passing away. His disposition was far closer to that of Webster and the Whigs in 1834 than to that of Clay and the party in 1841. To Tyler, parties were rightly composed of gentlemen, who placed principles above expediency and personal honor above the demands of organization. To remain independent, he had abandoned the Democrats in 1834. Discovering that year that the Democrats were using the Bank issue "for mere party purposes . . . without reference to the good of the Country" and that he had "fallen" into the "company of political speculators," he had lamented to a friend: what "is an honest man to do?" Whig "sharpers," Tyler concluded, made fewer demands than Democratic "gamblers." and so he defected.[5] The passing years had merely ossified Tyler's gloomy view of political parties. When he abruptly became president, he privately hoped to return the Republic to the arcadian days of Jefferson, when gentlemen scorned "faction" and relied solely on the "virtue and intelligence of the people."[6] Tyler's understanding of party—which coincided remarkably with that of the long-gone Federalists—was wildly out of touch with the realities of 1841. A fundamental change had taken place; both parties had realized themselves as organizations, and even the most independent Whigs had belatedly accepted the need for party discipline.[7]

---

[4] Oliver Perry Chitwood, *John Tyler: Champion of the Old South* (New York: D. Appleton-Century Co., 1939), pp. 205–6; Robert J. Morgan, *A Whig Embattled: The Presidency under John Tyler* (Lincoln: University of Nebraska Press, 1954), pp. 6–10.

[5] Tyler to Littleton W. Tazewell, June 23, 1834, Tyler Papers, LC.

[6] Tyler to Rives, April 9, 1841, Rives Papers.

[7] Joel M. Silbey, *The Shrine of Party: Congressional Voting Behavior, 1841–1852* (Pittsburgh: University of Pittsburgh Press, 1967), pp. 52–55, 62–66. Thomas B. Alexander finds the cohesion of Whigs in Congress in the early 1840s impressive, though less so than that of the Democrats. See his important *Sectional Stress and Party Strength: A Study of Roll-Call Voting Patterns in the United States House of Representatives, 1836–1860* (Nashville: Vanderbilt University Press, 1967), chap. 4.

Despite such basic differences between Tyler and his party on a national bank, Webster and many other Whigs initially hoped that the potential dispute might be resolved by means of a face-saving device. In April, Webster urged Tyler to accept the Whig view of the presidency and to consider the cabinet and the president as jointly comprising the executive. Tyler could put the question of a national bank to a cabinet ballot, allow himself to be outvoted, and defer to the judgment of his "constitutional advisors." But Tyler was no more willing than Harrison had been before him to accept this evisceration of his office, and he rejected the proposition the moment Webster made it.[8] Webster then offered another expedient. Tyler, as a states'-rights senator from Virginia, had accepted the view that a state legislature had the right to instruct its senators how to vote. Might not the president consider himself "instructed" by the majority of 1840 to endorse a national bank?[9] Tyler denied that the election had been a referendum on a national bank and refused to consider himself instructed on the issue.

Yet, if Webster and his colleagues in the cabinet were the first to know that harmony between the president and his party would not be easy, they were also among the first to recognize that Tyler was eager to work with the Whigs if he could do so with honor. Tyler reassured the cabinet and all Whigs that he meant to remain one of them. He conspicuously rejected Democratic "lures" to get him to desert the Whigs, and, through April and May, made the White House a Whig haven.[10] Knowing that Clay's friendship was critical, the president took special steps to please the Kentuckian by making appointments designed to satisfy the senator.[11]

More important for party harmony, Tyler seemed ready to concede that "expediency" made some kind of new bank unavoidable. The president made clear, both in his quasi-inaugural message to Congress in April and in a long, frank letter to Clay later that month, that he could not approve an "old-fashioned" national bank.[12] But he did struggle to

---

[8]Frank G. Carpenter, "A Talk with a President's Son," *Lippincott's Monthly Magazine*, 41 (1888):418; Leonard Dinnerstein, "The Accession of John Tyler to the Presidency," *Virginia Magazine of History and Biography*, 70 (October, 1962):449.

[9]Webster to John Davis, April 16, 1841, Davis Papers.

[10]John C. Clark to Rives, May 8, 1841, Rives Papers; [Joshua] Bates to Thomas Wren Ward, May 18, 1841, Thomas W. Ward Papers, Massachusetts Historical Society, Boston (hereafter cited as MHS); Tyler to Berrien, April 12, 1841, John M. Berrien Papers, Southern Historical Collection, University of North Carolina, Chapel Hill.

[11]Tyler to Clay, April 30, 1841, in *The Letters and Times of the Tylers*, ed. Lyon G. Tyler, 3 vols. (Richmond, Va.: Whittet & Shepperson, 1885), 3:94 (hereafter cited as *Letters of the Tylers*).

[12]James D. Richardson, comp., *A Compilation of the Messages and Papers of the Presidents, 1789-1905*, 11 vols. (Washington, D.C.: Bureau of National Literature and Art, 1907), 4:39; Tyler to Clay, April 30, 1841, *Letters of the Tylers*, 3:92-94.

come up with a bank that both he and the party could live with. In the end, Tyler reverted to a scheme originally proposed by Tennessee Democrat Hugh Lawson White in 1832. White's plan evaded the constitutional issue of whether Congress had a right to charter a national bank anywhere which could create branches everywhere. Congress would simply charter a bank in the capital, where it had undisputed legislative jurisdiction, and the Washington bank would create branches in the sovereign states which gave permission for the branches to enter.[13]

Unfortunately, most Whig editors and congressmen mistook Tyler's civilities for pliability and they underrated his determination to resist an "old-fashioned" bank—a bank which assumed the right of Congress to create a national bank and designate its branches wherever Congress wished. Whigs who paraded various proposals before Tyler in the White House interpreted his polite silence as consent, and Clay in particular took Tyler's amenities as a sign that the amiable Virginian would ultimately capitulate on the bank question.[14]

Not until Clay, who had been at home in Kentucky from April to mid-May, returned to the capital on the eve of the special congressional session did he realize how far apart he and the president were on the bank issue. Confident that he could win or force Tyler over to an authentic national bank, Clay interviewed the president a few days after his arrival. Their discussion began civilly, but, as Tyler and the Whig leader of Congress pressed their respective views of a bank, the gulf between them became obvious. Neither yielded, and Clay's insistence on what Tyler regarded as an "old-fashioned bank" finally goaded the president into asking if he must yield all his principles and the consistency of his entire career to Clay's demands. Clay apparently answered candidly: Tyler must. Then go, Tyler bristled to Clay, to your end of the capital and "perform your duty . . . as you shall think proper. So help me God, I shall do mine at this end . . . as I shall think proper."[15]

Clay was now alarmed and wrote to an intimate on June 11 that the Whigs faced "a crisis as a party." He regarded Tyler's bank proposal as

[13]Tyler to Rives, May 8, 1841; and Rives to Tyler, May 15, 1841; Rives Papers. See also George Rawlings Poage, *Henry Clay and the Whig Party* (Chapel Hill: University of North Carolina Press, 1936), p. 38. Webster had endorsed an identical provision for state approval of the branches of a national bank in 1834. In his proposal for a new bank that year, Webster declared himself ready to approve a bank charter which provided that "no branch of the bank [would] be established in any State, unless by permission of its legislature." Daniel Webster, "Speech to the Senate," January 20, 1834, *The Writings and Speeches of Daniel Webster*, ed. J. W. McIntyre, 18 vols. (Boston: Little, Brown & Co., 1903), 6:245 (hereafter cited as *Writings*).

[14]Clay to H. B. Bascom, May 10, 1841, Miscellaneous Clay Papers; Allen to Rives, April 14, 1841, Rives Papers.

[15]Poage, *Henry Clay*, pp. 39–40. Lyon Tyler reconstructed this conversation from "family tradition." *Letters of the Tylers*, 2:34.

absurd, and confessed he was exhausted with the long train of fiscal "experiments" which Jackson had begun in 1834. More important, Clay now gave credence to rumors rife in the capital that Tyler meant to use the bank dispute to supplant the senator as Whig leader or to begin a new political party of "moderates."[16] Clay had no intention of submitting his program, or the Whig principle of congressional supremacy, or his own hegemony, to a veto by Tyler and his small band of states'-rights comrades in Congress. Policy, party, and personal interest all required that he battle Tyler, even at the risk of a veto and a breach between the Whigs and their president.

Webster and the Whig cabinet took a more charitable—and for the moment a more accurate—view of Tyler's principles and purposes, and, when the president divulged his bank plan to the cabinet, they decided to support his scheme.[17] The cabinet members, of course, had a personal interest in avoiding a party division which would cost them their posts. But most regarded Tyler's dilemma as sincere, his wish to remain a Whig genuine, and his plan workable.

Webster was fully aware of expected Whig objections to Tyler's bank proposal. Those Whigs who were eager for a powerful national bank to pump new credit into the economy or to underwrite speculation would find the restrictions Tyler required enfeebling. Those Whigs who thought Congress had the authority to create a bank and bank branches wherever it wished would find Tyler's constitutional qualms obnoxious.[18]

Nevertheless, Webster supported Tyler's bank plan. He believed Tyler's proposed bank would provide the country with minimal economic stability and would survive partisan attack. In 1841, such a bank to check "excess" by "gentle and quiet means" was exactly what he favored.[19] He thought it pointless to pursue the constitutional issue. The task of the Whigs was to get "*something . . . done.*" Webster believed the cabinet had learned from Tyler "exactly, what can be done, and *all* that can be done." The choice was "*getting no Bank*" and "breaking up the Administration" or approving a compromise and preserving the party.[20]

[16] Clay to Robert P. Letcher, June 11, 1841, John Jordan Crittenden Papers, Duke University Library, Durham, N.C.; Clay to Henry P. Carey, June 11, 1841, Conaroe Collection, Historical Society of Pennsylvania, Philadelphia (hereafter cited as HSP).

[17] Tyler's "Statement" on the bank controversy of 1841, *Letters of the Tylers*, 2:67-70; Rufus Choate to John Davis, June 27, 1841, Davis Papers; William B. Campbell to David Campbell, July 8, 1841, David Campbell Papers, Duke University Library, Durham, N.C.

[18] Webster to Hiram Ketchum, July 17, 1841, *Writings*, 16:348-49.

[19] Webster to Ketchum, July 16, 1841, *ibid.*, p. 347.

[20] Webster to Ketchum, [July, 1841], *ibid.*, p. 351.

Whether the bank the cabinet endorsed would have worked is dubious. As critics were quick to observe, the District of Columbia was an implausible place to locate a national bank. The business of Washington was politics; the business of commerce was centered in New York and Philadelphia. Critics also questioned whether state assent to bank branches would come as readily as Webster and others claimed. Democrats had, after all, made opposition to a national bank their party creed, and the Tyler proposal opened the way for long, uncertain battles over bank branches in almost every state. Even if most of the battles were won, the cabinet plan did not stipulate whether states could tax the branches of the bank, and hence opened the way for later, more hostile legislatures to seek to tax the branches out of existence. Many capitalists doubted that such a bank could achieve its goal of reviving financial stability and credit.[21] Webster's position was and remained, however, that capitalists ultimately would subscribe to the proposed bank and that, if the institution faltered "for want of any particular power," Congress could alter the bank the next winter. The "urgent necessities of the country" required the Whigs to "try such a bank as we can agree upon and can establish."[22]

Of more immediate importance than the doubts of financiers, though, were the political forces working against Whig acceptance of the cabinet proposal. Like Clay, most Whigs had little concern for the president's honor,[23] and most favored immediate creation of a strong national bank. Even Southern Whigs, who had originally joined the party as dedicated to states'-rights as Tyler, had mellowed in their attitude toward a central bank. Shaken by the depression and the collapse of cotton prices on the international market, many Whig planters and merchants from the South were coming round to the view that a flourishing domestic market—lubricated by a strong national currency—was indispensable to their prosperity.[24] An overwhelming majority of Whig congressmen and editors from all sections preferred a strong bank.[25]

[21] Nathan Appleton to Rives, June 7, 1841, Rives Papers; Edward Cruft to George Newbold, June 8, 1841, George Newbold Papers, New York Historical Society, New York, N.Y. (hereafter cited as NYHS); George Curtis to James F. Simmons, June 14, 1841, James F. Simmons Papers, LC; *New York Herald*, June 15, 24, 1841; *New York Commercial Advertiser*, June 16, 1841; *Boston Atlas*, June 23, 24, 1841.

[22] Webster to Ketchum, July 17, 1841, *Writings*, 16:351.

[23] Davis to Webster, April 23, 1841, Daniel Webster Papers, LC.

[24] Charles G. Sellers, Jr. ("Who Were the Southern Whigs?" *American Historical Review*, 59 [January, 1954]:335-46), notes the increasing dependence of Whig planters on Southern merchants, who in turn favored more fluid cash arrangements than did the planters.

[25] Party cohesion on the bank issue was strong among Whigs of both houses of the Twenty-seventh Congress. See Silbey, *The Shrine of Party*, pp. 52-53; and Alexander, *Sectional Stress*,

Against this uncommon resolve of Whig congressmen and cadres, and against the near-paranoid determination of Clay to see his personal plan triumph, Webster and the cabinet had only minimal and unstable advantages. They had the temporary trust and support of a weak president. They had his unpopular but potent threat to veto any stronger bank. They had the blessings of a few Whig newspapers, including the influential, if placid, *Washington National Intelligencer*. Most important, though, they had support from a small group of Whigs in the Senate who opposed an "old-fashioned" bank. The slim Whig majority in the Senate included a handful whose defection would doom any Clay measure.[26]

To Webster fell the difficult and thankless work of persuading his colleagues that they must swallow the bank proposed by the president. Webster's main obstacle was that most Whigs simply disbelieved that Tyler would dare to flaunt their wishes.

The sultry weeks of June and July in Washington made few of the sweltering congressmen more reasonable about the bank dispute, and Clay encouraged Whig bravado. All of the Kentuckian's maneuvers and statements exuded confidence that the president would yield. Clay drew out Tyler's views by soliciting a bank proposal from Secretary of the Treasury Thomas Ewing in early June. Ewing submitted the plan endorsed by Tyler and the cabinet to the Congress, whereupon Clay promptly arranged for carefully chosen House and Senate committees to recommend his own plan over Ewing's. Clay's bill called for a bank established in Washington, which would have the unqualified power to establish branches and perform banking functions wherever it wished. Intense pressure fell on Whig holdouts in the Senate to accede to Clay's bank bill.[27] Meanwhile, all intimations that the president might veto the bill were suppressed or brushed aside. Some denied that Tyler had

---

pp. 38–48. For evidence of overwhelming Southern Whig support for the party's position on the bank, see Silbey's appendix on the "Finance" scale position of Southern Whig congressmen, *The Shrine of Party*, pp. 155–65. Alexander computes the percentage of Whigs from the South Atlantic and South Central states who voted with the party on roll-call votes in the House of Representatives. Southern Whigs in the Twenty-seventh Congress consistently voted with the party on critical votes dealing with Whig bank bills. See Alexander, *Sectional Stress* pp. 155–59, Table 27–8, especially the " 'Yes' Percent" of South Atlantic and South Central Whigs for the following crucial votes: roll-call code numbers 25, 61, 63, 64, 65, 82, 83, 84, 85, 86, 117. Votes 65 and 86 were the final ballots on the two bank bills of the session.

[26] Using roll calls, newspapers, and letters, Poage has brilliantly dissected the fragile parliamentary position of the Whig majority in the Senate; See his *Henry Clay*, 41–42, 46–47. Whigs in and out of Congress were fully aware in June that they lacked the numbers in the Senate to pass a strong bank bill; see, for example, the *New York Herald*, June 21, 1841.

[27] Poage, *Henry Clay*, pp. 43–46; *New York Herald*, June 21, 1841.

hinted at any such step; others intoned that senatorial independence rendered speculation on the president's views out of order.[28]

Webster's newspaper and congressional spokesmen confronted these false hopes with insistence that the Ewing bill would work and that Tyler would veto any other. The pentultimate expression of the Webster-cabinet position came on July 2, when Rufus Choate, Webster's replacement in the Senate, predicted that the Clay bill would never become law. Choate, a distinguished constitutional lawyer, added that he saw nothing in the original Ewing proposal that surrendered Congress' theoretical power to establish a national bank. Choate further declared—speaking with all the authority of the representative of the mercantile and manufacturing interests of Massachusetts—that he was confident the Ewing bank would gain the necessary subscription of funds from the nation's capitalists.

Reinforced by similar editorials in pro-Webster papers and by private missives that Tyler "cannot—& will not sign" Clay's bill, Choate's arguments punctured the aura of hope Clay had sought to create for his bank and goaded the Kentuckian into a venomous counterattack. Cross-examining his fellow senator as one would a witness in court, Clay demanded to know the source of Choate's certainty that Tyler would veto Clay's bill. Choate insisted that his was a judgment based simply on "notorious and . . . decisive indications" and that delicacy allowed him to divulge no more, but Clay had made his point. The issue transcended the bank; congressional Whigs allegedly faced a full-fledged crisis of executive tyranny.[29]

Despite the confrontation of Clay and Webster's Senate spokesman, which openly broadened and exacerbated the issue between the Whig party and the Whig president, the debate changed no votes, and Clay remained short of the necessary Senate majority to pass his bank bill. The stalemate of early July seemed to mark the juncture for Webster to act as conciliator between the congressional Whigs and the president. He had remained loyal to Tyler throughout the crisis[30] and had used his small but critical influence to thwart Clay's plans and rebut attacks on the president. Dismayed and exhausted, many congressional Whigs seemed ready to accept a compromise along the lines of the Ewing bill

[28]U.S., Congress, *Congressional Globe*, 27th Cong., 1st sess., 1841, app., pp. 355–61.

[29]*Ibid.*, p. 145.

[30]Silas Wright to Van Buren, June 21, 1841, Martin Van Buren Papers, LC; Rufus Choate to Davis, June 27, 1841, Davis Papers. Choate reported that "Mr. Webster particularly and the President are on the best of terms."

and to get on with the rest of the Whig program.[31] Though some murmured, few yet believed that Tyler was a "tyrant," and Webster hardly thought that his party would manufacture a break from the president on the "usurpation" issue when accommodation on a bank was possible.

Webster did what he could to end the stalemate. He, other cabinet members, and all available officeholders continued to ply Whig congressmen with pleas to accept the Ewing bill. Finally, on July 16 and 17, the Whig secretary of state appealed publicly to the Whigs of Congress and to the country to support compromise. In two letters released to the Whig press, Webster insisted that some bank compromise was inevitable, and that the plan proposed by the secretary of the treasury was a fair one. Admittedly, the Ewing bill sacrificed the "useful" power of a national bank to create branches at will, but was the power in question "absolutely essential"? Would a bank without it be "good for nothing"? Was it better that the Whigs "should have no bank"? Those who seemed in "such hot haste to ride rough-shod over the . . . opinions of the President" thought yes. But Webster begged his comrades to accept a bank plan that was *"practicable* and *attainable."* The "one salvation of the Whig party," Webster pleaded, was *"union,* immediate UNION," behind the Ewing compromise.[32]

But it was Clay, not Webster, who broke the Whig deadlock. As Webster appealed for party compromise, Clay appealed for party loyalty, and by July 23 the skillful senator not only had regained control over the wavering among Whig regulars but had finally maneuvered the remaining intransigents into line.

Bold steps brought Clay mastery. The bulk of the Whig press, following the line of their Washington correspondents, issued denials that Clay was dictatorial and exonerated his ardor on the grounds that he and the party were "surrounded" by *"treachery."* Tyler and his friends were plotting to *"break up"* the Whig party, Whig papers alleged. The defeat of the bank and other measures would prove the party unable to redeem *"its solemn pledge to the people,"* and the Whigs would crumble in impotence.[33] When intimidation failed to move the Whig recalcitrants, Clay took spurious but decisive steps toward accommodation. He made known his intention to offer a "compromise" amendment but kept the details of his measure from states'-rights senators. Secrecy was

---

[31] Poage, *Henry Clay*, p. 58.
[32] Webster to Hiram Ketchum, July 16, 17, 1841, *Writings*, 16:354–51.
[33] Poage, *Henry Clay*, pp. 59–61.

wise, for Clay's actual proposal conceded precious little. His amendment did permit state assent to bank branches, but it also stipulated that the assent of a state would be "presumed" unless its legislature, acting within an allotted time, explicitly denied permission for the bank to branch in its domain. In principle, Clay's was a major concession to state review of federal law. In practice, his amendment required unanimity among the three branches of any state government to reject a bank branch. A state governor, house, or senate in favor of a bank branch could block rejection and permit state assent to be "presumed." When Congressman John Minor Botts of Virginia sounded Tyler out on Clay's plan, he rejected it as a deception. But Botts apparently misled the Whig caucus into thinking Tyler approved the Clay "compromise." The president's "pledge" and Clay's pressures worked, and the Whig caucus accepted the Kentuckian's solution.[34]

Once the Clay compromise was made public, it became evident that Tyler would dissent, but Clay was now in control of his party. Meeting again, the Whig caucus considered the probability of a veto and decided to force the issue. The consent of the holdouts apparently was won through an understanding that, should Tyler veto Clay's compromise bill, the party would pass the bank plan endorsed by the cabinet and the president six weeks before. The clear design was to discredit Tyler once and for all. Approval of Clay's bill would doom him with the Democrats. A veto of Clay's bill would isolate him from the Whigs, sensitive as the party was to abuse of the presidential veto. Whatever the outcome, the Whig principle of congressional supremacy would prevail. Either the Whigs would win their bank or they would yield to Tyler's alternative bank plan under duress and out of solicitude for the country. The caucus finally agreed, and the Clay measure passed the Senate on July 27 by a vote of 25 to 24, succeeding because of the absences or reluctant yeas of three Whigs opposed to the measure. The Whigs had at last legislated a national bank.

II

Passage of the Clay bank bill had consequences that were greater than the Whigs had calculated. Designed either to secure a good bank or to gain a lesser one while discrediting the president, the Whigs' action left Tyler with the sense of a man betrayed. Advice from fellow states'-rights men to trust no Whigs and to make no concessions, advice once

[34] *Ibid.*, pp. 63-66.

rejected, now seemed painfully justified. The cabinet which he had trusted had proved its impotence. Embittered, Tyler not only pondered a veto but for the first time weighed the possibility of casting his lot with a new party. Not just Clay's bank, but the whole, futile process of conciliating the Whigs came under review. In such a mood Tyler edged toward withdrawal of his support for the Ewing bank bill[35] —support on which the congressional Whigs had counted.

In the circumstances, the influence of Webster and the cabinet with the president plummeted. Privately, Webster yearned for Tyler to reconcile the Clay bill with his scruples—the administration would then "go on swimmingly"—but, to preserve what favor he had with the president, Webster voluntarily agreed to advise on the issue only if asked.[36] He was consulted little, and between Senate passage of Clay's bill on July 25 and Tyler's final decision around August 11, he had almost no inkling of the outcome. Hopeful but isolated throughout the critical two weeks, Webster, as late as August 10, though Tyler might sign.[37] Tyler's apparent indecision gave grounds for Webster's hopes, but the president's agony was feigned. Tyler's son reported that his father had never been "ass" enough to consider approval, and Tyler himself later told his cabinet he had postponed an immediate veto largely to retain their support.[38] The cabinet, however, convinced that Tyler's dilemma was authentic, sought one more time in a five-hour meeting on August 11 to persuade Tyler to sign. Tyler seemed to waver under the force of their arguments, but Ewing left the session "sick at heart," and even Webster emerged "almost discouraged." Two days later Webster's son reported that a veto was certain. The cabinet had failed.[39]

The real scope of the failure of the cabinet to reconcile the president and congressional Whigs did not become evident, however, until word leaked on August 15 of the substance of the impending veto message. Under the influence of his Virginia advisers, Tyler had hardened his stand. His objection to the Clay bill now came not only "on the *old trouble of Branches*," as Fletcher Webster and most other Whigs antici-

[35]Tyler to N. Beverly Tucker, July [25], 1841, Tyler Papers, LC.

[36]Webster to Everett, July 29, 1841; and Webster to Caroline LeRoy Webster, August 8, 1841; *Writings*, 18:106-8.

[37]R. M. Blatchford to Seward, August 8, 9, 10, 1841, Seward Papers.

[38]Poage, *Henry Clay*, p. 70; "The Diary of Thomas Ewing, August and September, 1841," *American Historical Review*, 18 (October, 1912):99.

[39]James Bowen to Seward, August 11, 1841; and Christopher Morgan to Seward, August 11, 1841; Seward Papers.

pated on August 13.[40] Tyler had found a more fundamental flaw. The Whig measure allowed the District and branch banks to make "local discounts," or, as Tyler understood and used the term, to make local loans.[41] Tyler objected to empowering bank branches to make loans. The power to lend permitted branches of the federal bank to compete for borrowers with banks chartered by the states—including many banks in the South which had actually been created, and were partly owned, by state governments. More important, in the past, the power of a national bank and its branches to lend had brought "enormous" inflation and had proved "a fruitful source of favoritism and corruption."[42] But, to Whigs, local loans were vital to any national bank which hoped to regulate the credit of the country. By increasing or curtailing its loans, a bank increased or reduced the amount of credit available. Seemingly, Tyler meant to eviscerate the regulatory power of a national bank. Under Tyler's new dictum, not only Clay's bank bill was vetoed. The Ewing bill, which had presumed a bank's authority to regulate the currency and had granted the power of local discount, now also was unacceptable.

Congressional Whigs, who caucused the night of August 15, now faced an unexpected and knotty problem. The original Whig strategy had called for prompt passage of the Ewing bill in the event of a veto, but word of Tyler's hardened position seemed to preclude the Ewing bank. After heated discussion, filled with acrimony against Tyler, the caucus resolved to ignore the rumors and hold Tyler to the bank measure he had sanctioned in June. If he vetoed "his own bill," the cabinet would resign and the president would be read out of the party. If he signed, Whigs believed that the difficulties of gaining state assent would quickly doom the Ewing bank and force Tyler to approve a measure similar to the one he had just vetoed.[43] Either way, Tyler would look like an idiot, and congressional Whigs would be vindicated.

With the president and his party bent on collision, only one slim hope for harmony remained. Tyler still wished somehow to avoid a rupture with the Whigs. In individual talks with Webster and other cabinet members on the morning of Monday, August 16, the day of his

---

[40] Fletcher Webster to Hiram Ketchum, August 13, 1841, Webster Papers, LC. Tyler did find the branching provision of the Clay bank bill unacceptable. See Tyler's "Veto Message, August 15, 1841," Richardson, *Messages and Papers of the Presidents*, 4:66–67.

[41] Tyler used interchangeably the terms "local discount" and "local accommodation." "Accommodation" was the ante-bellum term for loan. Richardson, *Messages and Papers of the Presidents*, 4:64–65.

[42] *Ibid.*, p. 65.

[43] Poage, *Henry Clay*, p. 79.

veto, he assured them that a bank was still possible. He asked for their help, and his plea won their tacit pledge not to resign. *"Cool & Steady* is the word," wrote Webster's son after his father reported on the morning's "gratifying" interview with Tyler.[44] Webster, more than eager to help in the work of harmony, had no specific plan to resolve the differences between Tyler and the Whigs but sensed that "good feelings" were critical. He had already planned a "man-party" for Monday evening to calm Whig tempers and he now redoubled his efforts. That afternoon he drafted an article for the next day's *Washington National Intelligencer* which called for Whig "calmness, considerateness and patriotism." He made a similar plea to the lubricated Whigs that evening. More "earnest and eloquent" than one listener "had ever heard him," Webster called for union to "restore and invigorate the Whig party."[45]

Webster's champagne succeeded in cooling Whig rancor for the moment, but of ultimate importance were the efforts of his cabinet colleague, John J. Crittenden, to devise a new bank plan. As Crittenden reviewed Tyler's veto, he detected a way out of the morass. The president had banned "local discounts," but Whigs could construe his meaning narrowly. They could interpret local discount to mean not all forms of lending but that one form of loan by which a bank gave a borrower its bank notes in return for interest and his promise to pay.[46] Such an interpretation of Tyler's language would permit a national bank to engage in other, slightly more complicated forms of lending. One such form, important to merchants who sought credit, was a bank's purchase of a bill of exchange. A bill of exchange was simply a written promise to pay later for goods already delivered. By getting a bank to purchase a bill of exchange, the merchant in effect got a loan which lasted from the time he delivered the goods until the date payment was promised on them. If Tyler accepted the subterfuge, Crittenden expected that the "moneyed transactions of men" would simply be "put into the shape of bills of exchange."[47] Bank branches with the power to deal in bills of exchange would be able to give, curtail, and control credit.

[44] Fletcher Webster to Ketchum, August 16, 1841, Webster Papers, LC.

[45] Harriet A. Weed, ed., *Autobiography of Thurlow Weed* (Boston: Houghton Mifflin & Co., 1883), pp. 508–9.

[46] Today, of course, banks give loans in the government-printed currency, the dollar. In the absence of a national paper currency, ante-bellum bankers printed and lent their own bank notes. Banks usually took out the interest due them in advance and allotted less than the full amount of the loan. Hence the term "discount" was used for "loan."

[47] Crittenden to Clay, August 16, 1841; and Crittenden to Chapman Coleman, August 25, 1841; Crittenden Papers, Duke. See also Poage, *Henry Clay*, p. 81. Poage implicates the entire

Crittenden moved to win Tyler's assent to his scheme. He first suggested to Clay that the Kentuckian draft a new bank bill which permitted branches everywhere to trade in bills of exchange. Though Clay declined, sensing that his authorship would only make the bill unpalatable to Tyler, he arranged for Alexander H. H. Stuart, a congressman from Virginia, to discuss the plan with Tyler.

Desperate for a graceful way out of his predicament and unaware of the subterfuge involved in the bank proposal, Tyler was enthusiastic. Penciling in one amendment, he told Stuart: "If you can be instrumental in passing this bill through Congress, I will esteem you the best friend I have on earth." Tyler would "sign it in twenty-four hours."[48] The president asked Stuart to see Webster at once, and with him to work out the details of the bill and seek its acceptance by the party. Stuart found Webster away from his lodgings, left his card, and sped to his congressional colleagues, who quickly agreed to the plan. John Berrien of the Senate and John Sergeant of the House made arrangements to discuss the new bill with Tyler the next morning.[49]

By the morning of Tuesday, August 17, however, Tyler's enthusiasm for the proposal had vanished, and the Whig conferees found him remote and vague. Just what had dampened Tyler's ardor is unclear. There is no evidence that he yet understood that the bill merely evaded the intent of his veto. More likely, his sense of mistrust and isolation, never far beneath the surface, was rekindled the previous night by the shouted insults of an antiveto "mob" on the White House porch.[50]

With Tyler's judgment now fluctuating by the hour, speed, reassurance, and the utmost tact were vital to putting the party-saving bank bill through. Webster and Ewing played a decisive role in calming the president and regaining his support for the new measure. At the cabinet meeting of Wednesday the eighteenth, they found Tyler by his own admission "bewildered," irritable, and inclined to postpone the whole bank matter. But patiently Ewing drew from the president his terms for a bank. He would accept a bill which authorized Congress to establish a bank and bank branches with the power "to deal in Bills of Exchange." Furthermore, if the proposed bank were confined to trading in bills of

---

cabinet in the Crittenden scheme, but Ewing's "Diary" and Webster's private "Memorandum" on the bank crisis suggest that neither shared in the origin of the proposals. Crittenden, and possibly Secretary of War John Bell, seemed solely responsible.

[48]"Statement" of A. H. H. Stuart, cited in *Letters of the Tylers*, 2:78-79.

[49]Poage, *Henry Clay*, pp. 80-81.

[50]"The Diary of Thomas Ewing," p. 99.

exchange, Tyler would approve a bill which created bank branches even "without assent of the States."[51]

Instantly Webster intervened to seal the bargain. In language certain to satisfy the states'-rights president, he told Tyler why he "would like such a bill." The power of local discount, which Tyler found "abominable" and "unnecessary" in a bank, Webster also found unnecessary and probably unconstitutional. The power of dealing in exchanges, which Tyler was willing to grant, Webster found "necessary" to any bank. Webster said that Tyler was wise in foregoing the requirement of state assent to bank branches, for the states could not deny Congress a constitutional power it already had or grant Congress a power it lacked.

Webster's approval of the new proposal reassured the president. Expressing "acquiescence in the views of Mr. Webster," he asked the cabinet to "see that the Bill should assume that form" and agreed from that point on to let the cabinet handle negotiations with the Whigs in Congress.[52]

Whether or not Webster thought the distracted president meant or comprehended his new commitment to a bank is open to question. Perhaps, as lawyers, Webster and Ewing believed that Tyler knew what he was doing when he bargained for his latest bank. Webster certainly went over the bank bill as if it were a contract; after the cabinet adjourned, he and Tyler scrutinized the proposal item by item. Webster could not help but notice, however, that the president hesitated even after he seemed satisfied with the bill. Tyler dispatched Webster to the capitol to "state" the changes that would win his signature—but only on the condition that Webster do so without "committing or pledging him" or "professing to speak by his authority."[53]

Webster moved swiftly to bring the congressional Whigs and the president together on the proposal Tyler had approved. By nightfall Webster had won Whig acceptance of the measure. He returned to the White House to confirm Tyler's commitment. The two men read over the plan together, Webster recalled, and attention "was of course particularly drawn to the provision" allowing the bank to deal in bills of exchange. Tyler "expressed no objection," nor did he make any "mention of the necessity of State assent." When the president did insist that

[51] *Ibid.*, pp. 100–101.

[52] *Ibid.*

[53] Webster's account of the negotiations is contained in his "Memorandum" on the 1841 bank crises, a manuscript in the Webster Papers, LC. Though undated, Webster's account was written during or soon after the events it describes. It was clearly meant to detail his role in the crises for posterity. As far as I know, it has not been cited before.

the measure not "be called a Bank," Webster "sat down at his call, struck out Bank & wrote the Title [Fiscal Agent] as it finally passed."[54] The President suggested "no other alteration whatsoever" and asked Webster to prepare a defense of the bank bill, presumably to be used in his message of approval. Webster immediately returned to Capitol Hill and secured the desired changes in the measure.[55] Despite Tyler's caution not to commit him, Webster confidently pledged that the president would approve the bill.[56]

To Webster, the fate of the measure now turned on the mood of the Whigs and the president. With minimal good faith and calm, Tyler would sign, and rupture would be averted. If tempers flared again, Webster could not speak for Tyler or the outcome.

Henry Clay shattered what calm there was when the Senate opened discussion of Tyler's veto of the Kentuckian's bank bill on August 19. Clay began his speech on Tyler's veto with restraint, but let himself go when Senator Rives of Virginia came to Tyler's defense. Compulsively, Clay vented all his rancor and suspicion. A cabal was at work in the capital. "Bitter, systematic, determined, [and] uncompromising," they schemed to break up the Whigs and "to form a third party."[57]

More decisive than Clay's outburst, however, was the disclosure on the afternoon of the nineteenth of a letter which confirmed all the warnings whispered to Tyler about the motives of the Whigs.[58] John Minor Botts, the hot-headed Whig congressman from Virginia, wrote an arrogant and disparaging letter about Tyler to the "coffee house" in Richmond, where such communiqués were customarily posted for all to read. Notwithstanding that "our Captain Tyler" was "making a desperate effort to set himself up with the *loco-focos*," Botts reported, the country would "get a bank bill." But the new bank plan pending before Congress would, Botts indiscreetly and perhaps inaccurately boasted, make Tyler "an object of execration with both parties"—"with the one for vetoing our bill . . . [and] the other for signing a worse one."[59]

---

[54]*Ibid.* Tyler asked also that the bank's capital be reduced from thirty million to twenty million. The final version authorized twenty-one million.

[55]*Ibid.* Both Tyler and Webster publicly denied that Webster had brought a copy of the bill for Tyler's scrutiny. See Tyler's "Statement," *Letters of the Tylers,* 2:98-99. Tyler needed the excuse of not having seen the final bill in order to exonerate his later veto of it; Webster felt obliged to support his chief. Webster's private "Memorandum" proves conclusively that Tyler did see and approve the bill before it went to Congress.

[56]Clay to Clayton, November 1, 1841, John M. Clayton Papers, LC.

[57]Poage, *Henry Clay,* pp. 73-77.

[58]*Letters of the Tylers,* 2:113-14.

[59]Botts's letter of August 16, 1841, is reprinted in *ibid.,* p. 112.

The Democratic press promptly published Botts's letter, and, when Tyler saw it, his frayed nerves snapped. So this was the upshot of all his efforts to appease the Whig party. Enraged, he burst into Webster's State Department office the next morning and ranted for an hour "of the ill-treatment which he recd. from Mr. Botts & other Whigs. He appeared full of suspicion & resentment," Webster recorded. "I began to fear another veto." By the twenty-third, Tyler had told everyone he could buttonhole that he would "have his right [arm] cut off, & his left arm too," before he would sign the new bank bill.[60] Compromise had collapsed. The end was near.

III

The next two weeks were the denouement to the disruption of the Whig party. On August 24 Tyler asked Webster to get the entire bank matter postponed, and Webster agreed to do what he could. He entreated every Whig who would listen and put his arguments into formal letters to the Whig senators from Massachusetts, which were published on August 25. In two letters Webster urged the Whig party to show its good faith by denouncing the Botts letter, by rebuking any "intimation" that Whigs sought "to embarrass the President," and by suspending the bank issue until the regular session of Congress in November.[61] Privately, Webster reported to his cabinet colleagues that Tyler was "deranged" on the bank question and won their temporary aid in trying to avert passage of the bill the president had initially approved.[62]

Webster's efforts to hold the party together failed. Clay pressed on with the bank measure, determined to settle the issue of personal and congressional supremacy once and for all. He now carried with him even the few Whigs who were still reluctant to ostracize the president. As Clay persisted, Tyler openly began to prepare for the resignation of his cabinet and for the replacement of Harrison's appointees with more congenial allies. Word of Tyler's cabinet negotiations added fuel to the view that he had planned treachery all along.

Desperate efforts by others to ward off disaster also failed,[63] and, after the Whigs passed what they claimed was Tyler's bank bill on September 3, disruption between the president and his party was certain. Webster and his cabinet colleagues faced their last, cruel choice. Should they stay or leave? Ewing, ruminating in his diary, probed the

[60] Webster," Memorandum," n.d., Webster Papers, LC.
[61] Webster to Messrs. Bates and Choate, Senators from Massachusetts, August 25, 1841, *Writings*, 16:355-56.
[62] Ewing to [Crittenden], December 6, 1842, Crittenden Papers, Duke.
[63] "The Diary of Thomas Ewing," pp. 110-11.

issues incisively. With the exception of Crittenden and Badger, he and the rest of the cabinet felt that Clay had provoked the breach with the president. Impervious to reason and oblivious to the consequences, Clay had plunged headlong to isolate Tyler and Webster and to win undisputed control of the Whigs. Despite Ewing's judgment that Clay's motives had been narrow and selfish, the Kentuckian's success seemed to leave the Whig cabinet no choice but to resign. Those who stayed after a second veto would be charged with vain "love of office." Worse, they would be forced to associate with the few friends Tyler had left, "persons whom we did not esteem and whose political principles were averse to ours . . . . We would be made the constant object of attack by the papers on both sides in politics, and probably be at last compelled to resign or be displaced, with injured characters, and minds sour and discontented."[64]

Understandably, Webster did not perceive the future as clearly as did Ewing. Sleepless and bitter, he saw only that Clay at every point had obstructed a settlement with the president. Quite rightly, he felt that he as much as Tyler had been the target of Clay's vendetta. If he left Tyler, he would bow to his rival, leave the wronged president in isolation, and complete Clay's work of destruction.[65] In office, at least, the secretary of state could get on with the unfinished diplomatic work of reconciliation with Great Britain—a task which also provided a plausible excuse for remaining. Perhaps, too, he could still serve as a bridge between the president and the Whigs. Just as unwilling as Tyler was to subordinate his personal will to the demands of party, Webster consummately understood the feelings of the president toward the ordeal of the past months.

Webster decided to cast his lot with Tyler. With the resignations of all his colleagues on Tyler's desk, he approached his leader on the afternoon of September 11 and raised the topic of his own future. Tyler was cordial but noncommittal, and finally Webster asked: "Where am I to go, Mr. President?"

"You must decide that for yourself, Mr. Webster," Tyler replied.

Seizing the opening, Webster answered: "If you leave it to me . . . , I will stay where I am."

Tyler rose, extended an open hand, and replied, "Give me your hand on that, and . . . I will say to you that Henry Clay is a doomed man from this hour."[66]

---

[64] *Ibid.*, p. 106.

[65] Manuscript diary of Phillip R. Fendall, September 23, 1841, Phillip R. Fendall Papers, Duke University Library, Durham, N.C.

[66] *Letters of the Tylers*, 2:121–22; italics omitted.

Whether Clay or Webster was doomed by the secretary's decision time would reveal. For the moment, Whig discipline and Clay's rule were transcendent. Never had Congress and the press of the Whig party been so united on issues or a single leader. Most Whigs expected the price of achieving that unity—the ostracism of John Tyler—to be minute. Webster had no more prescience than others, but throughout the ordeal he intuitively suspected otherwise. Ominous confirmation of his judgment came almost instantly. Among the first communications of the repudiated president to his secretary of state was an inquiry about the practicability of annexing the slaveholding Republic of Texas.[67]

[67]Tyler to Webster, October 11, 1841, Webster Papers, LC.

VIII

OUTCAST

THE SOLE SURVIVOR of the original Harrison cabinet, Webster, in electing to remain with Tyler, embarked on one of the great gambles of his career. The secretary of state was now not only dedicated to restoring amity between the United States and Great Britain. He was also determined to see the rebuked administration vindicate itself before the country and regain the leadership of the Whig party. As partisans on both sides obstructed his goals, Webster increasingly saw his venture as a higher test—a test of "practical statesmanship" against the "rancor, recklessness, & animosity" seemingly endemic to party politics. Webster meant to prove that "really patriotic feeling," that "candor, moderation, & conciliation," could conquer the "elements of discord" which parties exploited and bring the nation a "repose and reconciliation" which partisanship deliberately denied it.[1] But the test

[1] U.S., Congress, *House Documents*, 27th Cong., 2nd sess., December 21, 1841, H. Doc. 20 ("Letter from the Secretary of the Treasury, Accompanied by a Draught of a Bill for the Establishment of a Board of Exchequer at the Seat of Government, with Agencies, &c."), p. 13; Webster to Everett, May 31 and August 25, 1842, Edward Everett Papers, Massachusetts Historical Society, Boston (hereafter cited as MHS); Webster to Fletcher Webster, November 12, 1842, Daniel Webster Papers, Dartmouth College, Hanover, N.H. The "letter" from Walter Forward, secretary of the treasury, was, in fact, written by Webster. Richard M. Blatchford to Seward, December 20, 1841, William Henry Seward Papers, University of Rochester, Rochester, N.Y.

of "statesmanship"—like Webster's earlier efforts to overcome the evils and trammels of party in 1825 and again in 1833—involved great risk. Success turned on a rebirth of moderation among the Whigs and on temperate action by the president. Over neither did Webster have control.

I

Whatever the president's purpose in the fall of 1841, Webster's clear interest, and almost impossible task, was to keep his ties with both Tyler and the Whig party. Loyalty to Tyler he demonstrated at once. The two had a "long and friendly" talk as soon as Webster asked to remain with Tyler, and shortly thereafter Webster wrote a rebuttal to the published recriminations of resigning cabinet members. Webster found the departures unwarranted and even implied they were part of a Whig plot to embarrass and isolate the president.[2] Privately, Webster informed officeholders that he would suffer no neutrals in the contest with Clay. "There was war," he told one Whig appointee; "Mr. Tyler must know his friends."[3] Meanwhile, Webster did his best to make the new cabinet acceptable to the Whigs. Initially, he sought to persuade Francis Granger of New York and Thomas Ewing of Ohio to stay on.[4] Failing that, he sought to convince Supreme Court Justice John McLean, a Whig of inflated stature because of his imagined following in the West, to come in as secretary of war.[5] McLean declined.

Tyler consulted Webster on the new appointments and apparently abided by their understanding that all should be Whigs of some stamp. Charles Wickliffe, leader of the anti-Clay Whigs of Kentucky, was named the new postmaster-general; John C. Spencer, a member of the anti-Clay Whig faction of New York, became secretary of war; Walter Forward of Pennsylvania was promoted from comptroller to secretary of the treasury. The secretary of the navy, Abel P. Upshur, and the attorney general, Hugh S. Legare, were Southern, states'-rights Whigs who had joined the party in the mid-1830s. No Democrats were asked

[2]Daniel Webster, "The Resignations from President Tyler's Cabinet," draft of an editorial for the *Washington Madisonian*, September 25, 1841, *The Writings and Speeches of Daniel Webster*, ed. J. W. McIntyre, 18 vols. (Boston: Little, Brown & Co., 1903), 15:137–39 (hereafter cited as *Writings*).

[3]Manuscript diary of Phillip R. Fendall, September 23, 1841, Phillip R. Fendall Papers, Duke University Library, Durham, N.C.

[4]Samuel Blatchford to Seward, September 12, 1841; and Weed to Seward, September 13, 1841; Seward Papers.

[5]John McLean to Webster, September 18, 1841, Daniel Webster Papers, George F. Hoar Collection, MHS.

or appointed to the group. Though the president exaggerated in claiming that his new officers, like their chief, were "all original Jackson men,"[6] those who wished Tyler well thought the cabinet had foiled the hotspurs of both parties. Thurlow Weed reported that the "new Whig Cabinet" took the ultras "*all aback*." The new appointments confirmed that "John Tyler is a good Whig and intends to be hereafter."[7]

Tyler coupled the naming of a Whig cabinet with an explicit appeal to the Whigs for a moratorium. Well aware that Whigs believed they had been betrayed, he asked them not to press their momentary "differences of opinion" to a final rupture. The Whig Congress, Tyler stated in his message vetoing the second bank on September 11, had distinguished itself by "an immense mass of labor at a season very unfavorable both to health and action"; the Whigs had passed numerous "laws . . . beneficial to the country." It had been Tyler's "good fortune and pleasure to concur with them in all measures except" the bank bill. Should "our difference on this alone be pushed to extremes"? The president's "anxious desire [was] that it should not be." Tyler solicited Whig suffrance until the regular session of Congress in November. Delay would give him "time to prepare and submit a definitive [bank] recommendation" of his own, and the party could then judge his fidelity. In the interim he asked only for Whig "moderation."[8]

But congressional Whigs were in no mood to be moderate, and on September 15 acted to bar any reconciliation with Tyler. The fifty or so Whigs who remained in Washington after the adjournment of Congress approved a "Manifesto" formally expelling the president from the party.[9] Though Tyler editors quickly noted that the Whig caucus represented only a fraction of the party,[10] most Whigs accepted the manifesto's verdict that Tyler was a traitor and the renewed appeal against "executive tyranny." The Whigs thus wrote off a new bank for the duration of Tyler's administration and chose instead self-exoneration and unity at Tyler's expense. Senator Silas Wright, a Democrat, wryly observed that the Whigs seemed "made for a minority."[11]

[6] Tyler to Thomas A. Cooper, October 8, 1841, Tyler to Tazewell, October 11, 1841, John Tyler Papers, Library of Congress, Washington, D.C. (hereafter cited as LC).

[7] Blatchford to Seward, September 12, 1841; and Weed to Seward, September 13, 1841; Seward Papers.

[8] James D. Richardson, comp., *A Compilation of the Messages and Papers of the Presidents, 1789-1905*, 11 vols. (Washington, D.C.: Bureau of National Literature and Art, 1907), 4:71-72; *Washington Madisonian*, September 11, 1841.

[9] *Boston Courier*, September 15, 1841; *Washington Madisonian*, September 16, 21, 1841.

[10] *Washington Madisonian*, September 16, 21, 1841.

[11] Silas Wright to Azariah Flagg, December 19, 1841, Azariah C. Flagg Papers, New York Public Library, New York, N.Y. (hereafter cited as NYPL).

None felt the ugly temper of the party more than Webster. Even those who acquiesced in his staying in the cabinet told him that he must quiet suspicions that "you intend to connect yourself permanently with [Tyler's] fortunes, to separate yourself from your late associates, & even to add your name & influence & personal aid in justifying him & condemning them." Unless Webster somehow made it "plain . . . that you retained your relations to the President at his request, in opposition to your own impulses, & only with a view to a temporary emergency," he would be treated with even "less indulgence" than Tyler.[12]

Webster, of course, did no such thing and paid heavily for his independence. His former friend and cabinet colleague, John Crittenden, thought Webster's decision to remain with Tyler inexcusable. He found it a "degradation," to be explained only by a "disposition . . . to cling to office with a spirit altogether ignoble in a man of his intellect & reputation."[13] Bostonians were no less severe; Webster clung to power, many thought, "because he is bankrupt in everything, pennyless [sic] & dependent."[14] By January, 1842, Crittenden reported that "Webster's condition" had become "even worse than Tyler's. . . . I hear him spoken of by members of Congress as one of the 'most profligate men in the Nation.' " "Clay and his clique," observed a Jacksonian editor at the end of January, hated Webster "more than . . . the Democrats."[15] Talk of Webster's treachery soon found its way into the columns of the pro-Clay Whig press. The message was the same everywhere. To be Tyler's friend was to be the Whigs' enemy. There was no middle ground.

Notwithstanding Whig rebuffs, to carve out a middle ground remained the strategy of Tyler and Webster. Tyler believed he could yet foil the partisans if he could devise a bank plan which compromised the demands of both parties. Acting with a resilience he had lacked in his months of strife with the Whigs, he prepared to "accommodate" his "views to [a plan] which is likely to unite the greatest numbers in its

---

[12]Winthrop to Webster, September 13, 1841, copy, Robert C. Winthrop Papers, MHS.

[13]Crittenden to Robert P. Letcher, September 13, 1841, John Jordan Crittenden Papers, Duke University Library, Durham, N.C.

[14]George Bancroft to William L. Marcy, November 4, 1841, Miscellaneous Letters, New York State Library, Albany.

[15]Crittenden to Robert P. Letcher, January 9, 1841, Crittenden Papers, Duke. See also John P. Kennedy to Robert C. Winthrop, October 16 and November 19, 1841, Winthrop Papers; Francis P. Blair to Jackson, January 18, 1842, *The Correspondence of Andrew Jackson*, ed. John Spencer Bassett, 7 vols. (Washington, D.C.: Carnegie Institute of Washington, 1926-35), 6:136 (hereafter cited as *The Correspondence of Andrew Jackson*).

support." Whatever his personal thoughs on hard money and paper currency—and he confessed that "society might have been much happier" without the system of credit—the president admitted by December that the "practical statesman" had "to look at things as they are, to take them as he finds them, to supply deficiencies and to prune excesses as far as" he could. For a "public man" to hew to private scruple in the face of the "inexpressibly great" need to regulate the currency would be "folly." Consulting and meditating through October and November, Tyler sought a bank proposal which would win acceptance from both parties or force both to bear the onus of delaying economic relief to the country for partisan ends.[16]

By December, Tyler had matured and his cabinet had approved a plan for a "Bank of Exchequer." The president asked Webster to draft the official administration defense of the compromise bank, and Webster, sitting down at his desk at six in the morning and not rising again until finished at two in the afternoon, returned a powerful document which went to Congress virtually unchanged on December 20.[17] It was time that the "ardent and intense political controversies" over a national bank be "brought to an end." It was time

that in relation to currency and exchange, individuals may know what they have to expect, or whether they may expect any thing, from the measures of Government. Doubt and uncertainty . . . constitute the worst of all conditions. They affect every man's means of living, and, instead of giving encouragement and applying a stimulus to individual exertion and effort, check the hand of industry, suppress the spirit of enterprise, and bring stagnation and paralysis upon the productive powers of the country.

Tyler's plan was designed "to give the country tranquility."[18]

Statesmanship and stability would begin, Webster continued, with the recognition of a single fact: neither a Bank of the United States nor the Sub-Treasury was practical "in the present condition of things." A return to the Sub-Treasury was "highly improbable"; and, given the "deplorable depression of general credit" and "the existing pressure in the money market," no "ordinary" national bank could gain the private subscriptions needed to fund it. The administration therefore offered a

---

[16]Tyler to Littleton W. Tazewell, October 11, 1841, Tyler Papers, LC; Richardson, *Messages and Papers of the Presidents*, 4:83; Tyler to Webster, October 11, 1841, Webster Papers, LC.

[17]R. M. Blatchford to Seward, December 20, 1841, Seward Papers; Daniel Webster, "Draft of a Message on the Exchequer, December, 1841," *Writings*, 15:144–47.

[18]*House Documents*, 27th Cong., 2nd sess., 1841, H. Doc. 20 ("Letter from the Secretary of the Treasury"), pp. 1–2.

plan which avoided "extremes on both sides" but nonetheless sought to achieve "the good designed by both."[19]

The proposed exchequer, like a national bank, accepted the government's responsibility to provide and supervise a sound paper currency. Though the initial scale of operations was small—$15 million—provision was made for its possible enlargement. The exchequer would be enacted by an ordinary law rather than be created by charter; Congress could expand or contract its activities by amendment at any time. Like a national bank, the exchequer would also be permitted to trade "to some extent" in the exchange of the states and thus to have a hand in regulating credit.[20]

But, in decisive ways, the administration plan was radically unlike a national bank. The exchequer and its agencies would be barred from making loans or engaging in the commercial speculations which had brought controversial profits and final ruin to the Bank of the United States. Furthermore, control of exchequer operations would fall neither to private bankers nor to politicians. Webster conceded the Democratic claim of the 1830s that the national currency could not be trusted to the hands of private bankers, who had a vested interest in maximizing loans and profits. They had proved that they would not curtail credit when necessary.

What was needed was regulation of the currency through apolitical public control. This the Tyler plan would provide by creating an "independent" board of commissioners to supervise the bank's activities. The commissioners would be men of "high character"; they would be appointed by the president with Senate approval and would be removable only for cause; and their terms would be staggered so that no president serving a single term could appoint the entire board.

Webster noted pointedly that the exchequer plan met all the old Jacksonian objections to the toppled Bank of the United States. Control rested always with the people because an exchequer act, created by conventional legislation, could be repealed or amended by Congress "at all times." "Congress will have created no corporation, it will have conferred no privileges or benefits, except on the public; it will have granted no vested rights to individuals." If a banking "measure may ever be accomplished, as the good sense, the fraternal sentiments, and the business necessities of the American people must lead them ardently to desire," if the country were ever "to enjoy tranquility in

[19] *Ibid.*, p. 2.
[20] *Ibid.*, pp. 3–11.

things nearly affecting men's daily labor and daily bread," Webster concluded, Congress should enact the exchequer proposal.[21]

The exchequer proposal revealed both the ingenuity and the limits of the "practical statesmanship" Webster hoped to revive in the 1840s. What was new and prophetic in the exchequer design was its independent board of supervisors, whose structure and purpose strikingly anticipated the federal regulatory agencies devised at the end of the nineteenth century. Webster seemed to sense that, if old-fashioned stewardship were to have any role in the future, it would have to operate out of bureaucratic bastions that seemed impregnable to sinister private influence. What was old and ultimately suspect in Webster's plan was his reliance on "high character" as the guarantee of selflessness in the exchequer board. The political reliability of personal "character" was doubted by the American public of 1841. Decades later, Webster's model for bureaucratic stewardship would prevail, but only after the public had been persuaded of the need for national regulation, and only with the emergence of experts having professional credentials for the autonomous supervision of public affairs.

So deft was the exchequer's blending of Whig and Democratic demands that it threw both parties into confusion. Neither party wished Tyler's scheme any success, but both were hard-pressed to find grounds on which to oppose it.[22] The dilemma was exactly what Tyler had counted on in his hopes of winning approval for the plan.

Some Whigs were reluctantly ready to try Tyler's plan. Many were having second thoughts about the break with the president and wondered if the party had not gone too far to placate the domineering Henry Clay. Others though the party must legislate some kind of bank and were tempted to "take the best we can get." The "people want something," admitted one Whig.[23] Even Whigs who scorned Tyler's appeal for "moderation" as political claptrap thought their party was obliged to give the exchequer a chance.[24]

The Whigs' response to Tyler's exchequer depended on Clay, however, and Clay meant to see the measure defeated—by Tyler himself.

[21]*Ibid.*, pp. 3-10, 11-12.

[22]*New York Commercial Advertiser*, December 10, 1841; A. H. Everett to John Davis, December 13, 1841, John Davis Papers, American Antiquarian Society, Worcester, Mass.; *Albany Evening Journal*, December 16, 1841; Wright to Flagg, December 19, 1841, Flagg Papers, NYPL.

[23]J. C. Bates to Nathan Appleton, December 11, 1841, Nathan Appleton Papers, MHS; Charles Hudson to Davis, December 22, 1841, Davis Papers.

[24]James Simmons to [unidentified correspondent], December 20, 1841, James F. Simmons Papers, LC.

Though he found little to like in the Tyler plan, Clay seemed reluctant, on the heels of the tempestuous special session of Congress, to spend his newly won hegemony by riding roughshod over the party again. He quietly let his doubts be known but gave other Whigs their freedom in judging the measure. When the House began to deliberate the proposal, Clay even arranged for the bill's investigating committee to include a majority of Democrats and pro-Tyler men. Silas Wright, who detected "Mr. Clay's game," thought it "one of the cunningest maneuvers of the Clay Whigs since they have had power."[25] Clay knew that the exchequer's only chance was to please everyone; Tyler's handful of supporters could hardly force the measure through. Clay counted on delay, a recovery of discipline among Democrats, inevitable alterations in the bill, and, finally, on new mistakes by the president to quash the exchequer and the "spirit of moderation" which momentarily lulled some congressmen.[26]

Clay's strategy, abetted by Democratic leaders who were unwilling to modify their bank creed, worked brilliantly. Month after month the exchequer proposal was stalled. House and Senate committees struggled vainly to compromise all views. Whigs in the House used pension bills and comparably urgent measures to delay consideration of the measure. Not until 1843 did the exchequer bill ever come to a vote.

Meanwhile, Tyler made the expected mistakes. The step that wiped out all hope of "moderate" Whig support came in July. With the exchequer bill still stalled in Congress, and with other efforts to obtain revenues for the nearly bankrupt federal government unsuccessful, Congress passed a new tariff bill. Even though Tyler opposed a high tariff, he was prepared to agree to the tariff increase in order to bail out the Treasury. But Whigs linked to the tariff bill a measure providing for the distribution of surplus Treasury revenues to the states. Given the state of the government's finances, the distribution project was little more than a symbolic sop to the party's Western Whigs. But Tyler had already told Congress that he opposed distribution. By linking the tariff and distribution measures, the Whigs deliberately placed the president in a predicament. Tyler refused to buckle, however, and on July 29 vetoed the combined land and tariff bill.

The Whigs were enraged, and even the moderates among them believed Tyler had cast his lot with the antidistribution Democrats. De-

---

[25]Wright to Flagg, December 19, 1841, Flagg Papers, NYPL.

[26]Webster to Everett, March 30, 1842, *Writings*, 16:367; *New York Herald*, December 13, 1841; A. M. Everett to Davis, December 13, 1841, Davis Papers.

fiantly the Whigs passed their land and tariff bill a second time. At this point Webster desperately intervened to prevent a second Tyler veto. He conceded that the "conduct of the Congress in uniting these two subjects" was "wholly indefensible." Nevertheless, he saw that another presidential veto would end all chance of further cooperation with the Whigs. "I would give almost my right hand," he told Tyler, "if you could be permitted to . . . *sign the bill.*"[27] Webster's plea notwithstanding, Tyler vetoed the bill again. Reluctantly the Whigs abandoned the land provision and passed the tariff, lest they be charged with bankrupting the government for partisan reasons.

But Whig hatred for Tyler was now implacable. Despondent, even Webster conceded that Tyler's two vetoes had destroyed all hope of conciliation with the party.[28] Clay's strategy of delay and inaction on the exchequer succeeded totally. Tyler's posture of moderation ceased, Clay's dominance was reassured, and Webster's mediating role was demolished. By the fall of 1842, Webster was faced with the choice he had struggled to avoid—that between resignation from the Tyler cabinet and apostasy to his party.

II

Webster confronted the stark choice between departure and party defection because by the fall of 1842 he had successfully achieved the main goal of his diplomacy—settlement of an enflamed border dispute between the United States and Great Britain.

Since becoming secretary of state, Webster's primary diplomatic purpose had been to eliminate disputes which threatened the twenty-five-year-old peace between Britain and the United States. The most immediate and intractable problem was the Maine-Canadian border. The Peace of Paris of 1783 had left unclear the exact line of demarcation, and repeated efforts to negotiate or arbitrate the line had failed. Left to the diplomats for fifty years, the conflict suddenly threatened to erupt into an unwanted war in the late 1830s, when frontier settlers on both sides of the border took the dispute into their own hands. The intermittent series of bloody clashes in the contested "Aroostock" region of

---

[27] Webster to John Tyler, August 8, [1842], *Writings*, 16:381.

[28] Cushing to William Schouler, September 19, 1842, William Schouler Papers, MHS; Samuel Blatchford to Seward, August 20, 1842, Seward Papers; Webster to Joshua Bates, May 16, 1842, letterpress copy, Thomas W. Ward Papers, MHS; Webster to Bates, July 16, 1842, copy, Webster Papers, Dartmouth; Webster to Everett, August 25, 1842, Edward Everett Papers, MHS.

Maine alarmed the entire northeastern section of the Canadian-American frontier by 1839. Only the hope of arbitration and timely military deployments had cooled passions temporarily.[29]

The arrest and trial of Alexander McLeod—a Canadian who drunkenly and falsely boasted of taking part in the burning of the American ship *Caroline* near Niagara Falls in 1837—stirred feelings anew and brought the two countries perilously close to war. Webster's reassurances to the British and McLeod's acquittal by a New York State court in October, 1841, eased the strain and paved the way for a determined effort by both nations to settle the northeastern border once and for all.[30]

The British took the initiative in the matter in January, 1842, by announcing the appointment of Alexander Baring, Lord Ashburton, as the special emissary to the United States who would negotiate the border dispute. The choice of Lord Ashburton—a member of the firm of Baring Brothers, the husband of an American heiress, and a personal friend of Webster—as head of the mission augured well for its outcome.[31]

From the moment of Ashburton's arrival, Webster was prepared to make substantial territorial concessions in order to secure peace. He regarded the area involved as worthless and Anglo-American unity as incalculable. The resumption of the flow of credit from abroad, the restoration of a sound American currency, and even the solvency of state and federal governments seemed to him to turn on the result of these talks.[32]

---

[29] Richard N. Current, *Daniel Webster and the Rise of National Conservatism* (Boston: Little, Brown & Co., 1955), chap. 6; Thomas LeDuc, "The Maine Frontier and the Northeastern Boundary Controversy," *American Historical Review*, 53 (October, 1947): 30–41; James Morton Callahan, *American Foreign Policy in Canadian Relations* (New York: Macmillan, 1937), pp. 161–84.

[30] Alstair Watt, "The Case of Alexander McLeod," *Canadian Historical Review*, 12 (June, 1931): 145–67. While Webster soothed the British, he also brought pressure on New York's governor, William Henry Seward, to release McLeod outright, and wrested from him a pledge to pardon McLeod if a jury convicted the Canadian.

[31] For the political changes in Britain which brought to power leaders who favored a peace-seeking mission, see Thomas LeDuc, "Lord Ashburton and the Maine Boundary Negotiations," *Mississippi Valley Historical Review*, 40 (December, 1953): 478. Precisely to create the best possible diplomatic climate for the talks, the British government circumvented its hostile, regular envoy in Washington, Henry James Fox, and chose the well-disposed Ashburton to lead the negotiations.

[32] For the vital importance of British credit in stimulating the American economy in the 1830s, see Peter Temin, *The Jacksonian Economy* (New York: W. W. Norton & Co., 1969). Though in 1839 Webster had received a substantial retainer from Baring Brothers, the mercantile house of Lord Ashburton, there is little reason to think the retainer altered his diplomacy. Webster had charted his position on the Maine boundary in a private memorandum in 1839; he was willing to give ground then and remained ready to yield land for peace in 1842.

But Webster knew that, to secure Senate ratification of any cessions of territory, he must first gain the acquiescence of Maine and Massachusetts—the states immediately concerned—to any agreement.[33] He proceeded skillfully and surreptitiously. He used his personal influence, private agents, and several thousand dollars of secret State Department funds to neutralize the hostility of Maine editors to border concessions.[34] Webster's propoganda coup set the stage for the selection of moderate men to represent Maine and Massachusetts at the talks. He then secured a "copy" of the map alleged to be Benjamin Franklin's own, which denoted the border agreed on in 1783 by a large red line. The "Red Line Map," which Webster kept secret from Lord Ashburton, gave most of the disputed territory to Britain.[35] When Maine commissioners balked at the concessions he proposed, Webster coolly divulged his copy of Franklin's "original" to them and noted that his proposal gave Maine far more land than it was entitled to. Webster warned the Maine commissioners that, if the boundary were not settled promptly, British agents might also discover the document and legitimately demand the whole of the disputed area. Webster's maneuver and British concessions finally won Maine's acquiescence. Having won the assent of the American negotiators to a compromise boundary for Maine, Webster reached a settlement on this subject with Ashburton with little difficulty.

The Barings gave Webster the retainer mainly to secure his good offices in getting delinquent American states to pay their debts to Baring stockholders. In 1840, and again in 1843 and 1844, the improvident Webster duly implored his countrymen to accept their obligations, pay their British creditors, and save their honor. Ralph W. Hidy, *The House of Baring in American Trade and Finance: English Merchant Bankers at Work, 1763-1861*, Harvard Studies in Business History, no. 14 (Cambridge, Mass.: Harvard University Press, 1949), pp. 283-84, 316. For Webster's views of the goals of the talks, see Webster to Everett, February 2, 1841, *Writings*, 18:99-100; T. W. Ward to Bates, May 16, 1842, letterpress copy, Ward Papers.

[33] Massachusetts was a party to the talks because, prior to 1820, Maine had been part of the Bay State.

[34] For a full and incisive analysis of the secret role of Webster, of his Maine agent, F. O. J. Smith, and of the secret funds of the State Department in setting the stage for Maine's acquiescence to the loss of territory, see Frederick Merk and Lois Banner Merk, *Fruits of Propaganda in the Tyler Administration* (Cambridge, Mass.: Harvard University Press, 1971), pp. 60-69, 72-76. For further evidence of Webster's skillful use of propaganda, see Richard N. Current, "Webster's Propaganda and the Ashburton Treaty," *Mississippi Valley Historical Review*, 34 (September, 1947): 187-200.

[35] Current, *The Rise of National Conservatism*, pp. 120-21. Critics have charged that the "Red Line Map" was a forgery, and that a map the British possessed—also secretly—was both more accurate and generous with American territory. Almost certainly Webster knew nothing of the other map during the negotiations; quite certainly he did not care. Peace, not accuracy, was his concern. The relatively easy division of the territory has struck most historians as a fair settlement of a nettlesome conflict. For Webster's move to dissuade Ambassador Everett from searching for other boundary maps, see Webster to Everett, June 14, 1842, Edward Everett Papers, MHS.

Attempts to negotiate other items of Anglo-American differences fared less well. Webster and Ashburton discussed the right of impressment, which had helped bring on the War of 1812 and which the British still technically claimed, and they spoke of joint British-American efforts to curb the African slave trade, but the result was a stand-off between the parties.[36]

Of more moment to Webster was his wish to settle, along with the boundary of Maine, the frontier of Oregon. Britain and the United States had jointly administered the Pacific territory since 1818; both countries claimed all of Oregon. Mounting American emigration to the region and mounting political use of the Oregon issue threatened to make it more explosive than the northeastern boundary. Webster, who thought as little of the wilds of Oregon as he did of the barrens of Maine, was eager to establish a frontier now and avoid acrimony later.

But, though Webster and Ashburton initially hoped to settle the Oregon dispute,[37] conflicting interests barred agreement. Webster, like many New Englanders, had become increasingly interested in the acquisition of an American port on the Pacific coast to facilitate the trade of East Coast merchants with the Orient.[38] The finest port on the West Coast—the harbor of San Francisco—belonged to Mexico, but two other harbors lay in the Oregon territory. One was at the mouth of the Columbia River, and the other, farther north, was at the juncture of the Strait of Juan de Fuca and the Pacific Ocean. The British were perfectly willing to accept the Columbia River as the Oregon boundary and to yield the United States the Columbia River port, but peculiar ocean and river cross-currents rendered the harbor virtually unusable. Hence, previous American negotiators had held out for the better port and for the disputed land between the Columbia and the more northerly boundary of 49° latitude. Ashburton had explicit instructions not to accept the forty-ninth parallel, largely because of heavy British fur-trading interests in the region and because of a preponderance of British settlers in the disputed territory.[39]

---

[36] For a discussion of the Webster-Ashburton talks and the African slave trade, see Hugh G. Soulsby, *The Right of Search and the Slave Trade in Anglo-American Relations, 1814–1862*, The Johns Hopkins University Studies in Historical and Political Science, vol. 51, no. 2 (Baltimore: The Johns Hopkins Press, 1933), chaps. 3 and 4.

[37] See the draft instructions from British Foreign Minister Lord Aberdeen to Lord Ashburton, February 8, 1842, Great Britain, Public Records Office, Foreign Office 5, vol. 378 (photostatic copy, LC).

[38] Norman A. Graebner, *Empire on the Pacific: A Study in American Continental Expansion* (New York: The Ronald Press, 1955), pp. 7–9, 63–64, 70–71, 88–89, 98–99.

[39] *Ibid.*, pp. 22–32; draft instructions from Aberdeen to Ashburton, February 8, 1842, Great Britain, Public Records Office, Foreign Office 5, vol. 378 (photostatic copy, LC); Freder-

Webster sought to break the impasse over Oregon in April, 1842, with a remarkable proposal. He suggested that the United States would be willing to accept the Columbia River boundary in return for British acquiescence to America's acquisition of the Port of San Francisco.[40] Though San Francisco belonged to Mexico, the Mexican government owed American citizens more than six and a half million dollars and had lagged in its payments.[41] Webster hoped that Mexico could be persuaded to cede San Francisco to the United States in exchange for America's assumption of Mexico's debt. But Webster made his offer under two false impressions. He thought that the British themselves hoped to acquire California from Mexico, or that Britain at least would obstruct any American attempt to do so; and he apparently thought that the Columbia River port was a poor but passable harbor.[42] Ashburton, knowing that his government had no current designs on California and doubting in any case that Mexico would cede any part of the area to the United States, readily assented to British nonintervention and optimistically reported home that "we shall probably get our boundary with the understanding I mention."[43]

Subsequent events, however, forced Webster temporarily to drop his offer of compromise on Oregon. An expeditionary force sent to survey the Oregon coast returned to the capital in June with a bleak appraisal of the Columbia River harbor, where the expedition had lost a ship.[44] Simultaneously, relations between the United States and Mexico plummetted in the face of an acidulous diplomatic exchange over alleged American aid to the Republic of Texas, which Mexico still considered a rebellious Mexican state.[45] With the prospects of obtaining San Fran-

---

ick Merk, "The Oregon Pioneers and the Boundary," *American Historical Review*, 29 (July, 1924): 682-84, 690-91, 699; and *idem*, "The Oregon Question in the Webster-Ashburton Negotiations," *Mississippi Valley Historical Review*, 43 (December, 1956); 379-404, reprinted in *idem*, *The Oregon Question: Essays in Anglo-American Diplomacy and Politics* (Cambridge, Mass.: Harvard University Press, 1967), pp. 189-215.

[40] Ashburton reported Webster's suggestion in a letter to Lord Aberdeen, April 25, 1842, Great Britain, Public Records Office, Foreign Office 5, vol. 379 (photostatic copy, LC).

[41] George Lockhart Rives, *The United States and Mexico, 1821-1848*, 2 vols. (New York: Charles Scribner's Sons, 1931), 1:431.

[42] Ashburton to Aberdeen, April 25, 1842, Great Britain, Public Records Office, Foreign Office 5, vol. 379.

[43] *Ibid.* For confirmation that the British government never seriously envisioned acquisition of California or San Francisco, see Ephraim Douglass Adams, "English Interest in the Annexation of California," *American Historical Review*, 14 (July, 1909): 752-63; *idem*, Adams, *British Interests and Activities in Texas, 1838-1846* (Baltimore: The Johns Hopkins Press, 1910); and Merk, *The Oregon Question*, pp. 205-15.

[44] Rives, *The United States and Mexico*, 2:11.

[45] Jose Maria de Bocanegra, Minister of Foreign Affairs of Mexico, to Webster, May 12, 31, 1842; Bocanegra to Waddy Thompson, United States Minister to Mexico, June 1, 2, 1842; and

cisco dimmed, Webster fell silent on an Oregon compromise. He readily accepted Ashburton's suggestion that the protracted length and the complexity of the Maine boundary talks precluded a settlement of the Oregon question in mid-1842 and agreed that the two governments would take up the northwestern frontier at a later time.[46]

With the conclusion of negotiations and the ratification of the Treaty of Washington by the Senate on August, 20, 1842, Webster's diplomacy reached its climax.

III

After the ratification of the Treaty of Washington, Webster's political interests called for his prompt resignation from the cabinet and a speedy return to the Whig fold. The negotiations with Britain had provided Webster's excuse for remaining as secretary of state; to stay longer would confirm the rumors of disloyalty that had dismayed his friends and delighted his enemies. Whatever political purpose there might have been in staying on, events had voided. The call for "moderation" had failed; in 1842, party lines were more rigid than ever. The political ostracism of Tyler and Webster seemed clear proof that the day of the public man was past. Gentlemanly independence was a luxury which disciplined party organizations no longer tolerated. The successful politician would work within his organization or perish outside it.

Yet, it was difficult for Webster to accept the equation of independence with apostasy and of party conflict with public good. Such a view challenged his understanding of proper politics and patriotism and demeaned the suffering of his struggle against partisanship. It also required that he slink back to his party as a supplicant, seeking forgiveness for his wayward course. Torn between what he knew the realities of 1842 required and his abomination of those realities, Webster delayed his resignation. In the eyes of the Whigs, hesitation convicted him of apostasy.

Webster knew quite well, by the fall of 1842, that he must soon leave the Tyler cabinet. Though his personal relations with the president

---

Webster to Thompson, July 8, 1842; in *Diplomatic Correspondence of the United States: Inter-American Affairs, 1831–1860*, ed. William R. Manning, 12 vols. (Washington, D.C.: Carnegie Endowment for International Peace, 1937), 8:487–92, 110–20.

[46]Ashburton reported that the verdict of the American coastal expedition "induces the government to hesitate about letting our boundary come down to the river." Ashburton to Aberdeen, June 29, 1842, Great Britain, Public Records Office, Foreign Office 5, vol. 379 (photostatic copy, LC). See also Joseph Schafer, "The British Attitude toward the Oregon Question, 1815–1846," *American Historical Review*, 16 (January, 1911): 293–94.

remained cordial, Tyler's unmistakable drift toward the Democrats made Webster's position untenable. Tyler had begun a wholesale removal of Whigs from office and, Webster's remonstrances notwithstanding, had replaced them all with "very bad" Democrats. Webster saw clearly what the future portended: the "President must hereafter look for support principally to that party which *did not bring* him into power." While Webster remained, he both impeded Tyler's re-union with the Democrats and implicated himself in Tyler's course. It "is easy to see, " Webster confided to his friend Edward Everett in late August, that Tyler's new interests "must lead to changes. . . . I do not expect to stay long where I am."[47]

Yet Webster was reluctant to leave, and he found in the mounting pressure from Whigs to sever his ties with Tyler an excuse to cling to power. Webster understood the Whigs' motives—their "wish for freer scope in their assaults upon the President."[48] But the secretary of state had "some degree of self-respect and some pride"; his "ill treatment" at the hands of those eager to hasten his departure made resignation tantamount to submission. No Whig, Webster later recalled, had been "attacked and villified" by other Whigs to the degree that he had. Even during the negotiations with Britain, "gross abuse" had spewed from the papers and "more especial friends of Mr. Clay."[49]

The judgment of Webster's friends carried more weight than that of his enemies, but they too concluded that, after the Treaty, "retire he certainly *will*—he *must*."[50] Webster, however, was determined not to be hurried. He would neither leave Tyler "with abruptness, nor join any party against him, when I do leave." You ask, then, he ruminated to Edward Everett in August, "what do I propose to do? Probably, nothing."[51] For the moment he planned only to return to his home in Massachusetts for a month and mull over his future.

Massachusetts, however, was hardly a tranquil place in which to make a decision, for the Whigs there were among the most eager to hasten Webster's departure from the cabinet. Their reasons, though, were scarcely such as to hurry the secretary of state.

Since the collapse of Webster's presidential candidacy in 1836, he had split with most of the other Massachusetts Whig leaders on the

[47]Webster to Everett, August 25, 1842, Edward Everett Papers, MHS.

[48]*Ibid.*

[49]Webster to R. P. Letcher, October 23, 1843, *Writings*, 16:413–15.

[50]Choate to Davis, July 19, 1842, Davis Papers; Richard M. Blatchford of New York, and Jeremiah Mason and Joseph Story of Boston, all fast friends of Webster, also expected him to resign promptly. Blatchford to Seward, August 20, 1842, Seward Papers; Charles Sumner to Nathan Appleton, July 27, 1842, Appleton Papers.

[51]Webster to Everett, August 25, 1842, Edward Everett Papers, MHS.

party's best course for the future. Webster, of course, had wished to continue his pursuit of the presidency; in his view, Clay and small cliques within the party had prevented a fair test of his merits before the voters. But other Massachusetts men had thought differently. In particular, Abbott Lawrence, powerful in the party by virtue of millions of dollars made as a textile manufacturer and long a political and financial patron of Webster, believed that Webster had had an honest chance in 1836 and had failed it. Lawrence thought Massachusetts Whigs should shift their support to Clay in 1840.[52] When Webster used his prestige and influence to thwart Lawrence and Clay and to turn the state to Harrison, Lawrence was bitter and determined not to let Webster frustrate his wishes and the interests of the state party again.

Webster's tenure with Tyler gave Lawrence his opportunity, for it steadily undermined Webster's standing in Massachusetts. Congressman Robert C. Winthrop reported as early as April, 1842, that Webster's connection with the turncoat president gave Massachusetts men "a hard time of it." Unable to support or denounce an administration Webster was linked to, "we have given satisfaction to neither Clay nor Tyler." In the fall, Harrison Gray Otis of Boston wrote that, though he thought Webster "never deserved so much of his country as at this moment . . . , popularity seems to fall from him like the dew from the wings of a duck."[53] By the time of the annual party convention in Boston in September, 1842, Lawrence had gained control of the state party.[54] Word went out that Massachusetts Whigs would be asked to endorse Clay for president; Webster's resignation was desired to give his tacit blessing to the movement.[55]

Webster, of course, did not intend to sanction what he could regard only as an insurrection and personal repudiation by his own state, and he dispatched a frank, private warning to Massachusetts leaders. "My advice to the Whigs of Massachusetts," Webster wrote on August 24, when advised of Lawrence's plans, "would be *by no means* to commit the State, at this moment, to anybody." "Next year" would be soon

[52]Everett to Winthrop, May 21, 1838, Winthrop Papers; Charles Francis Adams, ed., *Memoirs of John Quincy Adams*, 12 vols. (Philadelphia: J. P. Lippincott & Co., 1876), 10:43. For a discussion of the Lawrence-Webster relationship, see Sydney Nathans, "Daniel Webster, Massachusetts Man," *The New England Quarterly*, 39 (June, 1966): 161–81.

[53]Winthrop to Everett, April 23, 1842, Edward Everett Papers, MHS; Otis to George Harrison, September 9, 1842, Harrison Gray Otis Papers, MHS.

[54]Webster, for example, found the columns of the *Boston Atlas*, once open to him at will, closed by mid-1842. On September 10 the *Atlas* came out for a Massachusetts endorsement of Clay. George W. Gordon to Fletcher Webster, July 13, 1842, George W. Gordon Papers, NYPL; *Boston Atlas*, September 10, 1842.

[55]*Boston Courier*, September 30, 1842.

enough for endorsements. On August 26, however, Webster back-tracked slightly. If the Massachusetts party felt compelled to touch on the presidency—"tho' they would do better to say nothing"—the state convention should simply resolve that, " 'if Mr. Clay shall be the leading candidate of the Whigs" in 1844, "they would support him cordially." "But to nominate him, or endeavor to *pledge* the Whigs of the State for him, would be little short of insanity. *He has no reasonable prospect of being elected.*" If Massachusetts and other states prematurely enlisted in Clay's cause, state elections would turn on his name. Webster predicted flatly that all such contests, including the pending gubernatorial race in Massachusetts, would "terminate disastrously." Pointedly Webster added: "I never had a stronger opinion upon any political question."[56]

The Whigs of Massachusetts ignored Webster's warning. The state convention met in Boston in September, 1842, and, under Lawrence's leadership and with Lawrence presiding, unanimously nominated Clay for president. To Webster the convention extended bland thanks and "the gratitude of his country" for his diplomatic success. Then it proceeded to upbraid Tyler and to proclaim between him and the Whigs of the Bay State a "full and final separation."[57] The barbed challenge of the convention was clear: was Webster a Tyler heretic or a Massachusetts Whig?

The convention's action galvanized Webster; his indecision of August became defiance. Webster's son undoubtedly spoke his father's thoughts in a scorching letter written after the Massachusetts meeting. The choice of Clay—"the great cause of all the insult and abuse which many Whig politicians and Whig papers heaped upon" his father—signaled an intent to "discard" Webster, to "give him up forever." "*Is this* the will and the wish of the people of Massachusetts? Are they all ready to rush into the support of the stranger and to sacrifice their own." Were "these six penny politicians to rule them and control them by such management?" "Are we to submit in silence. Has not my father one friend left . . . ? Is all—all forgotten?"[58]

Infuriated by the endorsement of Clay, the senior Webster resolved to defend his entire political course in a speech Bostonians had earlier asked him to make on the treaty with England.[59] Anxious to know

---

[56] Webster to Francis P. Healy, August 24, 26, 1842, Webster Papers, MHS.

[57] *Boston Courier*, September 16, 1842.

[58] Fletcher Webster to Healy, September 24, 1842, Webster Papers, MHS.

[59] Webster to C. P. Curtis, September 15, 17, 1842, *Writings*, 16:383–84. Webster first sought to postpone the assembly. "I rather dread the occasion," he confessed to Curtis. But by

whether he meant to sever himself from the president, the city awaited his September 30 speech apprehensively. "His most intimate friends cannot anticipate what he will say," reported Harrison Gray Otis. "He is I hear *sore*."[60]

Readying his notes for the speech, Webster quickly jotted down some headings related to his recent negotiations and wrote on the blue letter paper "Treaty" and "impressment." Then he left a large space and in an unusually heavy hand wrote "Pause," underlined it, and added an exclamation mark. Resuming a rapid scrawl, he continued: "my personal condition. . . . Acted on my own judgment. *I shall do so again.*"[61]

From the skimpy jottings, Webster gave a speech which was a masterpiece of rebuke, threat, and solicitation. To those who expectantly awaited his decision on remaining in the cabinet, the secretary of state announced: "Gentlemen, I shall leave you as enlightened as I found you. I give no pledges, I make no intimations, one way or the other." To his bitter critics, he declared: "I am, Gentlemen, a little hard to coax, but as to being driven, that is out of the question." To those who accused him of keeping his job out of ambition, he lashed back: "I have no attachment to office. I have tasted of its sweets, but I have tasted of its bitterness."

Then he softened. "There is a delicacy in the case, because there is always delicacy and regret when one feels obliged to differ from his friends. . . . [But a] public man has no occasion to be embarrassed, if he is honest. . . . Himself and his feelings should be to him as nobody and as nothing."[62]

Turning to those who had recently met in convention, Webster warmed again. Did they have "any authority to speak in the name of the Whigs of Massachusetts" for any purpose other than that of making nominations for state offices? "I have not been informed of it." Then who were they to commit the Whigs of the whole state? "I am a Whig, I have always been a Whig, and I will always be one," he reminded them heatedly; "and if," he added, with a glance toward Abbott Lawrence, "there are any who would turn me out of the pale of that communion, let them see who will get out first."[63]

---

the seventeenth he was ready for combat: "I do not see how the meeting can well be got rid of, and therefore the time may as well be fixed. . . . I must say something."

[60] Otis to George Harrison, September 26, 1842, Otis Papers, MHS.

[61] *Ibid.*

[62] *Writings*, 3:124–25.

[63] George Frisbie Hoar, *Autobiography of Seventy Years*, 2 vols. (New York: Charles Scribner's Sons, 1903), 1:135.

As to the convention's declaration of a full and final separation from the president of the United States, Webster demanded, "what does it mean?" Did it mean that Massachusetts Whigs would not support the president under any circumstances? Would Massachusetts Whig Edward Everett, currently minister to England, leave his post? "And in regard to the individual who addresses you,—what do his brother Whigs mean to do with Him? . . . If I choose to remain in the President's councils, do these gentlemen mean to say that I cease to be a Massachusetts Whig?" Webster threw down the gauntlet. "I am quite ready to put that question to the people of Massachusetts."[64]

Webster concluded with ringing praise for Tyler's administration. His exchequer was the best financial plan of the era—far superior to the "obsolete idea" of a national bank. The Secretary of State even defended Tyler's tariff vetoes, which he privately thought ruinous. Webster shifted the blame to Clay, who had set the fuse for the crisis with his compromise of 1833.

Though Webster knew that Tyler was speeding toward union with the Democrats, he ventured a final prophecy, which was perhaps designed as much to call the president back as to chasten the Whigs. "I believe that among the sober men of this country, there is a growing desire for more moderation of party feeling, more predominance of purely public considerations, more honest and general union of well-meaning men of all sides to uphold the institutions of the country." For the promotion of such objects, he for one was quite ready "to act with sober men of any party, and of all parties."[65]

But, despite Webster's talk of moderation, bitterness saturated his speech. In fact, as Harrison Gray Otis had detected, a wounded and thwarted Daniel Webster had "committed himself beyond his original programme." After reading the address, it was plain to Otis where Webster had "meant to have off." But, "full of black choler on account of Clay, and of his treatment by part of the Whig press," the speaker "boiled over, heated and inspired with false confidence by the applause of his auditors."[66] Webster's elliptical notes, and his later statements to his son that his Faneuil Hall strictures "were forced upon me," that "I could not withhold them," lend support to Otis' judgment.[67]

Angry as it was, Webster's speech was more than a vindictive attempt to unsettle the Whigs and destroy his rivals. As he later told his son, the

---

[64] *Writings*, 3:126–28.

[65] *Ibid.*, pp. 139–40.

[66] Otis to Harrison, October 25, 1842, Otis Papers, MHS.

[67] Webster to Fletcher Webster, November 12, 1842, Webster Papers, Dartmouth.

Faneuil Hall address spoke his "deepest and most honest convictions" about the menace of party. Webster's newest experience of ostracism, recalling earlier exclusions as a Federalist, then as an "aristocrat," and now as a Tyler Whig, had brought him again to the judgment that partisanship was something alien, recklessly divisive, and lethal to the country as well as to himself. "My attachment to the true Whig principles is undiminished," he affirmed to his son, but "I desire to see more of candor, moderation, and conciliation, in political matters . . . among men . . . of all parties."[68]

Yet the hopes of Webster's speech and letters flew in the face of reality. Webster knew better than any that the president regarded the experiment of conciliation as over. He knew, even as he tardily sanctioned a vague coalition of "moderates," that Tyler had abandoned an independent political course for alliance with the Democrats. And he knew that the Whig party, which after 1840 seemed swollen by recruits who had nothing of the "conservative principles of the [party] in them, but whose object . . . appears to be to cut and thrust at every thing which now exists," was infected with partisan frenzy.[69]

While the chagrined Abbott Lawrence thought that only a "*little knot* of men" would follow Webster after he made his "unfortunate . . . Speech,"[70] Webster's fusillade in fact threw the state party into disarray. Webster's "best friends" regarded his "tirade" as "eminently injudicious," and reported that he had "done great harm." Even Webster's long-time acquaintance Joseph Story noted that his philippic "did great mischief to the Whig party, & somewhat divided them."[71] The next month the Whigs met with a rare defeat at the hands of Massachusetts Democrats. Webster's adversaries, now even more embittered, did not regard the speech or the election as a triumph for him,[72] but the secretary of state returned to the capital with a sense of vindication.[73] He would continue in the Tyler cabinet.

[68] *Ibid.*

[69] Webster to Everett, August 25, 1842, Edward Everett Papers, MHS.

[70] Lawrence to Crittenden, April 5, 1844, Crittenden Papers, LC.

[71] Otis to Harrison, October 25, 1842, and July 1, 1843, Otis Papers, MHS; Story to R. Peters, November 27, 1842, Thomas Cadwalader–Richard Peters Papers, Historical Society of Pennsylvania, Philadelphia (hereafter cited as HSP).

[72] Winthrop to Everett, December 10, 1842, Edward Everett Papers, MHS.

[73] *Writings*, 16:384–85; George Ticknor Curtis, *Life of Daniel Webster*, 2 vols. (New York: D. Appleton & Co., 1872), 2:146–47.

IX

NO EXIT

T HROUGHOUT THE WINTER of 1842/43 Webster persisted in the delusion that "moderation" would yet carry the day. Whig defeats in the fall elections of 1842–"quite deserved"–encouraged him. As "was forseen," he wrote Everett, "blight and mildews afford the same auspices for good crops, as Mr. Clay's name does for . . . party success. I suppose the Whig party may be regarded as now broken up." Without "entirely new leaders," the Whigs "can never again be rallied. A vast portion of the moderate & disinterested, will join in support of the President; & there is reason to think some portion of the other party . . . will take a similar course."[1] As late as February, 1843, Webster assured a Whig congressman from Massachusetts that "the day of dogmatism, & domination, is passing rapidly off."[2]

In fact, there was little foundation for Webster's hopes. There were some who sensed that the issues of the 1830s had become sterile, who saw the two parties as competing for nothing more than patronage, and who wished politics to face new problems or simply to leave citizens and business alone. But in the early 1840s these diverse dissidents re-

---

[1]Webster to Everett, November 28, 1842, Edward Everett Papers, Massachusetts Historical Society, Boston (hereafter cited as MHS).
[2]Webster to Winthrop, February 6, 1843, Robert C. Winthrop Papers, MHS.

mained small in number—and they remained unenamoured of John Tyler. Tyler's use of the patronage system especially offended them. No previous president had depended so exclusively on patronage as a source of loyalty, and no president came to use the patronage so immoderately in order to lure political support.

Webster's political position rapidly deteriorated. Despite the secretary of state's appeal at Faneuil Hall, Tyler remained cold both to the Whigs and to moderation and continued his pursuit of the Democrats.[3] Neither the president nor anyone else read the disparate contests of 1842 as a referendum against partisanship—the Whig party had simply lost to the Democratic party. Webster's Faneuil Hall phillipic and his decision to linger with Tyler changed nothing but his chance for a graceful exit, which they severely diminished.

I

One other avenue for the secretary of state's departure did emerge, however. It promised not only to save Webster the ignomy of a resignation under pressure but to thrust him again to the forefront of politics. This avenue was diplomacy.

Despite the success of the Treaty of Washington, Webster had by no means resolved all the issues between Britain and the United States. Indeed, the most politically volatile issue—the boundary of the Oregon Territory—remained unsettled, even after the Webster-Ashburton negotiations.[4]

The need and opportunity for new steps to resolve the Oregon dispute became evident by late 1842. American emigration to Oregon was mounting daily, and politicians had begun fulminating for American absorption of the whole region.[5] Some senators even suggested the dispatch of a military force to occupy the disputed area. Exceedingly anxious to hasten a settlement, the British in mid-October requested that talks on Oregon begin at once and suggested that the American government authorize its envoy in London, Edward Everett, to initiate the negotiations.[6]

[3] Webster to Everett, October 31, 1842, Edward Everett Papers, MHS.

[4] See Chapter VIII of this volume.

[5] Frederick Merk, "The Oregon Pioneers and the Boundary," *American Historical Review*, 29 (July, 1924): 682–84, 690–91, 699.

[6] The note of October 18 from Lord Aberdeen to Minister Henry James Fox was received and read to Webster on November 15. Fox to Aberdeen, November 15, 1842, Great Britain, Public Records Office, Foreign Office 5, vol. 377 (photostatic copy, Library of Congress,

Webster reciprocated British concern over Oregon, but, in response to the British overture, indicated that he would not "at this moment" recommend that Everett lead the prospective negotiations. In a matter of days it became clear that Webster had decided to direct the proposed talks personally, either as head of a special mission to London or as Everett's replacement as minister to England.[7]

Webster knew from his experience in adjusting the Maine frontier that the success of any boundary negotiations turned on domestic politics. Expansionist and partisan frenzy seemed to make Senate approval of American concessions in Oregon improbable. Webster therefore inquired immediately whether the British had any new "offer to make" which improved on the rigid, earlier proposals.[8] Detecting no flexibility, the secretary of state concluded that no territorial compromise would pass the Senate if Oregon were treated by itself. Oregon would have to be made part of a broader diplomatic package which would include concessions needed to win Western and Southern support for a settlement.

By early 1843, part of the package Webster hoped would bring domestic support for an Oregon compromise included the annexation of California.[9] Webster had quite tentatively mentioned acquisition of a part of California when he and Ashburton initially discussed the Oregon boundary in mid-1842. Then Webster had hinted that he might accept the boundary of the Columbia River and yield to Britain the disputed territory and superior harbor between the Columbia and the forty-ninth parallel to the north, on the condition that the British would not interfere with American attempts to acquire from Mexico the port of San Francisco.[10] Worsened relations with Mexico had led Webster to drop

Washington, D.C. [hereafter cited as LC]). See also Everett to Webster, October 17, 1843, Edward Everett Papers, MHS; and Everett to Webster, November 8, 1842, U.S., State Department Dispatches, Great Britain, vol. 50, National Archives, Washington, D.C.

[7] Fox to Aberdeen, November 15, 1842, Great Britain, Public Records Office, Foreign Office 5, vol. 377 (photostatic copy, LC). In a letter to Everett two weeks after receipt of the British overture, Webster reported that Tyler was not "disinclined" to send a special mission to England to negotiate on Oregon. Webster to Everett, November 28, 1842, Edward Everett Papers, MHS. This portion of Webster's letter is omitted in the published version of the correspondence in *The Writings and Speeches of Daniel Webster*, ed. J. W. McIntyre, 18 vols. (Boston: Little, Brown & Co., 1903), 18:153–56 (hereafter cited as *Writings*).

[8] Fox to Aberdeen, November 15, 1842, Great Britain, Public Records Office, Foreign Office 5, vol. 377 (photostatic copy, LC); Webster to Everett, November 28, 1842, *Writings*, 18:153–54.

[9] Webster to Everett, January 29, 1843, *Writings*, 16:393–96.

[10] Ashburton to Aberdeen, April 25, 1842, Great Britain, Public Records Office, Foreign Office 5, vol. 379 (photostatic copy, LC); Norman A. Graebner, *Empire on the Pacific: A Study in American Continental Expansion* (New York: The Ronald Press, 1955), pp. 131–32;

all talk of his remarkable scheme by June, 1842.[11] After the new British overture on Oregon in November, however, Webster revived and modified his plan. He expanded the territory sought of Mexico from San Francisco to all of Upper California; he also insisted on British "good offices," rather than mere British neutrality, in persuading Mexico to accept the exchange.[12] Webster naturally expected the acquisition of California to placate many Western opponents of compromise in Oregon.

By the first month of 1843 Webster had also come to endorse, as part of the same proposed diplomatic arrangement with Britain, a reciprocal reduction of American and British tariffs.[13]

Webster had known since mid-1842 of informal talks about a mutual Anglo-American reduction of duties. The conversations had all taken place between a private American citizen, Duff Green, and sundry British officials. Green, a sometime Democrat, a full-time defender of slavery, and a close friend and adviser of John C. Calhoun, had gone abroad on business matters and as an unofficial emissary of President Tyler. In August, 1842, Green sounded out the British foreign minister on a commercial agreement which would lower the tariffs of both countries. Green proposed that Britain cut duties on Western-grown corn, hogs, lard, and other goods enough to open a new market for these products. The *quid pro quo* would be a permanently low American tariff on British manufactured goods.[14]

Though Webster knew of Duff Green's tariff project, he did not support it until late 1842.[15] The September confrontation with his protectionist backers in Boston quickened Webster's interest in Green's conversations, and the British initiative on Oregon galvanized Webster to link cuts in the tariff with an Oregon boundary settlement.[16] A

Frederick Merk, *The Oregon Question: Essays in Anglo-American Diplomacy and Politics* (Cambridge, Mass.: Harvard University Press, 1967), pp. 205-7.

[11] Merk, *The Oregon Question*, pp. 207-15; George Lockhart Rives, *The United States and Mexico, 1821-1848*, 2 vols. (New York: Charles Scribner's Sons, 1913), 2:11.

[12] Webster to Everett, January 29, 1843, *Writings*, 16:393-96; Fox to Aberdeen, February 24, 1843, Great Britain, Public Records Office, Foreign Office 5, vol. 391 (photostatic copy, LC).

[13] Frederick Mrek suggests that the Oregon-California package and the Oregon-commercial treaty package were alternatives for bringing about a settlement of the Oregon boundary question. Frederick Merk and Lois Banner Merk, *Fruits of Propaganda in the Tyler Administration* (Cambridge, Mass.: Harvard University Press, 1971), pp. 18-19.

[14] Duff Green to Mrs. Duff Green, September 1, 1842, Duff Green Papers, LC.

[15] Green to Mrs. Green, September 17, 1842, *ibid.*; Everett to Webster, November 3, 1842, Edward Everett Papers, MHS.

[16] Webster to Everett, November 28, 1842, Edward Everett Papers, MHS.

treaty which would cut the tariff as it compromised the Oregon boundary stood a good chance of gaining Southern support.

By January, 1843, the secretary of state had thus found a fitting occasion for retirement. He anticipated a central role in the negotiations to divide Oregon, annex California, and reduce the tariff, in talks that would take place in London under his tutelage. Webster undoubtedly calculated that success in this effort would endear him to hitherto lukewarm sections of the country. The South, which had always sought freer trade, would be buoyant—and grateful for a cut in duties. Hopefully, the West, with its surplus crops spilling into the new British market and its appetite for land sated by California, would be in Webster's debt as well.[17] Webster would balance off the probable loss of protectionist backers with gains from depressed Eastern shipping interests, which were then thirsting for added tonnage and which craved the acquisition of the port of San Francisco.[18]

But it is doubtful that Webster saw the treaty solely as a means to depart the cabinet and enhance his political marketability. It was equally an opportunity to prove the virtue of "practical statesmanship." The settlement of issues by reasoned negotiation would defuse and shame partisan politics.[19] With expansionist sentiment and sectional conflict neutralized, parties would be denied the frictions they fed on. Diplomacy would yet bring Webster triumph and his country repose.

II

Webster's wish to negotiate a territorial and commercial treaty with Britain had only the qualified support of the president. By early 1843, Webster and Tyler were working increasingly at cross-purposes.

Tyler clearly stood to gain much from Webster's treaty plan, but only if it succeeded. Reduction of the tariff and the acquisition of California would win praise from the Democratic allies Tyler sought, even if they were negotiated by a former Federalist. But the prospect that Webster would succeed was remote. There was no reason to think

---

[17] As Frederick Merk has shown, those who thought reduced British duties on Western crops would aid the Western American farmer were wrong. Closer to the British Isles, European wheat-growers benefited, as some contemporaries predicted. Frederick Merk, "The British Corn Crisis of 1845–46 and the Oregon Treaty," *Agricultural History*, 8 (July, 1934); 110–12, 119.

[18] Graebner, *Empire on the Pacific*, pp. 131–32.

[19] If "our most mischievous spirit of party could be laid, I have no doubt a proper adjustment of all disputes respecting the [Oregon] territory might readily be effected." Webster to Everett, January 29, 1843, *Writings*, 16:394.

Mexico would cede California to the United States. Diplomatic relations between the countries remained cool throughout 1842 and were chilled further in January, 1843, by the news that a force led by an American naval captain had occupied Monterey, California, under the erroneous impression that a war had begun.[20] There was almost as little reason to hope that a commercial treaty, even if negotiated, would win approval from a Senate which had hitherto been hostile to almost every act of the Tyler administration.

Far more urgent and practical to Tyler than Webster's scheme were goals he knew Webster opposed: the annexation of Texas and rapprochement with the Democrats. Tyler had first mentioned annexation to Webster in October, 1841, when he wrote of the "bright . . . lustre" and "wonderful results" acquisition of Texas would bring.[21] The president had found Webster, who represented New England constituents opposed to the extension of slavery,[22] unresponsive. Nevertheless, Tyler had briefly pursued the matter of annexation. The president instructed the new American minister to Mexico, Waddy Thompson, to sound out the Mexican government on a possible "cession" of Texas—which Mexico still claimed as a territory—to the United States.[23] Such a gesture would clear away one obstacle to annexation, the fear of war with Mexico. Advised of Tyler's scheme and of Thompson's initial optimism,[24] Webster again sought to discourage the project.[25] What

[20]Waddy Thompson to Webster, January 30, 1843; and Tyler to Webster, February 26, 1843; Daniel Webster Papers, LC. See also Webster to Thompson, January 17, 1843, U.S., State Department Instructions, Mexico, vol. 15, National Archives, Washington, D.C.

[21]Tyler to Webster, October 11, 1841, Webster Papers, LC.

[22]Kinley J. Brauer, *Cotton versus Conscience: Massachusetts Whig Politics and Southwestern Expansion, 1843–1848* (Lexington: University of Kentucky Press, 1967), pp. 38–48.

[23]Waddy Thompson to Tyler, May 9, 1842, in *Diplomatic Correspondence of the United States: Inter-American Affairs, 1831–1860*, ed. William R. Manning, 12 vols. (Washington, D.C.: Carnegie Endowment for International Peace, 1937), 8:485. Like Webster, Thompson and Tyler hoped to exploit Mexico's heavy indebtedness to American citizens. Webster hoped that Mexico might see fit to cancel her debts by ceding the port of San Francisco; Tyler and Thompson hoped they could arrange American assumption of Mexican debts in return for Texas. Thompson reported to Tyler on May 9 that he had spoken with Mexican leader Santa Anna and had "little doubt that I shall be able to accomplish your wishes." Thompson added that he thought Mexico might be willing to cede California as well as Texas to the United States.

[24]Thompson to Webster, April 29, 1842, U.S., State Department Dispatches, Mexico, vol. 11. In this dispatch to Webster, Thompson revealed that he thought Mexico might cede both Texas and California to the United States. Guessing at the New Englander's probable interest in the port of San Francisco, Thompson hastily added that he believed California was the more valuable territory because of its harbor. But, in his May 9 letter to Tyler, Thompson confided that the supreme value of acquiring California was that it would "reconcile the northern people" to the annexation of Texas.

[25]Webster to Waddy Thompson, June 27, 1842, in *The Letters of Daniel Webster, from Documents Owned Principally by the New Hampshire Historical Society*, ed. Claude H. Van

would have happened to ties between Webster and Tyler had Mexico been persuaded to yield its claim to Texas is conjectural. Likely difficulties were averted temporarily when relations between Mexico and the United States soured in mid-1842 and when Tyler consequently muffled the Texas question.

By 1843, time was running out for the president to exploit the Texas issue and to win Democratic support. To negotiate for Texas, the president needed a secretary of state whom he could trust to do his bidding.[26] To lure Democrats, Tyler needed to rid himself of Webster, whose presence many Democrats used as an excuse to decline the president's overtures for union.[27]

The conflict of views and interests began to tell on relations between Webster and Tyler. Careful observers noted a "want of harmony" between the president and his secretary of state.[28] Moments came when they barely spoke to each other.[29] The two men never discussed their estrangement directly, but by early 1843 Webster privately brooded that he could no longer even guess what "the President will do, or will not do, in any given case . . . for he is a man whose conduct is governed by no intelligible principle."[30] Meanwhile, Tyler made it clear through intermediaries that Webster had outlasted his usefulness.[31]

It was mainly to speed Webster's exit from the cabinet, then, that Tyler indulged Webster's wish to negotiate a territorial and commercial treaty with Britain. The two men devised a plan to send Webster to England to arrange the proposed treaty, but members of the House Committee on Foreign Relations indicated that they would not approve

---

Tyne (New York: McClure, Phillips & Co., 1902), pp. 268-70. In this careful reply to Thompson's dispatch of April 29 and to Thompson's letter to Tyler of May 9 (which Tyler showed to Webster), the secretary of state warned that "in seeking acquisitions . . . lying at a great distance from the United States, we ought to be governed by our prudence & caution," especially when "large Territorial acquisitions are looked for." "Nevertheless," Webster added, "the benefits of . . . a good Harbour on the pacific [are] so obvious, that to that extent, at least, the President strongly inclines to favor the idea of a treaty with Mexico." Webster's notable silence on Texas and his encouragement of talks to gain the port of San Francisco made it clear where he stood on the Texas annexation issue.

[26] Rives, *The United States and Mexico*, 1:506-7, 556.

[27] Glyndon G. Van Deusen, *Henry Clay* (Boston: Little, Brown & Co., 1937), p. 177; Levi Woodbury to [unidentified correspondent], April 26, 1843, Daniel Webster Papers, Dartmouth College, Hanover, N.H.

[28] Fox to Aberdeen, February 25, 1843, Great Britain, Public Records Office, Foreign Office 5, vol. 391 (photostatic copy, LC).

[29] John Pendleton Kennedy to Robert C. Winthrop, April 30, 1843, Winthrop Papers.

[30] Fox to Aberdeen, March 8, 1843, Great Britain, Public Records Office, Foreign Office 5, vol. 391 (photostatic copy, LC).

[31] H. Shaw to Webster, February 28, 1843, Webster Papers, LC.

funds for a special mission,[32] and Webster took the group's veto as an indication of the sentiment of Congress.[33] Next Tyler tried to make Webster the regular minister to England by appointing the current minister, Edward Everett, to the new post of emissary to China. Webster, amid denials to his old friend that he had plotted for Everett's "overthrow," awkwardly hinted that he would like Everett to make way. Everett offered to resign,[34] but declined to go to China, and so closed the door on a timely vacancy for Webster.

Tyler's remaining alternative was to induce the British to send to the United States a commission for negotiating the treaty. Duff Green sailed back to England in May, 1843, assured the British that Tyler and Webster deeply desired a tariff and Oregon settlement, and implored Sir Robert Peel's Tory government to rush a commission to Washington.[35]

The British, however, were cool to the proposal, for circumstances which might earlier have made the Peel ministry receptive had changed. In 1842, three successive poor crops, industrial distress, and mounting pressure for a lower British tariff on grain had spurred interest in the American idea. American crops, American markets, and a favorable Oregon agreement might have brought relief to the harassed government. By mid-1843, crops and business had improved, and those who agitated for free trade in Britain abandoned the strategy of reciprocal tariff cuts by treaty for unilateral British reductions.[36]

Even if British domestic pressures had still favored a special mission, the government of Sir Robert Peel almost certainly would have hesitated, disillusioned as it had become with the Tyler administration. The British grew especially unhappy with the president after December, 1842. In his message to Congress that month, Tyler had failed to divulge the recent British initiative on Oregon and, indeed, had made it

---

[32] A special mission served two purposes. It avoided the problem of displacing the regular envoy to Britain, Edward Everett, from his post. It also allowed the president to name Webster as the head of the mission during the congressional recess—and thus to delay for some months the need for senatorial approval of Webster's nomination. Fox to Aberdeen, February 24, 1843, Great Britain, Public Records Office, Foreign Office 5, vol. 391 (photostatic copy, LC).

[33] Webster to Caleb Cushing, February 24, 1843, Caleb Cushing Paper, LC; Webster to Everett, February 25, 1843, Edward Everett Papers, MHS; diary of John Quincy Adams, February 25, 1843, Box 44, John Quincy Adams Papers, MHS; Charles Francis Adams, ed., *Memoirs of John Quincy Adams*, 12 vols. (Philadelphia: J. P. Lippincott & Co., 1876), 11:327–30.

[34] Webster to Everett, March 10, 1843, Webster Papers, LC; Webster to Everett, March 29, 1843, Edward Everett Papers, MHS; Everett to Webster, September 16, 1842, *ibid.*

[35] Green to Sir Robert Peel, May 24, 29, 1843, copies; Green to John Tyler, May 31, 1843, copy; Green to Peel, June 6, 17, 1843, copies; Green Papers, LC.

[36] Thomas P. Martin, "Free Trade and the Oregon Question," in Arthur H. Cole, A. L. Dunham, and N. S. B. Gras, eds., *Facts and Factors in Economic History* (Cambridge, Mass.: Harvard University Press, 1932), pp. 478–79.

seem that John Bull was dragging his feet and must be prodded. Charitably, the British ambassador saw in Tyler's deceit a maneuver to stir a sense of alarm and to generate support for a special mission; nonetheless, he was offended.[37] More offensive still was Tyler's attempt to win public acclaim by putting an overly favorable gloss on parts of the Webster-Ashburton treaty and the published correspondence dealing with impressment and the slave trade. Tyler sought to make it seem as if the British had dropped the right of impressment and abandoned the right to stop and inspect suspected slavers—when in fact the British had surrendered neither claim. Prime Minister Sir Robert Peel publicly repudiated Tyler's interpretation of the treaty.[38]

Finally, Peel doubted in any case that the Senate would now ratify any new treaty negotiated by Webster and the Tyler administration. Wary of making concessions which might only be spurned, Peel believed that the "miserable motives of personal resentment and party interest by which men in the United States are influenced occasionally in deciding on the gravest Questions" made "Caution and Reserve doubly necessary." Emissary Duff Green consequently found Peel courteous, smiling, and absolutely noncommittal on a mission.[39]

While Webster had had his doubts about British enthusiasm for a treaty as early as January, 1843, neither he nor Green fully saw that Peel's government had chilled toward it. As Webster prepared to resign, he still appeared to expect the British soon to appoint a commission to negotiate the Oregon boundary.[40]

III

In April, 1843, Webster prepared to leave the Tyler administration. He "lingered" in the capital for some weeks, hoping vainly for some word about the negotiations and his own future, but none came.[41] By

---

[37]Fox to Aberdeen, January 29, 1843, Great Britain, Public Records Office, Foreign Office 5, vol. 391 (photostatic copy, LC).

[38]James D. Richardson, comp., *A Compilation of the Messages and Papers of the Presidents, 1789-1905*, 11 vols. (Washington, D.C.: Bureau of National Literature and Art, 1907), 4:195-96; Fox to Aberdeen, February 25, March 10, 1843, Great Britain, Public Records Office, Foreign Office 5, vol. 391 (photostatic copy, LC).

[39]Peel to Lord Ripon, April 24, 1843, quoted in Wilbur Devereux Jones, *Lord Aberdeen and the Americas* (Athens: University of Georgia Press, 1958), pp. 26-27. See also Green to Tyler, May 31, 1843, copy; and Peel to Green, May 31 (copy) and June 20, 1843, Green Papers, LC.

[40]George Ticknor Curtis, *Life of Daniel Webster*, 2 vols. (New York: D. Appleton & Co., 1872), 2:176; Green to [Tyler], May 17, 18 (copies), and 31, 1843, Green Papers, LC.

[41]Alexander H. Everett to Mrs. Edward Everett, April 23, 1843, Alexander H. Everett Papers, MHS.

April 23 he reported to Edward Everett that his continuance in the administration "in the present posture of things" was impossibly "awkward."[42] Tyler was bombarded with "constant intimations" that when Webster left "there would no longer be any obstacle, between the president, & the hearty support of what is called the Democratic party." Webster thought most of the talk came from "greedy office seekers," that the president had no chance of nomination from either party, and that his use of the patronage had created a "feeling of disgust in the Country." During his last days in office Webster sought again to persuade Tyler that "moderate Whigs . . . are the only friends he has"; that the Democrats "will certainly cheat him." But sadly Webster reported: "he cannot be convinced of this truth."[43] Unable to persuade Tyler to revive his pursuit of Whig "moderates" and unwilling to join Tyler in his pursuit of Democrats, Webster at last decided to leave the cabinet. He submitted his resignation on May 8.

Even after his resignation, Webster did not abandon hope that the British would yet dispatch a special mission, and with that expectation he cautiously forwarded the idea of a tariff treaty to a wider public.[44] Speaking to a group of Baltimore merchants, he suggested that such an arrangement with Britain would relieve the nation's current agricultural depression. The United States, of course, would have to match lower tariffs with an "adequate consideration"—meaning low duties on British manufactures. Yet this prospect ought not to alarm American manufacturers, Webster added, for their enemy was not the low tariff but the fluctuating tariff. "Change and the apprehension of change . . . unnerves every workingman's arm in this country. . . . Changes felt or changes feared are the bane of our industry." A commercial treaty would bring the tariff permanence, Webster stressed, and would relieve the many sufferers who had besought him to " 'cool us or freeze us; warm us, heat us, scorch us—do what you please, but make your purpose known, and stick to it!' "

Several days after the speech, a group of Boston merchants hailed the proposal of a tariff treaty and the prospect that Webster would negotiate it. They sent Webster a public letter which, anticipating an "adjust-

---

[42] Webster to Everett, April 23, 1843, Edward Everett Papers, MHS.

[43] Webster to Everett, April 28, 1843, Edward Everett Papers, MHS; Webster's draft of an editorial for the *Washington National Intelligencer*, May 12, 1843, Daniel Webster Folder, New York Public Library, New York, N.Y.

[44] Earlier, Webster had tested sentiment for Anglo-American tariff negotiations in Boston. Boston's "Protective Men" found Webster's ideas "very dangerous"; the city's free-trade merchants relished Webster's suggestions. Winthrop to Everett, May 16, 1843, Edward Everett Papers, MHS.

ment of preliminaries in the important question of the settlement of international trade," expressed hope that "some commission was contemplated by which these matters might come under your management and control, either at Washington or elsewhere."[45] The speech and the letter, Duff Green later told Peel in London, were parts of predetermined "arrangements . . . whereby powerful influences in the several states of the Union [were acting] in concert in favor of a treaty with England."[46]

Though Webster's speech was unusually foggy and tentative, editors and politicians quickly saw the point—and the point, one Bostonian reported, "produced a great sensation throughout the country." Few were enthusiastic. Whig papers in Washington, Philadelphia, and New York attacked the plan.[47] John C. Calhoun thought that Webster's proposal "was too sudden, and early. The papers in various parts of the Union were not prepared to take their ground." Calhoun reported that the *Charleston Mercury*, in the heart of the free-trade South, thought the proposal had come too late. The next Congress would be Democratic and could then arrange a tariff to its liking—without Webster's help. "Mr. Webster's object in the scheme," Calhoun suspected, "was to divide and distract the anti Tariff interest."[48]

Massachusetts protectionists were aroused. Abbott Lawrence's immediate response was regret that "Mr. Webster should have shadowed forth such a plan," and when he later discovered Webster's full complicity his regret became anger. He "has lent himself to Southern folly," Lawrence bristled. "So it is—and I believe he is *Politically doomed.*" John Davis, the Whig governor defeated in 1842, said sourly that "such nonsense requires more weight of character than he possesses to recommend it."[49]

IV

Webster had once more misread the mood of the president and of the two parties. The limited interest Tyler had affected in an Anglo-Ameri-

[45] *Writings*, 13:158-59; *Washington National Intelligencer*, May 27, 1843.

[46] Green to Peel, June 17, 1843, copy, Green Papers, LC.

[47] C. G. Greene to Duff Green, July 1, 1843, *ibid*. C. G. Greene noted that the *New York Tribune* was hostile to the speech. See also the *Washington National Intelligencer*, which was critical, and which reported further criticism expressed in the *Philadelphia Inquirer*.

[48] John C. Calhoun, June 7, 1843, quoted in J. Franklin Jameson, ed., "Correspondence of John C. Calhoun," American Historical Association, *Annual Report, 1899* (Washington, D.C.: Government Printing Office, 1900), 2:537; C. G. Greene to Green, July 1, 1843, Green papers, LC.

[49] Lawrence to Nathan Appleton, August 16, 1843, Abbott Lawrence Papers, Houghton Library, Harvard University, Cambridge, Mass.; Lawrence to Everett, October 3, 1843, Edward

can settlement of the Oregon boundary and the tariff waned with Webster's departure from power. Tyler's unofficial emissary in Britain, Duff Green, repeatedly begged for some official statement that the American government would welcome new diplomatic talks.[50] As long as his credentials to speak for the president were in doubt, Green wrote Tyler on May 31, he could not interest Sir Robert Peel in sending a commission to the United States.[51] For two months Tyler ignored Green's entreaties; finally, in late July, the president destroyed all chances of new negotiations being led by Webster. In a message meant for the eye of the British prime minister, Tyler wrote that any proposal coming from Duff Green was strictly "the emanation of his own mind." Green was "invested with no authority" whatsoever "to speak in the name of [his] Government."[52] Diplomatically, Tyler was far more interested in Texas[53] than in Oregon or the tariff;[54] politically, he was far more concerned with pleasing Democrats than with aiding Webster.

But, even if Tyler had favored Webster's scheme for a diplomatic negotiation of political issues, it is improbable that either party would have approved such a settlement. "Moderation" was the enemy of Whigs and Democrats alike in 1843, for both groups were convinced that discipline and clear party demarcations would bring victory in 1844. The Democrats' commitment to discipline was legendary, and

---

Everett Papers, MHS; John Davis to John P. Bigelow [July], 1843, John P. Bigelow Papers, Houghton Library, Harvard University, Cambridge, Mass.

[50]Green to Tyler, May 17, 31, 1843, copies, Green Papers, LC.

[51]Green to Tyler, May 31, 1843, copy, *ibid.* The evidence suggests that, from the first, neither Tyler nor Webster fully trusted Green, and, hence, that neither was willing to designate him an official spokesman of the president. Both Tyler and Webster described Green's mission as that of a "private citizen" to sound out British sentiment on a commercial treaty. Tyler to Everett, April 27, 1843; and Webster to Everett, April 28 and May 12, 1843, Edward Everett Papers, MHS.

[52]Tyler to Everett, July 21, 1843, copy, Edward Everett Papers, MHS. Tyler instructed Ambassador Edward Everett to be "perfectly explicit . . . with Sir Robert Peel" on the subject of Green's limited authority.

[53]Tyler's interest in Texas, first expressed within a month of his expulsion from the Whig party, was galvanized in July, 1843. That month Duff Green reported alarming rumors of a "plot" by the British to recognize Texas' independence in return for an agreement by the Texas Republic to abolish slavery. Tyler instantly made the acquisition of Texas—with slavery intact—the exclusive goal of his diplomacy. Texas without slavery might become a vast sanctuary for fugitive slaves from states of the Deep South. The vigor with which Tyler pursued annexation after mid-1843 was undiminished by the exposure of Duff Green's rumor as a false supposition. See Merk and Merk, *Fruits of Propaganda*, pp. 21, 96–97.

[54]Tyler told Calhoun in 1843 he had concluded that time and emigration favored American claims in Oregon, and so he had done nothing to hasten a settlement of the dispute. Tyler to Calhoun, October 7, 1845, quoted in Rives, *The United States and Mexico*, 2:12. Corroboration came from the British, who complained of no administration response "whatsoever" to their overtures for an Oregon settlement. Fox to Aberdeen, September 12 and December 13, 1843, Great Britain, Public Records Office, Foreign Office 5, vol. 393 (photostatic copy, LC).

Clay had formally stated the revised Whig view in mid-1842. "Of all the springs of human action," he told an audience at Lexington in June, "party ties are perhaps the most powerful." Once he had supposed that self-interest was more potent than partisan allegiance. But experience had shown that on party command "whole communities" would abandon "their long cherished interests . . . , and turn around and oppose them with violence." Whigs must yield to the times; "unless they [were to] stand by and sustain their leaders," regardless of private views, party "division" and "destruction" would follow.[55] Politicians regarded as vital the two issues Webster sought to neutralize, the tariff and expansion. Southern Whigs had increasingly been brought to concur in the need for a high tariff and were as hostile as Northern protectionists to Webster's tardy gesture of appeasement.[56] Democrats, for their part, increasingly turned to territorial expansion as a political appeal and could hardly favor Webster's effort to lance the issue.

Far better than Webster, the British understood that domestic political conflicts could not be reconciled by treaty. Even as Tyler quashed all hope of luring a mission from London, he stated his administration's wish eventually to "harmonize" American "*sectional* interests" by diplomacy. "The truth is," Tyler had confided to the American ambassador, "that the Country is tired of seeing all its great interests made the playthings of ambitious leaders. It wants quiet and repose; its best interests require permanence and indestructibility."[57] But British ministers judged that, unless diplomacy could achieve "speedy and decisive" results, diplomacy itself could become the plaything of ambitious leaders and "leave matters worse than it found them."[58] In the proposed venture, the worst was almost certain to happen.[59] Webster was

[55] Henry Clay, "Speech at Lexington, Ky., June 9, 1842," *The Works of Henry Clay, Comprising His Life, Correspondence, and Speeches,* ed. Calvin Colton, 10 vols. (New York: G. P. Putnam's Sons, 1904), 2:587.

[56] Joel H. Silbey, *The Shrine of Party: Congressional Voting Behavior, 1841–1852* (Pittsburgh: University of Pittsburgh Press, 1967), pp. 52–53, 155–56; Thomas B. Alexander, *Sectional Stress and Party Strength: A Study of Roll-Call Voting Patterns in the United States House of Representatives, 1836–1860* (Nashville: Vanderbilt University Press, 1967), pp. 44–48.

[57] Tyler to Everett, July 21, 1843, copy, Edward Everett Papers, MHS.

[58] Everett to Webster, January 2 and April 26, 1843, *ibid.*

[59] Hence, far preferable to the British than a new special mission to the United States—and the risk of a spectacular diplomatic failure—were secret negotiations through the regular ambassadors. But the British found Tyler unwilling to permit talks to go through American Ambassador Edward Everett, whom the president seemed to mistrust, and equally reluctant to deal with British Ambassador Henry James Fox, who was thought hostile to the United States. Fox to Aberdeen, September 12, 1843, Great Britain, Public Records Office, Foreign Office 5, vol. 393 (photostatic copy, LC).

"a great man for great things," but, in the partisan frenzy of American politics, almost "any thing he might do would be rejected by the Senate."[60] Prime Minister Robert Peel refused absolutely to subject the trade of two great nations and the fate of two Pacific empires to "the vortex of party."[61] Between the hostility to his proposal at home and the refusal of the British paragon of moderation, Webster waited vainly for Peel's commission. It could not have eased Webster's disappointment to know that his mission had been finally rejected because of American partisanship.

[60]Joshua Bates to T. W. Ward, May 29, 1843, Thomas W. Ward Papers, MHS.
[61]Everett to Webster, October 3, 1843, Edward Everett Papers, MHS.

EPILOGUE

DANIEL WEBSTER,
MASSACHUSETTS MAN

WEBSTER HAD TO RETREAT. The reality was that partisanship was not at an ebb but at an apex. Discipline was never stronger; division was never sharper. Parties welcomed the clarity of conflict. Step by step, Webster returned to Whig orthodoxy, and, as he did so, he learned the price of apostasy.

Webster vowed to return at his old rank; others were equally determined that he would begin at the bottom. The party regulars won much, and, as the summer of 1843 turned into fall, they wrung from Webster concession after concession. He resigned from the Tyler administration; he returned to party policy; finally, he withdrew from the contest for the presidency.

I

Not until the fall of 1843 did Webster end a graceless summer of indecision and isolation. Since his resignation in May, he had sullenly refused to make any overtures of conciliation toward estranged comrades in the capital and the state. He withdrew in silence at Marshfield and allowed the two major Whig papers of Boston to debate the propriety of his intransigence.[1] For Massachusetts Whigs, Webster's silence

---

[1]*Boston Atlas*, June 3, 18, 1843; *Boston Courier*, June 29, 1843.

215

was exasperating. The party had to unite to recapture the governorship from the Democrats, and it certainly had to speak with one voice to have authority in national councils. More than anything he could have done, Webster's silence diminished the influence of his rivals and effectively hobbled his challengers.[2] Even as the latter reported to Clay that Webster was without influence in the state and received the Kentuckian's plaudits on their liberation, Clay wrote off any reward for Massachusetts.[3]

By September, however, Webster had resolved to abandon isolation and rejoin the Whigs. His political hegira had been long, and after a twelve-year journey he found the White House as distant as ever. He decided to abandon the ways of a presidential aspirant and to return to the mores of a Massachusetts politician. One by one, he retraced his steps. As he did so, he discovered the cost of his journey.

Webster sought to regain his old stature by convincing Whig regulars of his orthodoxy. In a speech delivered at a great September agricultural fair in Rochester, New York, Webster repledged himself to the protective tariff. Listeners there who knew of his Baltimore speech might at first have thought he was renewing his appeal for a tariff treaty, for Webster spoke forcibly of the "duty of Government" to open new markets for farm products. Webster's revelation was that the new market was not at all the British market; rather, what farmers needed was a "near market, a *home* market." The government's duty, therefore, was to see to it that consumption, employment, and industry grew at home. But, Webster asked, how could Americans expand their industry without a high tariff? "It is a misnomer to talk about the protection of manufactures; that is not the thing we want or need: it is the *protection of the agriculture of the country*!"[4] Whigs at once understood the speech to be a repudiation of the ideas Webster had advanced in Baltimore and thought it a "capital *Tariff* speech."[5] The

---

[2] John Davis to J. P. Bigelow, [July], 1843, John P. Bigelow Papers, Houghton Library, Harvard University, Cambridge, Mass.; Winthrop to Everett, July 12, 1843, Edward Everett Papers, Massachusetts Historical Society, Boston (hereafter cited as MHS); *Boston Courier*, November 28, 1843.

[3] Clay to Porter, September 17, 1843, Peter B. Porter Papers, Buffalo Historical Society, Buffalo, N.Y.; Davis to Clay, October 14, 1843, Henry Clay Papers, Library of Congress, Washington, D.C. (hereafter cited as LC).

[4] Speech at State Agricultural Fair, Rochester, N.Y., September 22, 1843, as reported in the *Washington National Intelligencer*, September 27, 1843, and reprinted in *The Writings and Speeches of Daniel Webster*, ed. J. W. McIntyre, 18 vols. (Boston: Little, Brown & Co., 1903), 13:181–82 (hereafter cited as *Writings*).

[5] Porter to Clay, September 25, 1843, John Jordan Crittenden Papers, LC.

antitariff *Washington Globe* characterized it as "sly, cunning . . . ingenious . . . covert . . . propitiating . . . insidious."[6] Beyond a doubt Webster had returned to protection.

Webster still hoped, however, to extract a price for his return to the Whigs. If he could not have the presidency in 1844, perhaps he could at least win the vice-presidential nomination on Clay's ticket. Success for that scheme was improbable at best, and the bungling of one of Webster's friends hastened failure. Strategy called for Webster's New York backers quietly to build support for the plan, and then to have their November state convention nominate him for vice-president. But Colonel James Watson Webb, editor of the *New York Courier and Enquirer*, "bolted out as he usually does, *half cocked*," and prematurely endorsed Webster.[7] Opposition was so great by the time of the convention that Webster's friends scuttled the scheme.[8]

In the meantime, Webster's backers had solicited Henry Clay's sanction for the plan, declaring that Webster was eager to reconcile differences, to support Clay for the presidency, and to be his running mate. Clay's reply was prudent and ironic. On a reconciliation, Clay wrote that he had done Webster no wrong, "and have therefore no reconciliation to seek." On the vice-presidency, the Great Compromiser could "enter into no arrangements, make no promises [and] offer no pledges to obtain" Webster's support. As for Webster's help, Clay would gladly receive it, of course—just as he would "that of any other American citizen."[9]

Webster could not extract a price for his return to the Whigs; he himself would pay. One expense soon realized was that he could not count on his state to return him to the Senate—much less to support him for higher office. Led by Lawrence, Webster's opponents in the party continued to subvert his position openly. Webster's struggle to regain authority in his own state party began in earnest immediately after the effort to make him the vice-presidential nominee collapsed. He discovered that even his old job of senator, held by his close friend Rufus Choate, was in danger. Webster had always assumed that, if he wished to return to the Senate, Choate would resign and the state legislature would re-elect him as a matter of course. Choate was quite

---

[6] *Washington Daily Globe*, October 6, 1843.

[7] Porter to Clay, October 11, 1843, Henry Clay Papers, LC.

[8] Porter to Clay, November 6, 1843, *ibid.*

[9] Porter to Clay, September 25, 1843, Crittenden Papers, LC; Clay's reply is quoted in Porter to Clay, October 13, 1843, Henry Clay Papers, LC.

willing to make way. But Webster found now that the legislature was likely to balk.[10]

So, at Andover, Massachusetts, in a speech ostensibly on "the respective duties of the national and state governments," Webster began the uphill struggle for the senatorship. He told friends beforehand that it would be "the greatest speech that he had ever made in his life." He would parade his orthodoxy, "explaining & sustaining all the great Whig measures of Tariff, U.S. Bank . . . etc. etc." He would justify his past course, showing "why he did not sooner resign the office as Secretary of State."[11] Webster did these things in the speech, almost methodically. Since he had never really strayed from his old views, he added, he owed and offered apologies to no one. His concluding declaration, however, suggested as much anxiety as defiance. "I close . . . by repeating the declaration made by me in another place, last year, that I am a Whig, a Massachusetts Whig," and "none shall have the power, now or hereafter, to deprive me of the position in which that character places me."[12]

Webster's Andover speech did not reinstate him with the Whig party. Sullen in tone and silent on Clay, it struck a stony audience as inadequate, both in its explanation of the past and in its revelation of the future. The question remained: Was Webster a Whig? Webster refused to make the one gesture all looked for as a sign of final obeisance—an endorsement of Clay. He would give no more than a hint of his future fidelity; the party demanded no less than a pledge.[13]

II

During this impasse, in the autumn of 1843, Webster found a different way to re-establish himself in the state and in the national Whig party. The Texas annexation issue, long smoldering beneath the political surface, provided Webster an alternative to humbling himself before his fellow Whigs.

---

[10] Abbott Lawrence to Francis Granger, March 2, 1844, Francis Granger Papers, LC; Webster to Jeremiah Mason, February 6, 1844, copy, Daniel Webster Papers, LC; *New York Journal of Commerce*, September 22, 1843.

[11] Porter to Clay, November 6, 1843, Henry Clay Papers, LC.

[12] Daniel Webster, "Speech at Andover, November 9, 1843," *Writings*, 3:159–85; see esp. pp. 160, 177–78, 180–85.

[13] The pro-Clay *Boston Atlas*, apparently expecting Webster to announce for Clay, gave the speech a great build-up. *Boston Atlas*, November 7, 8, 9, 10, 1843. Professor Moses Stuart, the friend who had arranged for Webster to speak at Andover, sought to explain away the audience's coolness. Webster's speech was all "truth & sober conviction & rational emotion," and

Webster, of course, had long been on record against the annexation of Texas. Hardly had Texas gained independence than men began to talk of adding the Lone Star State to the Union. But, to Webster, even in May, 1836, annexation talk raised the specter of "new causes of embarrassment, & new tendencies of dismemberment."[14] In 1838 Webster had publicly denounced "anything that shall extend the slavery of the African race on this continent."[15] In 1841 he had spurned John Tyler's suggestion that annexation would throw a "bright . . . lustre" around their administration[16] and had struggled for two futile years thereafter to find more moderate issues and allies for himself and the isolated president. Conviction hence bulked large in Webster's mounting concern in late 1843 over rumors that Tyler was negotiating a treaty of union with Texas. Satisfied by winter that the rumors were true, Webster privately sought to alarm the Whigs of the state, and through them to alert the country.[17]

Leading Massachusetts Whigs resisted Webster's warnings about Texas, however, and, as Webster perceived their reasons, he saw the way to regain power without humiliation. Linked closely to Henry Clay, leaders of the state party shied away from forcing an issue so potentially embarrassing to him.[18] Clay, a slaveholder from Kentucky, would be hurt, no matter what stand he took on Texas. If against annexation, he would lose friends in the South; if for it, he would alienate many Whigs in the North; and, if equivocal, he would lose votes in both sections. Victory in 1844 would be jeopardized if Webster's rumors were true. Even his friends preferred to think he brought false tidings. They suspected that Webster's effort to induce Massachusetts Whigs to warn the country was a design to destroy the State's standing with Clay and perhaps Clay himself.[19] In fact, Webster had all but given up at-

---

the audience had responded in kind with "silent murmurs of the mighty deep." Nonetheless, Stuart felt obliged to ask Webster for further clarification on his reasons for staying with Tyler, and suggested that they be put into a pamphlet and published. Moses Stuart to Webster, November 11, 1843, Webster Papers, LC. Stuart knew "*there is more* in the case than you have developed" and suggested that more "light is needed" among Whigs.

[14]Webster to Everett, May 7, 1836, Edward Everett Papers, MHS.

[15]*Writings*, 2:206-11.

[16]Tyler to Webster, October 11, 1841, Webster Papers, LC.

[17]*Boston Courier*, November 27, 1843; Webster to Everett, November 30, 1843, Edward Everett Papers, MHS; Webster to Ketchum, December 2, 1843, Daniel Webster Papers, Dartmouth College, Hanover, N.H.; Webster to Charles Allen, December 9, 1843, Webster Papers, George F. Hoar Collection, MHS; George Ticknor Curtis, *Life of Daniel Webster*, 2 vols. (New York: D. Appleton & Co., 1872), 2:230-35.

[18]*Boston Atlas*, January 6 and February 18, 29, 1844.

[19]*Ibid.*, January 6 and February 28, 1844.

tempts to thwart Clay for 1844[20] But, detecting the fears of Clay's friends in Massachusetts and the vulnerability behind it, he carefully began to use the Texas issue to undercut their power.

Self-interest thus reinforced conviction about the Texas issue, and through the winter and spring of 1844 Webster carefully orchestrated the Texas danger to regain his position in Massachusetts. Though the faction led by Abbott Lawrence was momentarily ascendant,[21] Webster could not move alone, or too fast, in exposing and condemning the plot in Washington, lest he open himself to the charge of overplaying the issue to embarrass Clay. Nor could he move too fast or too intensely without running the risk of being linked with abolitionists, or with the small but potent Liberty party, a group that included many breakaway Whigs. What Webster did was stay one step ahead of the Lawrence faction through the spring, issuing private warnings in November, a public letter in March. At each point, he first got denials, then grudging recognition.[22] In this way, Webster ingratiated himself with the younger, rising politicians in Massachusetts who had already spoken out against annexation. He had found both a worthy cause and a convenient means of driving an entering wedge into the state Whig organization. His tactics previewed the uses Northern politicians would make of such issues as annexation, slavery, and expansion in the late 1840s and 1850s.[23]

[20]Webster to T. S. Curtis, January 17, 1844, Webster Papers, MHS. On March 30, 1844, the *Boston Courier* denied that Webster fought annexation to thwart Clay.

[21]Among those Whigs loyal to Lawrence were former Governor John Davis, Congressman Leverett Saltonstall, *Boston Advertiser* editor Nathan Hale, and one-time governor Levi Lincoln. Also siding with Lawrence, despite personal ties to Webster, were Robert C. Winthrop, Nathan Appleton, and Joseph Story.

[22]*Boston Atlas*, January 6, February 28, 1844. The *Atlas* denounced the "most silly, idle and ridiculous rumor" that there was "some serious intention" of negotiating a treaty of annexation. "We pray our Whig friends of Massachusetts not to allow themselves to be deceived" by "bugbears ... conjured up to frighten them." See also the *Boston Courier*, March 22, 30, 1844. The *Atlas* was forced to admit the truth of the rumors on March 22, and vowed at once to "resist" annexation "with the last drop of our blood." Lawrence also joined the bandwagon in March. Lawrence to Weed, March 21, 27, 1844, Thurlow Weed Papers, University of Rochester, Rochester, N.Y.; Lawrence to James Simmons, March 25, 1844, James F. Simmons Papers, LC. A somewhat similar line of analysis of Webster's stance toward annexation was suggested by Professor Robert F. Dalzell, Jr., in a paper, "Webster and the Anti-Texas Movement in Massachusetts," presented at the April 18-20, 1968, meeting of the Organization of American Historians.

[23]What became the rift between the "conscience" and "cotton" Whigs of Massachusetts is discussed in the early chapters of Kinley Brauer's important *Cotton Versus Conscience: Massachusetts Whig Politics and Southwestern Expansion, 1843-1848* (Lexington: University of Kentucky Press, 1967). Webster's continuing attempt to straddle the factions is analyzed in David Donald, *Charles Sumner and the Civil War* (New York: Alfred A. Knopf, 1960), pp. 148, 157-58.

Events brought Webster perhaps more success than he wished. As he had predicted, John Tyler presented the Senate with a treaty for the annexation of Texas. Moreover, the treaty, and indeed the whole question of annexation, was by virtue of a complex set of circumstances presented in a way almost guaranteed to inflame Northern sentiment. John C. Calhoun, newly appointed Tyler's secretary of state, once more linked Southern interests with the acquisition of Texas; votes on the treaty, he vowed, would be a test of proslavery sentiment. Calhoun's statement thus ensured defeat of the treaty. As Webster had prophesied, Northern antislavery sentiment was so aroused that even established Whig leaders, swept along by the current, spent 1844 following Webster's lead and denouncing Tyler, the treaty, and all efforts to annex Texas. What might otherwise have been a triumph of conviction and politics, however, was marred by two flaws. The anti-annexationist Whig party lost the election of 1844, and the annexation of Texas—with consequences fully as calamitous as Webster had feared—occurred in the last month of John Tyler's administration.

III

The election year 1844 should have been a Whig year. United as never before on a nominee, the Whigs for virtually the first time seemed as a party to reflect the main current of popular sentiment and political action. If most voters remained cold to the notion of stewardship implicit in the old Whig program of a national bank, a high tariff, and federal internal improvements, many were beginning to reconsider the merits of federal largess and the federal promotion of economic activity. The depression of 1837–43 had palsied the private credit which had funded the explosion of internal improvements in the thirties and which would be needed to finance the vastly more expensive projects of the future, the railroads. The temporary glut in the foreign market for cotton and wheat had revived interest in the old idea of fostering growth of the home market through the tariff. Increasingly, the country seemed responsive to the promotionalism Whigs explicitly stood for,[24] responsive to rapid and dramatic expansion of the economy, backed, if necessary, by government as well as by private enterprise.

But the Whig party went down to defeat in 1844, felled by the new issue of Texas—the issue unleashed and exploited by John Tyler in response to his earlier isolation by the Whigs.

[24]See, for example, Clay's speech in Raleigh, N.C., April 13, 1844, as reprinted in the *Boston Daily Advertiser*, July 10, 1844.

Few Whigs could find fault with Webster's performance in the campaign of 1844. When the Whig convention chose Clay as its standard-bearer in May, Webster gave his prompt endorsement, and hit the campaign trail for the party in 1844 as hard as he had in 1840.[25] Staying in the North, he focused on the issues of the tariff and Texas and took a strong orthodox line. The Whigs were for the tariff and against annexation, unequivocally.[26] If Webster's references to Clay were only correct and often absent, wise politics as well as personal feeling dictated his tack. There was no reason to remind Northerners that the anti-annexationist Whig ticket was headed by a Kentucky slaveholder whose stand against annexation wavered during the campaign.[27]

Like many Northern Whigs, Webster sensed late in the 1844 contest that the vote would be close. The Texas issue had made the outcome uncertain, and Webster's fears led him and others to experiment with a new issue, that of nativism. Northern cities were increasingly troubled by the influx of immigrants, who by and large voted Democratic, and the Whigs of Philadelphia had successfully exploited native-American fears in winning a city election in the spring of 1844. National Whig leaders divided on the use of nativist tactics. Moral objections aside, assaults on the immigrant could galvanize many who had not voted in the past to take to the polls and vote Democratic.[28] An anxious Daniel Webster, however, favored political nativism and encouraged it particularly upon the Whigs of New York City, where he had uncommon influence.[29]

---

[25] *Boston Courier*, May 6, 1844; *Boston Atlas*, May 10, 1844. During the campaign Webster spoke in Boston, Portsmouth, New Hampshire, Trenton, Springfield, Albany, Philadelphia, and New York City. Robert Winthrop reported that Webster "did wonders" in the "great battle." Winthrop to Everett, October 15, 1844, Edward Everett Papers, MHS.

[26] See, for example, Webster's speeches in Philadelphia and Albany, *Writings*, 3:217-74; and at Springfield, Trenton, and Peperell, Mass., *ibid.*, 13:239-46, 276-300.

[27] Clay was also rather effectively pilloried by Democrats as a profligate and blasphemer. Such charges did not endear him to the Northern voters, who were most earnest on the slavery issue. For protest against Democratic tactics, see the *Boston Courier*, September 24, 1844.

[28] *Boston Atlas*, May 13, 1844; *Boston Daily Advertiser*, July 29, 1844; Clay to Theodore Freylinghuysen, May 22, 1844, Henry Clay Folder, New York Public Library, New York, N.Y.; A. H. Bradford to Hamiltion Fish, January 19, 1844, Hamilton Fish Papers, LC; Seward to Clay, November 7, 1844, copy, William Henry Seward Papers, University of Rochester, Rochester, N.Y. See Ray Allen Billington, *The Protestant Crusade, 1800-1860: A Study of the Origins of American Nativism* (New York: Macmillan, 1938), pp. 131-32, 150-58, 193-211; and Louis Dow Scisco, *Political Nativism in New York State*, Columbia Studies in History, Economics, and Public Law, no. 13 (New York: Columbia University Press, 1901), pp. 24-28, 30-33.

[29] Hamilton Fish to John M. Berrien, October 17, 1844, copy, Fish Papers. The drift toward nativism by the Whigs of New York City is traced in Scisco, *Politcal Nativism*; see esp. pp. 39-60. Nativist appeals in the Whig press of Massachusetts are found in the *Boston Courier*, October 25 and November 2, 1844; and in the *Worcester National Aegis*, July 17 and November 20, 1844.

In all these activities throughout the fall of 1844, Webster acted in good faith and as a good Whig. But, to the small extent that he could still influence Whig strategy, his efforts did harm as well as good. The campaign he led in the North against the annexation brought a predictable reaction from the South. The election became to many Southerners a referendum not just on Texas but on the Southern way of life. The unexpected Southern reaction forced Clay to soften and qualify his opposition to Texas, while his effort at appeasement weakened him in the North. Webster and other Northern Whigs were forced to explain that the Kentuckian had not really changed his views, and they were prodded to embrace the diverting issue of nativism. That issue had an impact especially in New York City, but not the impact Webster wished. Fearful of disfranchisement or worse, thousands of the city's foreigners flocked to the polls and overwhelmingly voted Democratic.[30] As it happened, Clay's loss in New York State by a margin of 5,000 votes cost the Whigs the election.

Webster was chagrined at the Whig defeat. "I feel sick at heart," he wrote a friend. "This free country, this Model Republic, disturbing its own peace, & perhaps the peace of the world, by its greediness for more slave Territory, & for the greater increase of Slavery!"[31] Publicly, he blamed the loss on the Democrats' manipulation of the immigrant vote, of men who were not yet "American in feeling, principle, character, and sympathy."[32] But privately he thought Clay's vacillation on Texas, coupled with a "general feeling" in the nation that Clay's "temper was bad—resentful, violent, & unforgiving," had cost the election.[33] Webster was no more conscious of having exacerbated the Texas and nativist problems of his party in 1844 than Clay was conscious of having set the stage for these issues by his deeds of 1841.

Webster tried to put the best face he could on the Whig defeat in a postelection address at Faneuil Hall, Boston, on November 8. Whigs had carried Massachusetts, and they had won in much of the rest of New England. When the returns were all in, they would carry New Jersey, Ohio, Maryland, Delaware, North Carolina, Georgia, Louisiana, Tennes-

---

[30] So judged New York Governor Seward, Clay, and, indeed, Webster himself. Seward to Clay, November 7, 1844, copy, Seward Papers; Clay to Clayton, December 2, 1844, John M. Clayton Papers, LC. On the defeat of Clay, see Webster's "Speech at Faneuil Hall, November 8, 1844," *Writings*, 13:303–5. For analyses of the impact of nativism and of the Liberty party appeal on the outcome of the election in New York, see Scisco, *Political Nativism*, pp. 46–52; and Lee Benson, *The Concept of Jacksonian Democracy: New York as a Test Case* (Princeton: Princeton University Press, 1961), pp. 113–14, 121–22, 137, 145–46, 165–85.

[31] Webster to Winthrop, December 13, 1844, Robert C. Winthrop Papers, MHS.

[32] Daniel Webster, "Speech at Boston," November 8, 1844, *Writings*, 13:303–5.

[33] Webster to Everett, December 15, 1844, Edward Everett Papers, MHS.

see, Kentucky, and Indiana. The party was not broken or destroyed; the Whigs remained "a glorious band." Whiggery and Americanism went hand in hand; soon the country must awake to the Democratic menace. No, Webster exclaimed, "All is not lost!"[34]

But for Daniel Webster—as for Henry Clay and many others who had wedded their political fortunes to the Whig cause after 1828—all was, indeed, very nearly lost. Though Webster would represent Massachusetts in the Senate for another half-dozen years, though some of his major senatorial labors still lay ahead, though he would make yet another feeble run for the presidential nomination, he had all but spent his force in both national and state politics. Only the great sectional crisis of 1850 would revive his authority. For Webster, more than for other members of his party, the debacle of 1844 was ironic—and tragic.

For Webster had grown with American politics during the 1830s; indeed, he had helped to shape the new order which now had brought about his ruin. Committed to an archaic Federalism during Andrew Jackson's terms in office, convinced that the few should rule the many, determined to instruct the voters rather than pander to their wishes, Webster during the early 1830s represented only the most extreme of the anti-Jacksonians who sought a return to the political style of George Washington. But, by 1837, depression, defeat, and personal circumstance had changed Webster. Still determined that issues must be presented to the people, still convinced of the need for sectional support in his quest for the presidency, he had nonetheless broadened his perspective. No longer need discussions of the issues be dull. No longer could the anti-Jacksonians appeal to the wealthy. No longer could presidential aspirants seek support only from their home sections. Webster began, in 1837, to lead his party to a consciousness of its role as a national organization. The campaign of 1840 merely carried his tactics of 1837 to their logical conclusion.

But, if Webster himself grew, and in his own political growth shaped the growth and metamorphasis of his party, the very moment of Whig triumph was ironically to bring his most bitter disappointment and greatest defeat. Again and again denied the presidential nomination he sought, he at last seemed likely, in Harrison's administration, to move to the center of party power, to dictate Whig policy. Harrison's death, however, knocked Webster from his new-found niche. The internecine

[34]Webster, "Speech at Boston," *Writings*, 13:301-5.

warfare of the Tyler administration, which destroyed a president and rent a party, left Webster a prophet with little honor in his own land.

Forced to return to the orthodox Whig fold, Webster in 1844 found himself bereft of influence, stripped of power, and compelled to re-establish his authority in his state, his section, and his national party. He would never entirely succeed; he would never again return to the happy heights of the short-lived Harrison administration. Ironically, by 1844, Daniel Webster had once again become what he had been in 1828: merely a Massachusetts man.

BIBLIOGRAPHICAL
ESSAY

T HIS ESSAY SEEKS TO SURVEY the materials that are most pertinent
to the study of Daniel Webster in the Jackson era. For the most
complete compendia of the vast secondary literature of the
Jackson period, see the bibliographical essays in Glyndon G. Van
Deusen, *The Jacksonian Era, 1828–1848* (New York: Harper & Row,
Publishers, 1959), and Edward Pessen, *Jacksonian America: Society,
Personality, and Politics* (Homewood, Ill.: The Dorsey Press, 1969).

Manuscript Collections

Because the most up-to-date guides to manuscript collections in the
United States list collections only by name and fail to index depositories, collections are here grouped by archives for the convenience of the
reader. Despite their limitations as sources for the systematic study of
political behavior, these manuscript collections have provided indispensable information on Webster and the party conflict of the Jackson
period.

The Massachusetts Historical Society in Boston contains invaluable
material on Webster and the Whig party in Massachusetts. Most of the
important letters in the society's various groupings of Webster papers
have been published, but one must check the printed letters against the

originals for occasional deletions of text that early editors thought superfluous or unfavorable to Webster. Edward Everett's voluminous papers are the best source for Webster's relations with the Whigs of his state and, as well, for Webster's reflections on the difficulties of the Tyler years. Slightly less valuable for state politics, though no less voluminous, are the letters of Robert C. Winthrop. Among the other collections containing valuable material on Webster and the activities of other Massachusetts leaders are the George F. Hoar Collection of Webster papers and the papers of John Quincy Adams, Charles Francis Adams, Nathan Appleton, John Bailey, Amos A. Lawrence, Amos Lawrence, Alexander H. Everett, Levi Lincoln, J. O. Sargent, William Schouler, and James W. Paige. The letters of Thomas W. Ward and Harrison Gray Otis illuminate Webster's financial and political straits of the late 1830s and early 1840s. The papers of Joseph Story, Webster's close friend and adviser, proved disappointing. For an account of Boston's response to Webster's politics of 1842–44, see the manuscript journal of Richard Frothingham. Valuable material on Democratic politics in Massachusetts can be found in the letters of George Bancroft and to a lesser extent in the society's small holdings of Martin Van Buren Papers.

Important papers held at the Houghton Library of Harvard University include small collections of letters of Daniel Webster, Abbott Lawrence, John P. Bigelow, and Joseph Story.

On file at the Boston Public Library is the correspondence of William Lloyd Garrison and of Theophilus Parsons, Jr., who guided the nomination of Webster through the Massachusetts Whig caucus in 1835.

The papers of John Davis, rich in material on Massachusetts politics in the 1830s and 1840s, are assembled in bound volumes at the American Antiquarian Society in Worcester, Mass.

The Dartmouth College collection of Webster Papers proved thin for the period from 1830 to 1844, but, among the letters it does have, one setting out Webster's political strategy in 1837 and a handful of others are invaluable.

Useful on Webster and Whig frustrations in New Hampshire politics are the Samuel Dana Bell, John P. Hale, Levi Woodbury, and Daniel Webster papers of the New Hampshire Historical Society, and the William Plumer Family Papers at the New Hampshire State Library. Both archives are located in Concord, N.H.

The New York Historical Society in New York City has a small and marginally useful body of Webster Papers. More valuable on Webster and the Whigs is the correspondence contained in the Luther Bradish and Daniel Ullmann collections. Useful on banking and Democratic politics are the society's holdings of Nicholas Biddle, Albert Gallatin, George Newbold, and Gulian C. Verplanck letters.

The New York City Public Library contains fragmentary holdings of occasional assistance, including the manuscript diary of James Gordon Bennett and a small number of letters of Henry Clay, Virgil Maxcy, Azariah C. Flagg, and Webster. The extensive papers of New York businessmen Arthur and Issac Bronson contain little on politics.

Extremely helpful at the Columbia University collection are the letters of Azariah C. Flagg, a leading Democratic editor from New York. Flagg often received informative missives from colleagues in Washington. Less useful are the John A. Dix Papers. Columbia's cache of Webster Papers concerns personal matters, and its most pertinent letters have been published.

Most useful of the limited material on this period in the New York State Library at Albany are the unsorted letters of William L. Marcy and the papers of Whig Congressman Daniel Dewey Barnard.

The University of Rochester, Rochester, N.Y., holds the invaluable correspondence of William Henry Seward and Thurlow Weed. Their own letters and those of their correspondents detail the search of New York Whigs for a winning presidential candidate through the 1830s, and the determined but fruitless efforts of Webster and Clay to win the aid of New York for their ambitions. The papers demonstrate the impact of New York Whigs on national Whig politics.

At the Buffalo Historical Society, Buffalo, N.Y., is assembled the correspondence between Peter B. Porter and Henry Clay. Though many of the letters have been published, the collection must be consulted for the light it sheds on Clay's plans and opinions throughout the period.

The Historical Society of Pennsylvania, Philadelphia, houses material especially useful for investigating the Whigs and the Bank of the United States. Best of the sources are the Nicholas Biddle Papers and the correspondence found in the Thomas Cadwalader–Richard Peters Collection. The papers of Roswell Colt, James Buchanan, George Mifflin Dallas, Henry Carey, and Lewis Coryell proved less rewarding. Also helpful on the Whigs were the Josiah S. Johnston, John Sergeant, Thaddeus Stevens, and especially the John B. Wallace letters.

The exceptional manuscript collection of the Library of Congress is, of course, indispensable for any study of the politics of the period. Of material pertaining to Webster, his correspondence is vital. Unpublished items include such critical documents as his private "Memorandum" on the bank crises of the Tyler administration. Next in importance on Webster and on his state party and the Tyler years are the papers of

Caleb Cushing. The records of Cushing's remarkable and varied life are preserved in more than 171 boxes of manuscript, to which there is a reliable index. The material found in the Henry Clay and Thomas Jefferson Clay collections is adequate; as in the case of the important John Jordan Crittenden Papers, many important items have been published. The John M. Clayton Papers contain valuable exchanges between Clayton and Clay, especially for 1841. For data on the Bank of the United States, finance in the 1830s, the intrigues of Whig politics, and the personal tragedy of an extraordinary gentleman-financier who hastened the end of his caste, the correspondence of Nicholas Biddle is without peer. The William C. Rives Papers are exceptional, both for the internal split in the Democratic party after 1837 and for the first six months of the Tyler administration. Letters of Whigs also of value include the Hale Family Papers and the Thomas Ewing, James Kent, Hamilton Fish, James F. Simmons, Thomas Corwin, Edward Curtis, Thaddeus Stevens, Joseph Story, John McLean, and James Watson Webb correspondence. The library's holdings of William Henry Harrison Papers are thin; most of the John Tyler Papers have been published. Among Democrats, easily the most valuable for an understanding of the political system and many of the personalities of the period is the collection of Martin Van Buren. Andrew Jackson's Papers are full of more heat than light; more illuminating are the letters of Levi Woodbury. The small collections of Duff Green and John C. Calhoun letters are of great value.

Material on the Whig party in the 1830s at the Alderman Library of the University of Virginia, Charlottesville, is understandably skimpy. The James Barbour, Robert M. T. Hunter, Benjamin W. Leigh, and David McCord papers, as well as the Morris Family and Tayloe Family papers, yielded some information.

At the Virginia State Library, Richmond, the Alexander H. H. Stuart Papers cast no light on the Virginia congressman's role in the Tyler-Whig bank negotiations of August, 1841. More helpful were the insights into the mood of Virginia politicians offered by the Littleton W. Tazewell Papers and the material on Anti-Masonry found in the William Wirt Correspondence.

The correspondence assembled at the Duke University Library, Durham, N.C., ranges widely. The important papers of John Jordan Crittenden, Kentucky senator and protégé of Clay, have been published only in part; the originals of Crittenden's letters, memoranda, and drafts of speeches must supplement the printed correspondence. David Campbell's Papers reveal much about the views of a Virginia Whig who was often in Washington. The manuscript diary of Phillip R. Fendall throws much light on the mood of Webster and the Whigs in the fateful winter of 1841. The papers of James Martin Bell, John R. Mulvany, and John Rutherford yield more information about business than about politics. In the Southern Historical Collection at the University of North Carolina, Chapel Hill, the Duff Green Papers proved disappointing; for the 1840–44 period, his day-by-day letters held at the Library of Congress seem complete.

The South Caroliniana Collection of the University of South Carolina, Columbia, contains originals or copies of all the manuscripts of John C. Calhoun. Calhoun's correspondence casts much light on his motives and hopes in the period, but must be supplemented by the smaller but revealing collection of his letters at the Library of Congress. The Waddy Thompson Papers proved disappointing for information about the California and Texas maneuvers of the Tyler administration. Of limited use were the James Henry Hammond and William Campbell Preston papers.

Public Documents

Congressional debates can be found in the *Register of Debates in the Congress of the United States* and in the *Congressional Globe*. The official *Journals* of the House and Senate record the votes on bills and amendments as well as their text. The House and Senate *Documents* for these years contain valuable information from executive department reports, committee reports, and committee hearings. The official communications of the executive are found in James D. Richardson, com., *A Compilation of the Messages and Papers of the Presidents, 1789–1905*, 11 vols. (Washington, D.C.: Bureau of National Literature and Art, 1907).

Useful material on the foreign policy of the Tyler administration is found in the records of the Department of State at the National Archives, Washington, D.C. The most important diplomatic correspondence is contained in State Department Instructions, Great Britain, vol. 15; State Department Dispatches, Great Britain, vol. 50; State Department Instructions, Mexico, vol. 15; and State Department Dispatches, Mexico, vol. 11. Almost all of the significant material on relations between the United States and Mexico is published in William R. Manning, ed., *Diplomatic Correspondence of the United States: Inter-American Affairs, 1831–1860*, 12 vols. (Washington, D.C.: Carnegie Endowment for International Peace, 1937). Valuable on the negotiations over Oregon is the volume *British and Foreign State Papers, 1845–1846* (London: Harrison & Sons, 1860). Indispensable for understanding Anglo-American negotiations over the Maine and Oregon boundaries are the Foreign Office files of the British Public Records Office. The most pertinent of these, Files 5 and 115, have been photostated, and copies are on deposit at the Library of Congress.

Published Correspondence: Diaries and Memoirs

Superseding all other collections of Webster's speeches and letters is Charles M. Wiltse, ed., *The Papers of Daniel Webster*, on microfilm (Ann Arbor, Mich.: University Microfilms, 1971), which became available too late for use in this study. The best published edition of Webster's works is J. W. McIntyre, ed., *The Writings and Speeches of Daniel Webster*, 18 vols. (Boston: Little, Brown & Co., 1903). Though important letters not available to McIntyre were left out, and portions deleted from Webster's letters by Fletcher Webster, supervisor of the first edition of his father's correspondence, were not restored, McIntyre's volumes are otherwise remarkably complete. The correspondence should be supplemented, however, by Claude H. Van Tyne, ed., *The Letters of Daniel Webster, from Documents Owned Principally by the New Hampshire Historical Society* (New York: McClure, Phillips & Co., 1902). Still useful are Fletcher Webster, ed., *The Private Correspondence of Daniel Webster*, 2 vols. (Boston: Little, Brown & Co., 1857), and Edward Everett, ed., *The Works of Daniel Webster*, 6 vols. (Boston: Little, Brown & Co., 1851).

Memoirs about Webster abound, and were compiled largely by men who knew him near the end of his life. Peter Harvey, *Reminiscences and Anecdotes of Daniel Webster* (Boston: Little, Brown & Co., 1882), is the most reliable. Surprisingly valuable, too, are the recollections of Webster's friends assembled in *Severty-second Anniversary of the Birthday of Daniel Webster, Celebrated by a Number of His Personal Friends, at the Astor House, in the City of New York, January 18, 1854* (New York: McSpeden & Baker, 1854). Caroline LeRoy Webster's *Mr. W. & I* (Binghamton, N.Y.: Ives Washburn, 1942) is merely a travelogue of Webster's trip to England in 1839.

Calvin Colton, ed., *The Works of Henry Clay, Comprising His Life, Correspondence, and Speeches*, 10 vols. (New York: G. P. Putnam's Sons, 1904), is the most complete extant collection of Clay's works, but will be superseded when James S. Hopkins and Mary W. M. Hargreaves, eds., complete their *Papers of Henry Clay* (Lexington: University of Kentucky Press, 1959-).

The speeches of John C. Calhoun are reproduced in Richard K. Cralle, ed., *The Works of John C. Calhoun*, 6 vols. (New York: D. Appleton & Co., 1853-55). Calhoun's letters are admirably edited by J.

Franklin Jameson, "Correspondence of John C. Calhoun," American Historical Association, *Annual Report, 1899* (Washington, D.C.: Government Printing Office, 1900), vol. 2. Both will be replaced when the new edition of Calhoun's speeches and correspondence, Robert L. Meriwether and W. Edwin Hemphill, eds., *The Papers of John C. Calhoun* (Columbia: University of South Carolina Press, 1959-), is completed.

Valuable as a source on Webster, the Whigs, and Massachusetts politics is Charles Francis Adams, ed., *Memoirs of John Quincy Adams, Comprising Portions of His Diary from 1795 to 1848*, 12 vols. (Philadelphia: J. P. Lippincott & Co., 1874-77). Adams loathed Webster, and his diary must be used with care. Other material pertaining to Webster and Massachusetts politics and be found in "The Rufus Choate-Warwick Palfrey Correspondence," *Essex Institute Historial Collections*, 69 (January, 1933): 81-87; William E. Lawrence, ed., *Extracts from the Diary and Correspondence of the Late Amos Lawrence* (Boston: Gould & Lincoln, 1855); and Samuel Eliot Morison, *The Life and Letters of Harrison Gray Otis, Federalist, 1765-1848*, 2 vols. (Boston: Houghton Mifflin, 1913).

Illuminating with respect to the interplay of Whig politics and the affairs of the Bank of the United States is Reginald C. McGrane, ed., *The Correspondence of Nicholas Biddle Dealing with National Affairs, 1807-1844* (Boston: Houghton Mifflin, 1919). McGrane's edition contains only a fraction of the voluminous Biddle Papers. An understanding of John Tyler and his administration is enhanced by careful use of Lyon G. Tyler, ed., *The Letters and Times of the Tylers*, 3 vols. (Richmond: Whittet & Shepperson, 1885). The letters are accurately reproduced and include correspondence and memoranda by all the parties to the Tyler-Whig conflict; the "times," as interpreted by Tyler's son, must be read with caution. The activities and thinking of Tyler's first cabinet are brilliantly illuminated by "The Diary of Thomas Ewing, August and September, 1841," *American Historical Review*, 18 (October, 1912): 97-112.

Valuable sources for Whig politics in New York, so important to both Webster and his party, are Harriet Weed, ed., *Autobiography of Thurlow Weed* (Boston: Houghton, Mifflin & Co., 1883); Jabez D. Hammond, *The History of Political Parties in the State of New York from the Ratification of the Federal Constitution to December, 1840*, 2 vols. (Syracuse, N.Y.: Hall, Mills & Co., 1842); and Allan Nevins, ed., *The Diary of Philip Hone, 1828-1851*, 2 vols. (New York: Dodd, Mead & Co., 1927).

Among the published sources on Democrats, the most important works include John Spencer Bassett, ed., *Correspondence of Andrew*

Jackson, 7 vols. (Washington, D.C.: Carnegie Institution of Washington, 1926–35); and John C. Fitzpatrick, ed., "The Autobiography of Martin Van Buren," American Historical Association, *Annual Report, 1919* (Washington, D.C.: Government Printing Office, 1920), vol. 2.

Newspapers and Periodicals

Whig and Democratic newspapers of the period are especially good guides to the changing tone and themes of party politics. Among the Whigs, in particular, the press had great power to bless or to veto the ambitions of party leaders. Among Boston newspapers, the *Boston Courier* consistently took the side, and often published the thoughts, of Webster. The Whig *Boston Atlas* and *Boston Daily Advertiser* were faithful partisans of Webster through 1836, but the pro-Harrison *Atlas* broke with Webster in 1838, as did the pro-Clay *Advertiser* shortly thereafter. The *Boston Daily Evening Transcript*, Whiggish in sentiment but less political than the other papers, is a good source for straightforward reports of meetings. The Anti-Masonic paper in the city was the *Boston Daily Advocate*. The two major Democratic newspapers of the state were the *Boston Morning Post* and the [Boston] *Bay State Democrat*.

The Whig organ in the District of Columbia, the *Washington National Intelligencer*, almost always held its columns open to Webster, who often used them, but it was largely neutral with regard to Webster's Whig rivals. Filled with material on Webster's effort to establish a Unionist party in 1833–34 is the *Washington Examiner*, whose life was as short as the abortive movement for fusion. Tyler's views in the conflict with the Whigs between 1841 and 1844 were represented by the *Washington Daily Madisonian*.

Among New York papers, the *New York Journal of Commerce* and the *New York Commercial Advertiser* were often friendly to Webster, while the *New York Star* favored Clay, and the *New York Courier and Enquirer* vacillated between them. The *New York Evening Post* spoke for radical New York Democrats, and the *New York Herald*, sympathetic to all who avowed laissez-faire policies, ran a critical and independent course. The *Albany Evening Journal* reflected the thoughts of New York Whig leaders Thurlow Weed and William Henry Seward.

The *Niles National Register* is an exceptional source for summaries of editorials from both the Whig and the Democratic press, as well as for excerpts from the proceedings of Congress and the meetings of party groups throughout the country.

The *North American Review*, published in Boston, occasionally contained articles by Webster, as well as other favorable pieces about him.

General Histories

Still astonishing for its breadth and detail is Frederick Jackson Turner, *The United States, 1830–1850: The Nation and Its Sections* (New York: Henry Holt & Co., 1935), which argues that the Jackson era was dominated by sectional rivalry and mounting Western influence. Countering with an interpretation of Jackson as the representative of the Eastern workingman is Arthur M. Schlesinger, Jr., *The Age of Jackson* (Boston: Little, Brown & Co., 1945). Stimulating and controversial, Schlesinger's account shows persuasively the rising influence in the Democratic party of men and ideas hostile to the vicissitudes of a market economy. Leonard D. White provides a thoughtful rendering of the period in *The Jacksonians: A Study of Administrative History, 1829–1861* (New York: Macmillan, 1954). Balanced and comprehensive one-volume treatments of the period include Charles M. Wiltse, *The New Nation, 1800–1845* (New York: Hill & Wang, 1961); and Glyndon G. Van Deusen, *The Jacksonian Era, 1828–1848* (New York: Harper & Row, 1959). Recent interpretative overviews which downgrade the importance of politics and which doubt significant divisions between Whigs and Democrats are Edward Pessen *Jacksonian America: Society, Personality, and Politics* (Homewood, Ill.: The Dorsey Press, 1969); and Douglas T. Miller, *The Birth of Modern America, 1820–1850* (New York: Pegasus-Western Publishing Co., 1970). The best recent studies of American party conflict are found in William Nisbet Chambers and Walter Dean Burnham, eds., *The American Party Systems: Stages of Political Development* (New York: Oxford University Press, 1967), and especially in the essay by Richard P. McCormick, "Political Development and the Second Party System."

Specialized Histories

The political, economic, and social ferment of the Jackson era has lured hundreds of historians and fostered an impressive array of monographs. Louis Hartz, *The Liberal Tradition in American: An Interpretation of American Political Thought Since the Revolution* (New York: Harcourt, Brace & Co., 1955), argues for a fundamental consensus of Whigs, Democrats, and, indeed, almost all citizens on political democracy and capitalistic enterprise. Marvin Meyers, *The Jacksonian Persuasion: Politics & Belief* (Stanford: Stanford University Press, 1957), finds differences between Whigs and Democrats. Meyer's intensive analysis of Jacksonian rhetoric reveals Democratic spokesmen yearning for the safety of an arcadian past and the sweets of a capitalistic future, while Whigs faced and favored the world of the marketplace with candid confidence. Lee Benson, *The Concept of Jacksonian Democracy: New York as a Test Case* (Princeton: Princeton University Press, 1961), finds more limited differences among politicians. Career-line analysis led Benson to conclude that leaders and followers of both parties differed little in background and shared a common egalitarianism. But parties did divide on whether state activity or state neutrality could best promote equality. Restating the case that men of wealth gravitated overwhelmingly toward the Whigs during the 1830s are Frank Otto Gatell, "Money and Party in Jacksonian America: A Quantitative Look at New York City's Men of Quality," *Political Science Quarterly*, 82 (June, 1967): 235–52; and Robert Rich, " 'A Wilderness of Whigs': The Wealthy Men of Boston," *Journal of Social History*, 4 (Spring, 1971): 263–76.

More recent studies of party conflict in the Jackson years stress the organizational imperatives which created and sustained the two-party system of the period. Focusing on the legislative behavior of congressmen and showing to different degrees the growth of party discipline are Joel H. Silbey, *The Shrine of Party: Congressional Voting Behavior, 1841–1852* (Pittsburgh: University of Pittsburgh Press, 1967); and Thomas P. Alexander, *Sectional Stress and Party Strength: A Study of Roll-Call Patterns in the United States House of Representatives, 1836–1860* (Nashville: Vanderbilt University Press, 1967). Election returns and state-by-state analysis of party techniques led Richard P. McCormick, in his *The Second American Party System: Party Formation in the Jacksonian Era* (Chapel Hill: University of North Carolina Press, 1966), to judge that competition to win the presidency revived the two-party system between 1824 and 1840. McCormick developed the same thesis in "Suffrage Classes and Party Alignments: A Study in Voter Behavior," *Mississippi Valley Historical Review*, 46 (December, 1959): 397–410; and "New Perspectives on Jacksonian Politics," *American Historical Review*, 65 (January, 1960): 288–301. Silbey, Alexander, and McCormick suggest that the organizational need to win the presidency and the organizational need to maintain discipline created unity within parties and division between parties quite apart from the sway of issues or the pull of common values.

The debate over differences between Whigs and Democrats, however, is by no means settled. David Hackett Fischer, in *The Revolution of American Conservatism: The Federalist Party in the Era of Jeffersonian Democracy* (New York: Harper & Row, 1965), suggests that the use of common techniques by two parties may belie basic differences in preference and values between them, and that, quite probably, the Whigs' reluctance to accept the changes of style and organization that winning required reflected a view that elites, and not the masses, should rule public affairs. Other studies similarly find significance in Federalist and Whig resistance to party organization; these works argue that, for many leaders, to accept party conflict was to deny social harmony, and to condone party loyalty was to violate individual conscience. See, especially, Michael Wallace, "Changing Concepts of Party in the United States: New York, 1815-1828," *American Historical Review*, 74 (December, 1968): 453-91; Ronald P. Formisano, "Political Character, Antipartyism, and the Second Party System," *American Quarterly*, 21 (Winter, 1969): 683-709; Lynn Marshall, "The Strange Stillbirth of the Whig Party," *American Historical Review*, 72 (January, 1967): 455-68; Richard Hofstadter, *The Idea of a Party System: The Rise of Legitimate Opposition in the United States, 1780-1840* (Berkeley and Los Angeles: University of California Press, 1969); and James Sterling Young, *The Washington Community, 1800-1828* (New York: Columbia University Press, 1966). It is doubtful that citizens shared these anxieties as much as party leaders did; for a thoughtful appraisal of the concept of deference in historical analysis, see John B. Kirby, "Early American Politics—The Search for Ideology: An Historiographical Analysis and Critique of the Concept of Deference," *Journal of Politics*, 32 (November, 1970): 808-38.

There is no recent general history of the Whig party, but older studies of the Whigs are able. E. Malcolm Carroll, *Origins of the Whig Party* (Durham: Duke University Press, 1924), is firmly rooted in archival and newspaper sources, and is a judicious work. Arthur C. Cole, *The Whig Party in the South* (Washington, D.C.: The American Historical Association, 1914), is a path-breaking study of the Whigs in that section. The best general study of the Whigs after 1840 is George Rawlings Poage, *Henry Clay and the Whig Party* (Chapel Hill: University of North Carolina Press, 1936). Necessary to any understanding of the Whigs in the North is Charles McCarthy, "The Antimasonic Party," in American Historical Association, *Annual Report, 1901* (Washington, D.C.: Government Printing Office, 1902).

Students of the Whig party must rely heavily on the biographies of its leaders. After Poage, the best treatment of Clay is Glyndon G. Van Deusen, *Henry Clay* (Boston: Little, Brown & Co., 1937). Clement Eaton, *Henry Clay and the Art of American Politics* (Boston: Little, Brown & Co., 1957), is a thoughtful, brief treatment. Albert Kirwan, *John J. Crittenden: The Struggle for the Union* (Lexington: University of Kentucky Press, 1962), is outstanding, as is Samuel Flagg Bemis, *John Quincy Adams and the Union* (New York: Alfred A. Knopf, 1956). Glyndon G. Van Deusen has written able biographies of three

New York Whig leaders: *Thurlow Weed: Wizard of the Lobby* (Boston: Little, Brown & Co., 1947); *Horace Greeley: Nineteenth Century Crusader* (Philadelphia: University of Pennsylvania Press, 1953); and *William Henry Seward* (New York: Oxford University Press, 1967). No student of the Whigs can overlook Thomas Payne Govan, *Nicholas Biddle: Nationalist and Public Banker, 1786–1844* (Chicago: University of Chicago Press, 1959). Though John C. Calhoun's link with the Whig party was always reluctant and tenuous, his career casts much light on the type of man and the kind of organization the Whigs had to hold together. Calhoun's thought and politics are luminously chronicled in Charles M. Wiltse, *John C. Calhoun*, 3 vols. (Indianapolis and New York: The Bobbs-Merrill Co., 1944–51). For new reflections on Calhoun's ideas and his troubled relationship with the States'-Rights party of South Carolina, see William W. Freehling, *Prelude to Civil War: The Nullification Controversy in South Carolina, 1816–1836* (New York: Harper & Row, 1966). Francis P. Weisenberger, *The Life of John McLean: A Politician of the United States Supreme Court* (Columbus: Ohio State University Press, 1937), is standard. Old but useful biographies of the first Whig president are Dorothy Goebel, *William Henry Harrison: A Political Biography* (Indianapolis: Historical Bureau of Indiana, 1924); and Freeman Cleaves, *Old Tippecanoe: William Henry Harrison and His Time* (New York: Charles Scribner's Sons, 1939). The best biography of the ill-fated John Tyler is Oliver Perry Chitwood, *John Tyler: Champion of the Old South* (New York: D. Appleton-Century Co., 1939). For Tyler's presidency the student should also see Robert J. Morgan, *A Whig Embattled: The Presidency under John Tyler* (Lincoln: University of Nebraska Press, 1954); and Robert Seager II, *And Tyler Too: A Biography of John & Julia Gardiner Tyler* (New York: McGraw-Hill, 1963).

Biographies of Democrats contain important material on the history of the Whig party. Robert V. Remini, *Andrew Jackson* (New York: Twayne Publishers, 1966), ably synthesizes the latest scholarship on Jackson, though the student must consult the older James Parton, *Life of Andrew Jackson*, 3 vols. (New York: Mason Brothers, 1860); John Spencer Bassett, *The Life of Andrew Jackson* (New York: Macmillan, 1928); and Marquis James, *Andrew Jackson: Portrait of a President* (Indianapolis: The Bobbs-Merrill Co., 1937), for the details and color of the president's life. Important for understanding both Jackson's appeal and the public standards which required the Whigs finally to find their own military hero is John William Ward, *Andrew Jackson: Symbol for an Age* (New York: Oxford University Press, 1955). Robert V. Remini, *Martin Van Buren and the Making of the Democratic Party* (New York:

238

Columbia University Press, 1959), stops before 1830. But James C. Curtis, *The Fox at Bay: Martin Van Buren and the Presidency, 1837–1841* (Lexington: The University of Kentucky Press, 1970), superbly analyzes the career of Jackson's harassed successor and illuminates all of national politics during the 1830s. Crucial for the tortuous route by which the Texas and slavery issues were formally intertwined in the last year of the Tyler administration is Charles Grier Sellers, Jr., *James K. Polk: Continentalist, 1843–46* (Princeton: Princeton University Press, 1966).

Studies of Daniel Webster

The career of Daniel Webster has tempted many biographers, including more than Webster's share of debunkers. George Ticknor Curtis, *Life of Daniel Webster*, 2 vols. (New York: D. Appleton & Co., 1872), is old in age and style, but the material it assembles and the perspicacity of the judgments it renders make it far superior to the usual official biography. Best among the biographies that rely almost entirely on Curtis are Henry Cabot Lodge, *Daniel Webster* (Boston and New York: Houghton Mifflin, 1883); and John Bach McMaster, *Daniel Webster* (New York: The Century Co., 1902). McMaster's narrative, though not adulatory, is pro-Webster. Lodge, one conservative senator writing about the life of another, offers genuine insights into Webster's philosophy and rhetoric. Claude Moore Fuess's *Life of Daniel Webster*, 2 vols. (Boston: Little, Brown & Co., 1930), is an able though eulogistic account of Webster's triumphs and trials. Richard N. Current's *Daniel Webster and the Rise of National Conservatism* (Boston: Little, Brown & Co., 1955) is analytical and interprets Webster's thought and career largely in terms of his efforts to serve New England economic interests.

Useful studies on special aspects of Webster's career include Robert Lincoln Carey, *Daniel Webster as an Economist* (New York: Columbia University Press, 1929); Everett Pepperrell Wheeler, *Daniel Webster: The Expounder of the Constitution* (New York: G. P. Putnam's Sons, 1903); and the major work on Webster as an advocate, Maurice G. Baxter, *Daniel Webster & the Supreme Court* (Amherst: University of Massachusetts Press, 1966). Persuasive on Webster's far-sighted understanding of the convergence of Western and New England interests is Peter J. Parish, "Daniel Webster, New England, and the West." *Journal of American History*, 54 (December, 1967): 524–49. Excellent on Webster, Jackson, and the nullification crisis are Norman D. Brown's "Webster-Jackson Movement for a Constitution and Union Party in 1833," *Mid-America*, 46 (July, 1964): 147–71; and *Daniel Webster and the Politics of Availability* (Athens: University of Georgia Press, 1969). Richard N. Current, "Webster's Propaganda and the Ashburton Treaty," *Mississippi Valley Historical Review*, 24 (September, 1947): 187-200, examines Webster's secret manuevers to win passage of the Treaty of Washington. A more comprehensive treatment of the same subject, based on the papers of Webster's secret agent in the Maine boundary negotiations, is Frederick Merk and Lois Banner Merk, *Fruits of Propoganda in the Tyler Administration* (Cambridge, Mass.: Harvard University Press, 1971). Webster's abortive efforts to negotiate the Oregon boundary are traced in Frederick Merk, "The Oregon Question in the Webster-Ashburton Negotiations," *Mississippi Valley Historical Review*, 43 (December, 1956), reprinted in Frederick Merk, *The Oregon Question: Essays in Anglo-American Diplomacy and Politics* (Cambridge, Mass.: Harvard University Press, 1967). Sydney Nathans, "Daniel Webster, Massachusetts Man," *The New England Quarterly*, 39 (June, 1966): 161-81, and Kinley J. Brauer, "The Webster-Lawrence Feud: A Study in Politics and Ambitions," *The Historian*, 29 (November, 1966): 34-59, examine Webster's trials as a sectional leader seeking to broaden his political base.

Thoughtful discussions of Webster's rhetoric are found in Wilbur Samuel Howell and Hoyt Hopewell Hudson, "Daniel Webster," in *A History and Criticism of American Public Address*, ed. Marie Kathryn Hochmuth, W. Norwood Brigance, and Donald Bryant, 3 vols. (New York: Longman's Green & Co., 1943-55), vol. 2; Clarence Mondale, "Daniel Webster and Technology," *American Quarterly*, 14 (Spring, 1962): 37-47; and Raymond A. Berner, "A Practical Look at 'Webster's Reply to Hayne,' " *Pennsylvania Speech Annual*, 16 (September, 1959): 22-28.

The best analyses of Webster's political and social thought are found in Major L. Wilson, " 'Liberty and Union': An Analysis of Three Concepts Involved in the Nullification Controversy," *Journal of Southern History*, 33 (August, 1967): 331-55; Major L. Wilson, "The Concept of Time and the Political Dialogue in the United States, 1828-48, "*American Quarterly*, 19 (Winter, 1967): 619-44; William R. Taylor, *Cavalier and Yankee: The Old South and American National Character* (New York: George Braziller, 1961); and Leo Marx, *The Machine in the Garden: Technology and the Pastoral Ideal in America* (New York: Oxford University Press, 1964).

No understanding of Webster or the Whig party is possible without use of the valuable studies on politics and social change in Massachusetts. Though it focuses largely on the Democrats, Arthur B. Darling's *Political Changes in Massachusetts, 1824-1848: A Study of Liberal Movements in Politics* Yale Historical Publications, no. 15 (New Haven:

Yale University Press, 1925), is invaluable. A useful overview of Massachusetts Whig politics is James Schouler, "The Whig Party in Massachusetts," *Proceedings of the Massachusetts Historical Society*, 50 (1916-17). The best study of Massachusetts politics before 1820 is James M. Banner, Jr., *To the Hartford Convention: The Federalists and the Origins of Party Politics in Massachusetts, 1789-1815* (New York: Alfred A. Knopf, 1970). Banner's work should be supplemented by William A. Robinson, *Jeffersonian Democracy in New England*, Yale Historical Publications, no. 3 (New Haven: Yale University Press, 1916); and Paul Goodman, *The Democratic-Republicans of Massachusetts: Politics in a Young Republic* (Cambridge, Mass.: Harvard University Press, 1964).

Outstanding on the fundamental economic and ideological changes in the Commonwealth of Massachusetts and in early nineteenth century America is Oscar Handlin and Mary Flug Handlin, *Commonwealth: A Study in the Role of Government in the American Economy, Massachusetts, 1774-1861* (New York: New York University Press, 1947). Suggestive too are Arthur M. Schlesinger, Jr., *Orestes Brownson: A Pilgrim's Progress* (Boston: Little, Brown & Co., 1939); David B. Tyack, *George Ticknor and the Boston Brahmins* (Cambridge, Mass.: Harvard University Press, 1967); and Martin B. Duberman, *Charles Francis Adams, 1807-1886* (Boston: Houghton Mifflin, 1961). Useful both on Webster and on New England Federalism is Lynn W. Turner, *William Plumer of New Hampshire, 1759-1850* (Chapel Hill: University of North Carolina Press, 1962). David Van Tassel, "Gentlemen of Property and Standing: Compromise Sentiment in Boston in 1850," *The New England Quarterly*, 23 (September, 1950): 307-319; Paul Goodman, "Ethics and Enterprise: The Values of Boston Elite, 1800-1860," *American Quarterly*, 18 (Fall, 1966): 437-51; and Robert Rich, " 'A Wilderness of Whigs': The Wealthy Men of Boston," *Journal of Social History*, 4 (Spring, 1971): 263-76, seek to fathom the deeds and motives of wealthy, largely Whiggish Bostonians.

Indispensable as sources on Webster and the Massachusetts Whigs from 1844 on are David Donald, *Charles Sumner and the Coming of the Civil War* (New York: Alfred A. Knopf, 1960); Kinley J. Brauer, *Cotton versus Conscience; Massachusetts Whig Politics and Southwestern Expansion, 1843-1848* (Lexington: University of Kentucky Press, 1967); Thomas H. O'Connor, *Lords of the Loom: The Cotton Whigs and the Coming of the Civil War* (New York: Charles Scribner's Sons, 1968); Frank Otto Gatell, *John Gorham Palfrey and the New England Conscience* (Cambridge, Mass.: Harvard University Press, 1963); and Richard H. Sewell, *John P. Hale and the Politics of Abolition* (Cambridge, Mass.: Harvard University Press, 1965).

INDEX

THE JOHNS HOPKINS UNIVERSITY PRESS

This book was composed in Baskerville text and display by
Jones Composition Company, Inc., from a design by Edward Scott. It
was printed by Universal Lithographers, Inc., on Warren's 60-lb. Sebago,
in a text color, regular finish, and bound by L. H. Jenkins, Inc., in
Holliston Roxite linen cloth.

Library of Congress Cataloging in Publication Data

Nathans, Sydney.
    Daniel Webster and Jacksonian democracy.

    (The Johns Hopkins University studies in historical and political science,
ser. 91, no. 1)
    Bibliography: p.
    1. Webster, Daniel, 1782–1852. 2. United States—Politics and
government—1815–1861. I. Title. II. Series: Johns Hopkins University.
Studies in historical and political science, ser. 91, no. 1.
E340.W4N17   973.5'092'4 [B]   72-10779
ISBN 0-8018-1246-1